T0304411

CAUGHT IN THE EYE OF THE STORM

URBAN REVITALIZATION IN TORONTO'S LAWRENCE HEIGHTS

JON CARELESS

FERNWOOD PUBLISHING

HALIFAX & WINNIPEG

Development editor: Errol Sharpe
Copyediting and text design: Brenda Conroy
Cover design: Evan Marnoch
Printed and bound in the UK

Published by Fernwood Publishing
Halifax and Winnipeg
2970 Oxford Street, Halifax, Nova Scotia, B3L 2W4
www.fernwoodpublishing.ca

Fernwood Publishing Company Limited gratefully acknowledges the financial support of the Government of Canada through the Canada Book Fund and the Canada Council for the Arts. We acknowledge the Province of Manitoba for support through the Manitoba Publishers Marketing Assistance Program and the Book Publishing Tax Credit. We acknowledge the Nova Scotia Department of Communities, Culture and Heritage for support through the Publishers Assistance Fund.

Library and Archives Canada Cataloguing in Publication
Title: Caught in the eye of the storm : urban revitalization in Toronto's Lawrence Heights / Jon Careless.
Names: Careless, Jon, author.
Description: Includes bibliographical references and index.
Identifiers: Canadiana (print) 20240424263 | Canadiana (ebook) 20240426460 | ISBN 9781773636887 (softcover) | ISBN 9781773637099 (PDF) | ISBN 9781773637105 (EPUB)
Subjects: LCSH: Public housing—Ontario—Toronto. | LCSH: Urban renewal—Ontario—Toronto. | LCSH: City planning—Ontario—Toronto. | LCSH: Housing policy—Ontario—Toronto. | LCSH: Racism—Ontario—Toronto. | LCSH: Classism—Ontario—Toronto. | LCSH: Lawrence Heights (Toronto, Ont.)
Classification: LCC HD7305.T68 C37 2024 | DDC 353.5/509713541—dc23

For Sabrina

Contents

Acknowledgements vii

Preface..ix

Acronyms.. xii

Introduction: Investigating Lawrence Heights...1

    Trends in Existing Research 4

    Urban Revitalization in Regent Park 8

    Objective of the Case Study.. 10

    Outline of the Case Study.. 11

    Timeline of Change in Lawrence Heights (1959–2020) 18

Chapter One: Origins of Lawrence Heights 21

    Settler Colonialism 24

    The Great Depression, Keynesianism, and Public Housing..................................27

    Public Financing of Lawrence Heights..33

    Born in Conflict...37

    Design and Layout of Lawrence Heights 41

Chapter Two: Race, Oppression, and Struggle 52

    Canadian Public Housing Under Fire.. 54

    Lawrence Heights in Focus... 56

    Political Struggles in Lawrence Heights.. 63

    Oppression and Stigmatization..71

Chapter Three: Neoliberalism and Revitalization in Lawrence Heights 82

    Neoliberalism and Social Housing... 85

    "Urban Revitalization" and Neoliberalism... 95

    Creating a Vision for "Revitalization"..101

    "Revitalizing" the Housing Supply 103

    Infrastructure and Financing 109

Chapter Four: A Community Wrestles with Change 116

    Grassroots Resistance to "Revitalization" 122

    Engagement Through LHION 126

    Neoliberalism and the Social Development Plan 129

    History, Housing, and Neoliberalism 133

    Community Safety and Solidarity 136

    Revitalization and Gentrification 142

Epilogue: Visions and Dreams 147

References 157

Index 169

Acknowledgements

This manuscript is a converted version of my doctoral dissertation, which I completed during my tenure as a graduate student in the Department of Politics at York University. Accordingly, I start by thanking my committee members, including my supervisors, Dr. Robert Latham, Dr. Karen Murray, and Dr. Carlo Fanelli, for their dedicated assistance. They improved the text greatly, bringing it to a point where conversion into a book was made possible. Further, I thank my thesis examiners, Dr. Roger Keil and Dr. Rebecca Schein, and my committee chair, Dr. Gerald Bareebe, for their incisive critiques and suggestions. Dr. Ethel Tungohan also deserves a sincere thanks for lending me invaluable advice on how to undertake this case study.

I also give a brief thanks to my friends and former colleagues Benjamin Johnson, Ryan Kelpin, Rimmy Rhiah, Grant Andersen, and Michael (Yiming) Ye for their companionship through the process of completing our degrees at York University. They were an always present source of levity during what was a long and sometimes challenging journey. I also thank my biological parents, David and Annette, my stepfather Henry, my sister Erin, her husband Matt, my niece and nephew (Grace and Finn), and my partner Sabrina.

Thanks to the Toronto Community Housing Corporation, which, by way of granting me a research agreement, helpfully lent me access to a trove of internal documents that were invaluable for my case work. I had the fortune of speaking with several urban planners, archivists, non-profit workers, and historians who provided me insights that would otherwise have remained unknown to me. I also extend sincere thanks to the staff at Fernwood Publishing, who have made this book possible. My editor, Errol Sharpe, has been endlessly supportive of this project since we met and has taught me a great deal about how to compose an effective book for a wider audience. I am immensely grateful, as well, to the three reviewers who took the time to closely examine an earlier draft of this work on behalf of Fernwood. Their comments were an invaluable resource for me. I would also like to thank my copyeditor Brenda Conroy, Lauren Jeanneau and the rest of her production and design team, and Anumeha Gokhale who did terrific work on the marketing and distribution end of things. Lastly, my gratitude goes to the people I met in the Lawrence Heights Inter-Organizational Network, who graciously allowed me to sit in on so many of their meetings. The tireless work they perform for their community continues to this day.

Preface

This book provides an analysis of the process by which an entire urban neighbourhood gets torn down and replaced wholesale. Since it opened in 1959, Lawrence Heights has been stigmatized, ignored, and burdened with labels people attach to public housing: dangerous, disordered, and unattractive. These viewpoints relegate Lawrence Heights to a place most people notice only when it appears in a newspaper. It follows that, when the announcement came in 2007 that Lawrence Heights would be getting the equivalent of a full-scale makeover, a "revitalization," most people may have responded — if they did at all — by affirming it as a welcome undertaking.

Before I began this project, I had never visited Lawrence Heights. I have never lived in public housing. As a white person who grew up in a quaint and well-advantaged suburb called Herring Cove, a former fishing village on the east coast of Canada, I remain far removed from the everyday experiences common to those living in Toronto's public housing. Since the 1970s, most of the tenant base in Lawrence Heights has shifted from being comprised mainly of people from Europe to being progressively drawn from the Caribbean, West and East Africa, Latin America, and Asia. These demographic changes have helped fuel stereotyping of public housing tenants, who not only are in lower-income brackets but are also racialized, encouraging people to ignore and fear Lawrence Heights. Such stigmatization is wedded into its architectural structure. For people driving along the Allen Road towards Yorkdale Mall, the housing structures that comprise Lawrence Heights are hidden behind an imposing concrete wall that winds around the whole neighbourhood, resembling a cage.

When I first visited Lawrence Heights in 2018, I was welcomed into a community meeting at the Unison Health and Community Services Centre, which sits on picturesque Flemington Road. It started a long running engagement, where I was permitted to witness challenging work being done by people committed to realizing their own vision for change to the extent it was possible. The conversations I bore witness to involved people solving problems. There were small things, like ensuring that correct labels for recycling are applied to bins in apartment buildings in underserved parts of North York. Bigger problems too. They discussed pressuring Ontario's provincial government to reverse its austerity-driven agenda. I had the privilege of speaking with local historians, urban planners, and representatives of organizations in Lawrence Heights. True to the objectives of critically reflexive research and in acknowledgement of my responsibilities to the people whom I was engaging with, I reported honestly on these events and supported the mission of those striving for change on their terms.

This book offers a story of the neighbourhood of Lawrence Heights, one that has yet to be given a detailed treatment in the existing scholarship on urban politics, much less that which is focused on "urban revitalization." Using documentary sources, I draw a chronological narrative to help us see how and why Lawrence Heights was built and how it became a so-called priority neighbourhood and to explain what is happening there now. Municipal policies often function here as barriers to obstruct anything beyond measured and controlled participation and interference by tenants in this major development process. This book will appeal to anyone with a general interest in understanding how persons possessed with limited resources and power effectively organize to realize a better future. Additionally, this text will benefit undergraduate and graduate level students who are interested in learning about urban revitalization in a Canadian context and, in particular, as it relates to policies that affect public housing areas in Toronto.

One truth that this book speaks to is how the governments erect barriers that can stall grassroots-led change. Governments direct resources toward lucrative investment opportunities and simultaneously hold a lid on conflicts that threaten societal hierarchies. For roughly the past four decades, governments in Canada and elsewhere have taken the view that markets and private sector entities can better serve people's interests than governments can and have supercharged this ideology by replacing public assets and services with market-based ones. This is the philosophy of neoliberalism. Neoliberalism has enjoyed the label of "conventional wisdom" among bureaucrats, city councillors, and planners alike. Their lasting belief in these ideals has underpinned the formation of a development partnership for phase one of the revitalization where the Toronto Community Housing Corporation, a social housing provider that lists the City of Toronto as its sole shareholder, has formed a contractual arrangement with two developer firms, Context and Metropia, which have joined to form one entity called Heights Development. Together, these organizations are deploying their resources towards reconstructing Lawrence Heights.

When grassroots energies, community-based or otherwise, get involved with the revitalization, they are typically forced to engage with — and even act as *one* with — the local government. To this point, such grassroot activity can typically involve various non-profit workers, tenants, and other volunteers carrying out work that could otherwise be done by city-employed bureaucrats, such as informing tenants about revitalization news, performing surveys, and public engagement work that helps affirm the government's agenda and bring it to completion. Grassroots work, though, can also involve compelling the same government to provide community members with access to and control over public resources that can be put towards fulfilling the goals and needs of tenants themselves. Ideally, grassroots entities are enabled to exert maximal democratic oversight over those public officials and the processes involved in the allocation and distribution of these resources. They do so under a shared belief that social problems are best resolved using collectivist solutions rather than market-driven ones, where there is a greater emphasis on democratic decision making and public oversight. Despite the power the government and capital wield, this book reveals that, in the case of the Lawrence Heights "revitalization," tenants and their supportive representatives have worked tirelessly to realize collectivist-driven solutions to issues facing their community. There is hope that what they are achieving will continue gaining strength as the project goes forward.

Acronyms

4Q	Bathurst-Lawrence Four Quadrants Neighbourhood Alliance
CH2	Maintenance Office
CMHA	Canadian Mental Health Association
CMHC	Canada Mortgage and Housing Corporation
CRC	Community Resources Consultants
ESL	English as a second language
GMM	General Membership Meeting
HCZ	Harlem Children's Zone
HOPE VI	Housing Opportunities for People Everywhere
HUD	US Department of Housing and Urban Development
LHION	Lawrence Heights Inter-Organizational Network
LHTA	Lawrence Heights Tenants' Association
MTHA	Metropolitan Toronto Housing Authority
NPM	New Public Management
OHC	Ontario Housing Corporation
OMB	Ontario Municipal Board
RGI	rent geared to income
SDP	Social Development Plan
SHRA	Social Housing Reform Act, 2000
TCHC	Toronto Community Housing Corporation
TESS	Toronto Employment and Social Services
TPS	Toronto Police Service
TTC	Toronto Transit Commission
UGC	Urban Growth Centre

Investigating Lawrence Heights

In May 2007, former City of Toronto councillor Howard Moscoe announced what is popularly termed an "urban revitalization project" in the public housing district of Lawrence Heights, the largest such project in Canada in terms of scale, comprising a 100 acre site (40.5 hectares) south of the Yorkdale Shopping Centre in North York. Lawrence Heights is double the size of Regent Park, another major public housing site, which sits farther south in inner-city Toronto. It so happens that Regent Park, too, is in the process of revitalization, one of the most talked about in the country, through the of the work of Toronto's largest social housing provider, the Toronto Community Housing Corporation (TCHC), with private sector partners.

The term "revitalization" communicates a message that political power and capital are being deployed to "liberate" a community in need of assistance. To this end, Lawrence Heights was labelled a "priority neighbourhood," along with twelve others defined by the City of Toronto in negative terms as having a high concentration of outdated public housing structures in disrepair. The tenants who live in Lawrence Heights, many of whom are Black and Brown, are stigmatized and isolated from the rest of the city. The area also lacks suitable roadways and social infrastructure and has an insufficient presence of commercial businesses. There are only four non-residential buildings on the entire site: the Flemington Road Public School, Unison Health and Community Services, the Lawrence Heights Community Centre, and the CH2 Maintenance Office.

In April of 2013, the TCHC formally announced its development partnership for phase one of the revitalization with Heights Development, a much publicized joint association between Context and Metropia. The revitalization is to culminate in the demolition of the 1,208 public housing units in Lawrence Heights. In their place will be newly built publicly subsidized units placed alongside an additional new 4,092 condominium and townhouse units to be privately owned. The publicly subsidized and privately owned units are to be indistinguishable from one another. As in Regent Park, an argument for situating the public and private housing units alongside one another is to encourage a greater melding of people from different income classes, which urban planners call "social mixing."

The original tenants in Lawrence Heights are moved into nicer homes while continuing to pay rent geared to their incomes, and they are expected to benefit from being brought into closer contact with new neighbours paying for similar looking housing at prevailing market rates. Here you have the TCHC, a local government agency, leveraging its publicly owned assets by selling or leasing portions of the land that comprises Lawrence Heights to private developers. The developers then help finance the reconstruction of what are considered dilapidated public housing structures, stimulating an influx of newly affluent residents and the building of new commercial businesses and public amenities in the area. Fundamentally, the objective is urbanization. They are using capital and political will to turn a district of inner-suburban modernist public housing into a space that better resembles contemporary urban centres in Toronto like the Distillery District or the St. Lawrence neighbourhood.

Beneath these liberatory-sounding intentions, such urban revitalization schemes can generate contradictory effects. Most prominently, the government may ignite gentrification, leading to the displacement of tenants who live in neighbourhoods characterized by having high proportions of social housing. The term social housing, in the context of this Toronto-centric case study, refers to rental housing units that are owned either by the TCHC "or on their behalf by a non-profit corporation, or a non-profit housing cooperative," and operated to provide accommodations to low-income individuals and families (Tong 2021, 131). Apart from facing a threat of physical displacement, the public housing tenants in Lawrence Heights may also experience the eradication of their social bonds and culture via gentrification. This can happen when upward pressure gets applied to rental costs for housing and commercial properties in and around these areas over time. Social mixing, too, can involve a form of moral supervision being imposed on public housing tenants by their newer affluent neighbours and would be done so under the veneer of creating a friendlier, diverse, and prosperous community. As Ute Lehrer, Roger Keil, and Stefan Kipfer (2010, 88) put it, "social mixing" is a code phrase of sorts, used to immerse racialized public housing tenants under a controlling form of normalcy that is rooted in marketization, self-reliance, and (generally) white, middle-class sensibilities.

The spectre of these contradictory effects has cast a pall over the existing tenants in Lawrence Heights. As a case study of change in Lawrence Heights, this book reveals new insights into how these people are confronting the re-shaping of their lives within the larger machinery of capitalism, namely the unceasing need to exploit new avenues for the accumulation of capital and the exploitative effects this search has on people affected by it. Doing so involves delving into the history and ongoing revitalization of Lawrence Heights, which has to this point been a neglected area for critical analysis. A historical narrative of Lawrence Heights documents how these tenants have long been afflicted by systemic oppression, racist and classist stigmatization, and the fallout from what has been governmental mismanagement and a withdrawal of public resources that could otherwise have been devoted to improving and maintaining their housing structures — rather than destroying and rebuilding them.

From there, the book looks at the ways in which tenants themselves have gotten involved in the Lawrence Heights revitalization. Such participation has tended to take two forms; tenants have either opposed the plan outright or have worked with and supported the government and developers towards convincing other residents to support the project. The perspective being offered in this book about tenant involvement in a public housing revitalization is that it is not a purely negative and hopeless endeavour, despite that being the impression one might get when reviewing existing debates on this issue.

What is crucial to understand is that the tenants involved in the revitalization, including their representatives in various community-affiliated organizations and networks, are doing this work to improve the quality of life in Lawrence Heights to the extent *that they are permitted to do so*. Within the scope of their involvement in the revitalization, Lawrence Heights tenants, community linked workers, and other volunteers are compelled to operate *as part of* the local government and abide by the rules and limits it sets for them. The imposition of these strictures helps ensure that the Lawrence Heights revitalization fulfills the official vision for change that the government, its developer partners, and the business class deem acceptable. That vision is to conform with the dictates of the pro-market philosophy of neoliberalism and to hold the predominately racialized tenant base fastened within existing social hierarchies.

Nevertheless, tenant involvement has sought to wrest important benefits out of the revitalization planning process, including priority job placements, assistance with moving costs, and funding for community programs, which fulfill demands expressed by tenants in the course of being surveyed by TCHC planners and other officials. Tenant involvement is not merely a procedural facet of revitalization planning. In the course of their work, tenants are pushing back against systemic forces that have long coloured the history of their neighbourhood and that are inextricably wound into the revitalization planning, namely colonialism, white supremacy, and the market-empowering logic of neoliberalism.

Trends in Existing Research

Substantial academic research has been devoted to excavating the experiences of tenants living in public housing districts undergoing revitalization. These accounts, broadly speaking, tend to conclude that revitalization does not remedy the despair experienced by such tenants. Rather, it serves to perpetuate it, keeping existing hierarchies of race and class intact while supporting the evolving operation of capitalism. Some authors zero in on the withdrawal of both senior level government support and public money for social housing construction, maintenance, and oversight over the last few decades. Such moves have precipitated the rise of entrepreneurial government strategies at the local level to redevelop social housing communities suffering from austerity measures by actioning redevelopments that rely on a questionable faith in social mixing (August and Walks 2018; Beswick and Penny 2018; Lavee and Cohen 2019).

An important concept lying at the centre of these events is the lasting predominance of neoliberalism, a guiding philosophy for governance and policy that sees the government empower market forces wherever it can. Marxist geographer David Harvey says that neoliberalism is about dominant classes re-establishing their position over lower ones, an effort to counteract and undermine the social equity that was wrought through the tumultuous post–World War II period in North America and elsewhere, including the civil rights movement, second wave feminism, stronger labour movements, and a relatively robust welfare state.

The social forces and institutions of this time were themselves undermined by capitalism's contradictions, fuelling socioeconomic crises, political corruption, and widespread alienation. These developments got entwined with globalization, post-industrialism, and the rising power of finance capital, out of which then radical ideas like neoliberalism[1] gained popularity in its eschewing of collectivism in favour of extreme individualism, self-reliance, and marketization.

Neoliberalism complemented the simultaneous rise in popularity of postmodern architecture and new urbanist planning doctrines during the late twentieth century. At the time, these movements were bolstered by a growing resistance to "ghettoizing" public housing and a recognition that the relocation of once robust blue-collar employment opportunities, postwar expressway construction and suburbanization were as much joint contributors to the hollowing out of inner cities as were lasting racist and classist prejudices. In this milieu, governments that formerly adhered to technocratic managerialism, where expertise and public resources were funnelled more generously into large-scale public works programs for the benefit of cities, began changing stances (Harvey 1989). These agents started shifting more towards entrepreneurial-style governance that would better empower markets by prioritizing civic boosterism, fostering development through public-private partnerships, and commercializing the inner city. More attention was to be paid to attracting tourists and interest from investors around the globe. These motives got accompanied by rising government commitments to multiculturalism, diversity, cosmopolitanism, and democratic urban planning strategies. Relatedly, this period saw urban planners wanting to create more walkable socioeconomically diverse communities with copious green space and residents performing informal surveillance on one another for everyone's collective benefit.

Novel schematics for urban revitalization also arose that were melded to the philosophy of neoliberalism. At the centre of such revitalization schemes is a motivation to "deconcentrate poverty," with public

---

1   Neoliberalism, according to David Harvey (2007, 2), refers to a set of political economic ideas and practices that suggests that human prosperity "can best be advanced by liberating individual entrepreneurial freedoms and skills within an institutional framework characterized by strong private property rights, free markets and free trade." To fulfill these ends, the government secures "the quality and integrity of money," establishes "military, defence, police and legal structures," and helps create markets in whatever avenues where they don't already exist (i.e., water, health care, etc.).

housing districts being a principal target. Between 1993 and 2010, the Housing Opportunities for People Everywhere (HOPE VI) program was deployed in the United States. HOPE VI was intended in to "transform public housing by demolishing large spatially concentrated developments and replacing them with mixed-income housing," where higher-income homeowners get encouraged to move into these same spaces (Fraser, Burns, Bazuin, and Oakley 2013, 525). Using the vernacular of neoliberalism, the US Department of Housing and Urban Development (HUD) lists the key elements of the HOPE VI program in a series of bullet points:

- Changing the physical shape of public housing
- Establishing positive incentives for *resident self-sufficiency* and comprehensive services that *empower residents*
- Lessening concentrations of poverty by placing public housing in nonpoverty neighborhoods and promoting mixed-income communities
- *Forging partnerships with other agencies, local governments, nonprofit organizations, and private businesses to leverage support and resources.* (HUD n.d., emphasis mine)

Proponents of HOPE VI insisted the program would replace highly concentrated poverty and high crime rates with private investment, higher property values, and jobs, with the thinking being that public housing tenants would be compelled to become self-reliant and be higher wage earners.

Underpinning the HOPE VI agenda was the social science thesis known as "neighbourhood effects." Drawing from influential texts like William Julius Wilson's *The Truly Disadvantaged*, first published in 1987, the neighbourhood effects perspective diagnoses concentrated poverty as a social ill that can be remedied by empowering the community itself through urban planning techniques. Robert Chaskin and Mark Joseph (2010, 301) summarize the neighbourhood-effects thesis:

Both compositional factors (e.g., concentrated poverty, housing quality, crime, residential stability) and aspects of social organization (e.g., collective efficacy, social networks, and organizational participation) have an impact on the well-being and developmental trajectories of neighborhood residents, especially children and youth. Second, community is invoked as a unit of belonging and action that can be mobilized to effect change, in which the resources, skills, priorities, and participation of community members can be drawn on to inform, shape, and contribute to solutions to social problems and efforts to improve neighborhood life as it is affected by both material circumstances and social dynamics.

By the 1980s, governments had begun aggressively cutting back on social spending, weakening formerly strong Keynesian welfare states. In Canada, reductions were made to transfer payments from the federal to provincial governments. Cities, in turn, were forced to operate with less government assistance. Substantial bureaucratic resources at the local level got poured into "community building" measures to help fill the gap, including "supporting resident participation, promoting collaboration among community-serving organizations, and fostering social interaction and networks of support among community members" (Chaskin and Joseph 2010, 301). This wording mimics the language of neoliberalism, new urbanism, and entrepreneurial governance that is part and parcel of efforts to de-concentrate poverty, including the revitalization of public housing communities, where emphasis is placed on self-reliance, democratic urban planning decision making, and displacing the responsibilities of government into the hands of non-profits, individual volunteers, church groups, and other networks. Indeed, the fingerprints of new urbanism, which came into vogue in the 1980s, are entrenched in urban planning doctrines today with their emphasis on creating walkable neighbourly communities with mixed land uses whose sectors, including housing, schools, shops, parks, and cultural centres, are all highly integrated with one another.

Exploratory studies of HOPE VI sites, however, found little interaction between different income classes (Lucio, Hand, and Marsiglia 2014, 893). More pointed critics assailed the program for further marginalizing public housing tenants, alleging that the government was effectively colonizing public housing sites for takeover by the middle class (Fraser, Burns, Bazuin, and Oakley, 2013). As Martine August (2014, 1318) says, HOPE VI was designed to fund mixed-income on-site redevelopment while using a voucher program to disperse lower-income residents elsewhere. In this regard, community members are encouraged to participate in the revitalization of their own disadvantaged neighbourhoods and risk becoming alienated to the extent that they cannot conform with the middle-class standards held by their neighbours in these newly mixed-income areas.

Urban Revitalization in Regent Park

In Toronto, the urban revitalization project unfolding in Regent Park has been the most publicized. Built over the 1940s and 1950s, Regent Park underwent a demographic shift beginning in the late 1960s, when immigration restrictions in Canada were gradually relaxed. Its demographic profile shifted from being mostly white, working-class Europeans in the mid-century period to becoming much more ethnically and culturally diverse, including Black, South Asian, Latin American, and Chinese to name a few. These public housing dwellers in Regent Park would find themselves subjected to now commonplace class- and race-based prejudices. Over time, as the city's public housing supply continued deteriorating, pressure was mounted on Toronto City Council to make changes, with a good deal of the pressure coming from Regent Park tenants themselves. The supposed remedy to these issues came in the form of an urban revitalization plan. Over multiple phases, the existing housing was to be torn down and replaced with expensive new units occupied by existing Regent Park tenants who continued paying rent geared to their incomes and who would live alongside indistinguishable units occupied by more affluent newcomers paying market rates. Urban revitalization sees the government joining forces with capital to alter Regent Park under the idea that public housing tenants living in a newly marketized environment will adopt the ethics of self-reliance and the middle-class sensibilities of those living in the new adjacent housing.

This strategy is put forward in lieu of alternatives that might avoid destroying and rebuilding the existing community while also addressing the systemic problems that afflict it. These problems include the substandard housing conditions brought on by welfare state retrenchment, safety issues, and drug use. August (2014, 1318) challenges policymakers "to look beyond the 'false choice' which presents gentrification and displacement as the only alternative to ongoing disinvestment and decay." In putting such false choices forward, local policymakers do what is common by colonial authorities throughout settler societies. Typically, we think of colonial power as something exerted outward by invading authorities against Indigenous Peoples, where the intent of the former is to steal and settle on the lands possessed by the latter, who in turn are coercively fitted into social hierarchies. Such authorities also turn inward and apply these same practices on marginalized groups within these settled societies, recolonizing spaces to make more money and hold existing hierarchies in place. To see public housing redevelopments as forms of recolonization requires us to understand colonization not as a past event but rather as an enduring structure meant to continually erase Indigenous Peoples and their cultures while maintaining a racial hierarchy (Wolfe 2006).

Regent Park tenants have striven to overcome their oppressive living conditions by getting involved in the revitalization as a conduit for change. A much-hyped feature of the revitalization planning, for instance, was the creation of the Social Development Plan (SDP), an initiative designed in lockstep with the neighbourhood-effects thesis, entrepreneurial governance strategies, and neoliberal philosophy. The Regent Park Resident Council, formed in 2002, was designated by the TCHC to lead the SDP, garnering them the Ontario Non-Profit Housing Association Tenant Achievement Award in 2003. Described by the TCHC as a "guide to building a successful, cohesive and inclusive community in Regent Park," the SDP "set the stage for community engagement and efforts to build an inclusive environment in Regent Park" (Brail and Kumar 2017, 3779). Endorsed by City Council in 2007, the SDP was intended to procure tenant-led actions on three fronts: public safety, employment and economic development, and community building. It put forward seventy-five recommendations to devote resources towards things like community gardens, maintaining newly built streetscapes, and broad-based interests like education, art programs, and tenant empowerment.

The scope of permissible tenant involvement in the SDP, and the Regent Park revitalization more broadly, has been to do what the government and its developer partner requires of them. Tenants have helped legitimize and ratify the plan, formed cooperative working relationships with the government, the TCHC, and assorted staff, and have worked as hired mediators, otherwise called community animators, between the plan's official decision makers and the multi-ethnic tenant base. The government has instrumentalized the energies of the tenants they hire who possess the desirable cultural cachet and neighbourhood connections to convince the wider neighbourhood to commit to the socially mixed redevelopment. These hard-working tenants, meanwhile, are striving to realize a better life while confronting the forces of neoliberalism, systemic racism, the prominence of the neighbourhood-effects thesis, and entrepreneurial-minded governments and related institutions that are intent on gentrifying and recolonizing the area for the middle class.

Objective of the Case Study

The objective of the case study is to analyze the unfolding urban revitalization in Lawrence Heights, a much lesser-known area than Regent Park, that is similarly inhabited by a diverse mix of multi-racial public housing tenants. We appraise the factor of tenant involvement in the planning for the revitalization on its own terms in order to present a more holistic picture of the case study, as opposed to folding such activity into a conclusion that the government and capital are coordinating every facet of the revitalization in a strictly top-down fashion. An intent of the book, then, is to draw a full-fledged dossier of Lawrence Heights, taking into account its origins, the historical context in which it arose, and identifying precursors that led tenants living there to energetically engage in the government-led revitalization program. Doing so helps us grasp what changes they are trying to produce and how they are being alternately supported, limited, and forced to conform with the dictates of those with more power.

During the early twentieth century, Italian Marxist philosopher Antonio Gramsci conceptualized political struggle as being wrought between competing hegemonic and counter-hegemonic social forces. Dani Filc (2021, 26) offers the following helpful distillation of this idea:

> A certain model of society becomes hegemonic when its worldview pervades all spheres of society: its institutions, its private life, its morality, its customs, its religion, and the different aspects of its culture. Or, to put it in Gramsci's words, hegemony "propagate[s] throughout the whole social sphere, causing, in addition to singleness of economic and political purpose, an intellectual and moral unity as well … creating in this way the hegemony of a fundamental social group over a number of subordinate groups."

We can identify the revitalization model being applied to Lawrence Heights as a hegemonic construct, as something that most people are inclined to see as a necessary venture, as assisting people in need, and which is "common-sense," as Gramsci might put it.

Putting the revitalization into motion is, nevertheless, a political process that gets invariably contested and altered as much as it gets celebrated and affirmed. Filc (2021, 24) also cites the adage from French philosopher Michel Foucault that resistance always "emerges 'where there is power,' adding that 'points of resistance are present everywhere in the power network,' and consequently 'there is a plurality of resistances.'" Tenants, in various respects, were energetic pursuers of revitalization. Others accepted that it was happening, perhaps with some reservations. Some people resisted it outright as a destructive plan. Persons living in Lawrence Heights who have worked with the city and other staff on the planning side of the revitalization have demonstrated a commitment to helping bring about change, which the government absorbed into its own operations, allowing it to eliminate any resistances and pressures for change that it deems impractical and unproductive. And yet, discussions have happened between public officials and tenant participants where the latter have committed to holding the former accountable to them and negotiating the terms of changes associated with the revitalization where possible. There is, in a sense, a plurality of resistances in action.

Outline of the Case Study

I once asked Roger Keil, professor of global sub/urban studies at York University, where new insights could be drawn that concern the application of urban revitalization models to different marginalized communities in Toronto, a subject Professor Keil has written about extensively. The answer he gave was Lawrence Heights. Like Regent Park, Lawrence Heights was built in the same postwar context but was stationed in what was then a remote section of North York, one of the six administrative boroughs of the City of Toronto. Parallels between the two cases are numerous, but they are also marked by important differences.

Prior to the construction of Lawrence Heights, the lands were possessed with numerous swamps and a rural community of devotedly Methodist farmers, following a long line of European settlers who originally captured the lands (including those on which Regent Park sits) from Indigenous Peoples, principally the Mississaugas of the Credit First Nation. After it was colonized, the area eventually became known for the Henry Farm, owned by George S. Henry, who served as premier of Ontario from 1930 to 1934. North York, furthermore, was then an inner-suburban outpost that could employ significant amounts of labour and capital towards infrastructure and real estate development. By the mid 1940s, the then-named Central Mortgage and Housing Corporation (CMHC, later Canada Mortgage and Housing Corporation) purchased the requisite lands, setting the process in motion by which Lawrence Heights would get built between 1955 and 1959 with federal and provincial support.

Despite having significant government backing, Lawrence Heights was met with significant public opposition from nearby Lawrence Manor, whose residents felt the added density would upset their cloistered rural lifestyle and threaten their property values. Those in charge of developing Lawrence Heights were put in the position of negotiating terms with Lawrence Manor residents, who saw the matter only in terms of how it was to affect them, never as something intended to give housing assistance to low-income families. The first issue of the *Lawrence Manor Gazette*, in February 1956, remarked, "Despite our best efforts, the low-rental project to the west of us was passed" (Lawrence Manor Ratepayers' Association 1956, 2). Once Lawrence Heights was finally developed and opened for occupation in 1959, homeowners in Lawrence Manor tended to shun the new tenants, even erecting a physical fence to keep distance between them and the public housing units.

Resting northwest of central Toronto, Lawrence Heights is bounded by four major streets: Yorkdale Road (northbound), Varna Drive (eastbound), Dufferin Street (westbound), and Lawrence Avenue (southbound). The neighbourhood consists of two areas bisected by the Allen Road expressway. If you walk east of Flemington Road, you encounter public housing complexes comprised of low- to mid-rise buildings broadly similar in design. Housing in the neighbourhood includes single houses, semi-detached houses, townhouses, and small walk-up apartment structures ranging from one to four stories in height.

Much of this housing is located in courts that are accessed from the ring road. Flemington Park is a 3.5 hectare park, distributed unevenly through the neighbourhood. Flemington Public School sits in the middle of the neighbourhood, and the Bathurst Heights Secondary School is on the southeast edge, on Lawrence Avenue West. Allen Road bisects Lawrence Heights; aside from Lawrence Avenue West, the neighbourhood has just two crossings — a bridge at Flemington Road and an underpass at Ranee Avenue (City of Toronto 2010a, 14).

For the first decades of its existence, Lawrence Heights was populated mainly by low-income families from Europe, with a predominant

Apartment housing in Lawrence Heights (photo credit: Ryan Kelpin)

share coming from the British Isles. The 1970s saw fluctuating immigration and labour patterns, increasingly restrictive choices for affordable housing, and manufacturing jobs shifting out of inner-city Toronto into North York and to other locales, with capital simultaneously getting invested in the burgeoning and precarious service sector in the inner city. These changes, in turn, helped stimulate similar demographic shifts in Lawrence Heights. By the early 2010s, much higher percentages of Lawrence Heights tenants were Indigenous or from Latin America or Southeast Asia, as well as elsewhere. Many of these tenants commute to and from their jobs within North York, inner-city Toronto, and the Greater Toronto Area.

Apart from being physically walled off for decades from homeowners in Lawrence Manor, Lawrence Heights tenants have faced similarly intensive stigmatization by a range of outsiders, as has been common for people living in Regent Park and other public housing districts in the city. As this book shows, condemnation against Lawrence Heights tenants has come repeatedly from the news media and government officials, and much less from other Torontonians. Such stigma has come in various forms, including large numbers of news articles that focus overwhelmingly on incidents of crime in the area and portrayals of Lawrence Heights tenants as criminals, suspects, persons of interest, and generally dangerous and abnormal.

These aspersions have become twinned with public statements from city officials who denigrate Lawrence Heights as a failing experiment and proposed urban revitalization as the antidote. Former city councillor Howard Moscoe declared in 2007 that "we're going to eliminate the (public housing stigma)" attached to Lawrence Heights (Vincent 2007a, E6). During a community meeting at a local school in Lawrence Heights, former TCHC chief executive officer Derek Ballantyne said to the audience that the "housing stock is in bad shape and needs to be replaced," adding that "by selling some of the land, the money can be used to reinvest in the revitalization" (Vincent 2007a, E6). Christopher Hume (2018) of the *Toronto Star* described the plan for Lawrence Heights as intending to weave this area "back into the city." New and sleek will replace outdatedness, isolation, and crime. The stigma itself, then, is a selling tactic for the revitalization, convincing people that it is the rational and common sensical path forward.

On the public financing end of things, the executive director of Toronto's Housing Secretariat (formerly the Affordable Housing Office) spells out the strategy by which redevelopment projects in Lawrence Heights and in other TCHC-managed housing sites get built:

> TCHC revitalization projects are typically structured in a manner where the cost to replace the aged TCHC units is offset by the profits from the market development and the sale of TCHC land. To ensure the financial feasibility of a revitalization project, the right balance of new TCHC replacement and market homes is needed. (City of Toronto 2020, 4)

In other words, the TCHC sells a portion of lands it controls to fund replacing the housing units it manages in lieu of accessing public money to do so. When the Housing Secretariat refers to determining the *correct balance* between constructing new TCHC controlled rent-geared-to-income (RGI) housing with those to be sold or leased at market rates, the idea is to refrain from building too much of the former, which would render the revitalization into a poor investment choice for private partners. Regent Park is made feasibly revitalized through the collaboration between the TCHC and its private partners, just as Lawrence Heights is being re-moulded through similar arrangements.

Reconfiguring Lawrence Heights into a specifically *socially mixed* development is of paramount importance for the government. It is the subsidized renters who get wrung through a newly intensified surveillance system, monitored not only by the police but by the moralizing guidance of new middle-class residents, who must be drawn "into these developments to capture enough ground rent to offset the costs associated with a devolved public housing program" (Fraser et al. 2013, 529). In this scenario, urban revitalization becomes the officially stated purpose, with colonization being the real and unstated one. As noted above, earlier case studies of socially mixed HOPE VI redevelopments suggest that cross-class ties are challenging to construct between public housing tenants and new residents, with limited interaction being the norm (Chaskin and Joseph 2011; Graves 2011). Further, say Fraser et al. (2013, 527), officials behind HOPE VI projects decline to even specify how such cross alliances and social networks would arise between the two groups, which these authors claim is evidence that the widening call for socially mixed redevelopments are nakedly purposed to "colonize former public housing residents to prepare neighborhoods for market reinvestment." Such areas can eventually become further gentrified, threatening the ability for existing residents to continue living there.

Like with Regent Park, the same concerns around gentrification and recolonization by the middle-class apply to what is underway in Lawrence Heights. Such anxieties swirl in tandem with other forces at work, including tenant involvement in the revitalization. Here too, tenants have conveyed a mix of resistance and support. Many of them spoke to city councillors, revealing a desire to live in homes that are more conventional and to have a chance to own rather than simply rent. Tenants and organizers have had intimate involvement in composing a social development plan rooted in creating, among other things, job opportunities for tenants, community arts and recreational programs, and enhanced public safety measures. Organizing of this kind does become absorbed into the local government, which sets the limits around what is politically possible and controls how money and other resources are amassed and distributed.

There is a storied history of mistreatment inflicted upon Lawrence Heights tenants by the public authorities that have managed the area, starting with the Ontario Housing Corporation (OHC) and its successor as of 2002, the TCHC. The inward facing design of Lawrence Heights, which lacks through streets, has worsened the isolation and stigma felt by its residents, people who are struggling to make ends meet while living in a highly expensive city. When the Toronto police force ratcheted up its assault on the illegal drug trade in the 1980s and 1990s, a disproportionate share of brutality was met upon Black and Brown Lawrence Heights tenants, as was the case in Regent Park and in other disadvantaged communities. Robyn Maynard (2017, 83) notes that "the economic subordination and abandonment of Black communities has acted in parallel with expanding the scope of racialized surveillance and punishment across the criminal justice system."

Lawrence Heights tenants and organizers have long taken care of their neighbours. They have also wrestled with paternalistic government management, which in recent decades has been eroded and made more ineffectual through the withdrawal of money and provincial support. The element of paternalism is deeply entrenched in the way governments manage public housing tenants, with a pretence of government-run housing being that the people living there are incapable of self-reliance.

In a paper from 1968, Albert Rose referred to a duality of moral environmentalism, where the belief among social reformers of that time was that slum conditions produce slum dwellers. Reformers thus opted to build public housing as proper machines for modern living under the belief that better housing would produce "better people." But these beliefs conflicted with the government's intensive surveillance of families that occupied public housing, revealing doubts among reformers as to whether it is the environment or individual morality that is responsible for producing slums and slum dwellers (Brushett 2001, 185).

As neoliberalism came into vogue, social reformers adapted to governments' preference for leveraging the private sector to deliver public goods, with the enablement of public-private partnerships as mechanisms to generate capital accumulation through the dispossession of public assets. Urban revitalization put a new twist on the old moral environmentalism strategy without resolving the contradictory attitudes lurking beneath it. To wit, public housing complexes get rebuilt into more profitable spaces with higher circulations of exchange value, and their occupiers' new middle-class neighbours become a new source of moral instruction and surveillance. From the standpoint of public officials, developers, urban planners, and other associated professionals, resolving the shortage of affordable housing in Toronto is not simply a matter of building a lot of cheap housing, whether it be social housing or otherwise, to shelter people in need. Housing developments, by and large, must be sound investment strategies, which leads those with the power to build to draw strict limits around what is allowable in terms of a development's design and the amount of money people have to pay to live in the units.

Such are the characteristic outcomes of what governments frame as "partnerships" with private sector entities. Politicians often describe such alliances as being an efficient means to fix costly problems, using capital from collaborative and wealthy companies and saving taxpayers the bill. It is not so much that these partnerships enable the government to contribute more to enhancing public goods in an environment where cost-cutting and budget balancing are of paramount concern. Rather, when governments and private sector entities team up, they must prioritize creating profitable investments above all else, superseding any altruistic motives that might benefit the common good. If such investments fail to generate profits for the capitalists involved and insufficiently contribute to economic growth, then they will be considered underperforming ventures. What can be surmised, then, is that when it comes to the objectives of public-private partnerships, regardless of whatever democratic aims are being pursued, they are first and foremost about making money and are not about doing what the public necessarily wants or needs.

Collectively, these statements attest to the social relevance of Lawrence Heights as a subject of investigation. Yet, as a case study of urban revitalization in Canada, Lawrence Heights has yet to receive any substantial attention. Some might say that the project is still being completed, making it challenging to draw firm conclusions. Assessments of Lawrence Heights that occur only after the entire district has been transformed will naturally make conclusions based on the totality of events. This approach can colour how one evaluates available data concerning these early stages, potentially underappreciating their significant impacts for the people experiencing the events up close. The rapidity and fragmentary nature of contemporary urban life sees political work happening in a multitude of societal creases. Research should not be limited to evaluating events that create lasting changes or that persist over a long enough expanse of time that they can be given a traditionally full retrospective account.

One could also say Lawrence Heights is simply less well known than the public housing areas that are in the inner city. People driving, walking, biking, or taking transit through the east end of Toronto are more likely to move past Regent Park, which sits not too far east from Bloor and Yonge Streets, comprising a cluster of arts and cultural organizations that is a tourist hub, a thoroughfare for workers and home to several University of Toronto buildings.

In contrast, Lawrence Heights is further up Toronto's grid-based transportation system. It sits buried on a slope near the Lawrence West subway station and Lawrence Allen Centre, a smaller and less traversed space compared to nearby Yorkdale Mall, another tourist locale. Compared to Toronto, North York is also comparatively bereft of cultural cachet and is largely ignored in existing scholarship on urbanization compared to the larger City of Toronto. Derided by many as a hovel, this lesser-known administrative district within the larger City of Toronto is peppered with strip malls, nondescript suburban housing, car dealerships, vacant lots, aged high-rise apartment buildings, and bland industrial warehouses.

There are also many working-class migrant families populating North York, many of whom live in the relatively lower-cost housing. Inner-suburban North York, much like Scarborough, also possesses many TCHC-controlled housing complexes, whose residents struggle against similar stigmas. Indeed, areas dense with social housing, like "Jamestown, Jane-Finch, Rexdale, and Malvern now conjure images of racialized poverty and gang violence" (August 2014, 1321). Jane and Finch, a widely diverse and majority Black and Brown community found near York University in North York, is perhaps the most stigmatized area in the city, with approximately 3,531 publicly subsidized housing units under TCHC management. Countless stories concerning neighbourhoods like these remain untold.

Before we delve into the case study chapters, we conclude this introduction by presenting a chronological picture of Lawrence Heights, lending us a coherent narrative of change that culminates with the present revitalization.

Timeline of Change in Lawrence Heights (1959–2020)

1959   Construction of housing complexes in Lawrence Heights is completed and opened to the public.

1961   Thirty-eight extra units added to Lawrence Heights but fall well short of what Metropolitan Toronto Council promised.

1965   Ontario Housing Corporation discusses building more public housing but encounters resistance from suburbs.

1966   North York Welfare Department publishes report about Lawrence Heights. Tenants alternately describe feeling satisfied with the physical housing quality and feeling alienated and isolated.

1967	Passage of the Immigration Act, stimulating inflows of people from wider numbers of countries and regions and solidifying a hierarchy of migrants.
1969	Former minister of transportation Paul Hellyer organizes Hellyer Task Force, which releases report critiquing Canada's public housing program.
1970	Ontario Federation of Citizens' Associations presses the OHC to turn over day-to-day management of public housing to tenant groups but is stonewalled.
1970–2004	Pre-"revitalization" news coverage of Lawrence Heights tends to play up stigmatizing view of the neighbourhood as being *disordered*.
1971	In response to protests, the Ontario government suspends construction of Spadina Expressway, which would have cut into affluent Toronto neighbourhoods. The Allen Road is permitted to split Lawrence Heights down the middle without public opposition.
1971	Multiculturalism Act passes, intended to stimulate inflow of high- and low-skilled workers in rising service sector and heighten immigration levels in areas outside Europe. Policy changes coincide with the reconfiguration of Toronto into a "global city," characterized by heightened services sector requiring inflows of workers from elsewhere.
1971–1986	Black households gradually become overrepresented in Ontario-administered public housing neighbourhoods, including Lawrence Heights, compared to the rest of the Census Metropolitan Area.
1972–1974	Federal Liberal government steers funding away from public housing towards other social housing forms. Provincial government maintains control over public housing administration.
1976	OHC follows federal government's example and winds down public housing construction due to negative public perceptions of it.
1995–2003	Mike Harris–led Ontario government institutes so-called Common Sense Revolution which helps intensify government's commitment to public sector austerity, low taxation, privatization, and public-private partnerships as strategies to enhance growth.

1997	Ontario passes City of Toronto Act (Bill 103) to facilitate Metropolitan Toronto amalgamation, dissolving the city's six constituent municipalities into a megacity version of Toronto.
1999	Toronto City Council report documents city's struggles to finance social housing expenses without necessary provincial support. Harris-led Conservatives institute cuts to Ontario cities for social housing, public transit, etc.
2001	Ontario Municipal Act is passed, creating new sphere of municipal responsibilities downloaded onto them by the province. Social Housing Reform Act (SHRA)passed same year, placing jurisdiction over social housing administration to cities.
2002	Approval given to Regent Park revitalization, commencing public-private partnership to raze and construct new housing, amenities, and infrastructure in this Toronto-based public housing neighbourhood.
2004–2020	News coverage describing the "revitalization" in generally positive terms. Other articles describe concerns over lacking infrastructure to support enhanced density.
2005	The Lawrence Heights Inter-Organizational Network forms as grassroots oriented collective of tenants and local organizations which becomes instrumental presence in revitalization planning.
2007	Lawrence Heights revitalization formally announced. The "new" Regent Park serves as blueprint. Planning discussions commence between city officials and tenants.
2008–2012	Major economic crisis strikes world economy followed by prolonged recession.
2011	Lawrence Heights revitalization secondary plan completed.
2015	Construction of revitalization phase one begins in tandem with ongoing "community engagement" between planners and tenants.
2020	COVID-19 pandemic slows construction as lockdowns take effect.

CHAPTER ONE

Origins of Lawrence Heights

The stigma attached to project living is also acute with some. To hear it referred to as "the jungle," "the camp," "poverty village" or simply "OH There!" hurts personal pride, makes them feel inferior and produces the depressing hopeless feelings that are the common attributes of alienation.
— W.R. Delagran (1966, 18) from *Life in the Heights*

W.R. Delagran was a social worker and member of the North York Welfare Department who published several reports for local officials during the 1960s. In the above passage from *Life in the Heights*, Delagran analyzed testimony from early residents of Lawrence Heights who expressed feelings of isolation and pain rooted in their awareness of being stigmatized for living in public housing. They speak to long-ingrained assumptions among Torontonians about Lawrence Heights. Now these assumptions are being re-tooled and repurposed by planners as messaging devices that communicate an urgency for "revitalization."

When planning for the Lawrence Heights revitalization started gaining traction in the early 2000s, statements from some officials and other interested parties revealed their belief in the need to break with the area's history and construct something new. Derek Ballantyne, once the chief executive of the TCHC, was quoted in the *Globe and Mail* declaring that the area needs to be "re-planned and rethought" (Campbell 2008, A10).

The original construction of Lawrence Heights and the plan to re-build it through the revitalization are likewise rooted in the recurring tendency for money and political power to extend into new avenues where more wealth can be generated. The settler colonial advance in Canada and Toronto spurred an influx of Europeans onto the same territories that the CMHC would eventually purchase to help facilitate the construction of Lawrence Heights in the mid-1950s. The government was responding to economic crises, persistent housing shortages, and the necessity for growth. One step it took to address these challenges was to devise public housing for low-income families, with the government dictating the terms and rules by which public housing tenants could live and to keep society organized according to race, class, and gendered hierarchies. Today, relations between the government and public housing tenants remain structured in much the same way, with people in Lawrence Heights having to deal with their neighbourhood being torn down and rebuilt under the government's auspices.

This case study is at its base a historical treatment of the political economy of Lawrence Heights. Political economy refers to the ways in which money and political power jointly influence the tendencies for people to struggle amongst each other for position in hierarchies that are characteristic of social life under capitalism. This chapter starts us on a historical accounting of Lawrence Heights, with the intent of understanding how it originated, and begins to explore how money and political authority have profoundly altered the course of the lives of people who have lived there.

Developing a historical account of a neighbourhood involves the author selecting certain facts to analyze so that a cogent narrative and argument can be presented. Any historical study, then, is necessarily selective in that there are countless other facts and stories that could be told about this same case study. The story behind the name "Lawrence Heights" is one example. It is derived from Lawrence Avenue, one of the four roads bordering the area. Lawrence Avenue was named after Jacob Lawrence, a farmer born in 1822 who settled in Upper Canada. Lawrence built a sawmill on the east side of the Don River in 1845, and for a two-year period (1854–1856) he bought and operated a tannery from a local character named James Davis. It was Davis who constructed and ran a guesthouse that was a favourite among Mackenzie rebels during the Upper Canada Rebellion of 1837–1838. Davis was once so floored by a speech given at a prohibition meeting that he went home and poured all his alcohol into his garden, subsequently forbidding it from his guesthouse, which then became known as the Temperance Inn. As for Jacob Lawrence, he sold his tannery to James Hugo in 1856 and then continued to work before dying years later in 1885. The story behind the namesake of Lawrence Heights is just one of countless others that can be excavated.

This chapter, meanwhile, looks specifically at the historical origins of Lawrence Heights, providing explanations for how and why it was built. It presents a selection of facts and analyses to make the case that settler colonialism is a societal force that helped underpin the original development of Lawrence Heights and that its lasting presence works to hold the people living there in especially oppressive positions in the social hierarchy. The story begins with the dispossession by white European settlers of several tracts of formerly Indigenous-held territory; ownership of these lands passed through a series of hands before eventually coming under public ownership by the Canadian government. In the mid-century years, these stolen lands became the site for constructing Lawrence Heights, which was to warehouse individuals and families struggling to afford the costs of living. These tenants were to find themselves afflicted for generations by precarious employment, low wages, poor housing conditions, and the stigma that comes with living in concentrated poverty. The burdensome conditions facing public housing tenants are entwined with the damaging inequities of capitalism and the related brutalities of white supremacy and settler colonialism. Dispossessed Indigenous Peoples have seen their cultures and ways of life progressively eradicated, fixing them into perilous conditions defined by oppression, lacking access to needed resources, and higher risk of homelessness, unemployment, and premature death. Public housing tenants in Lawrence Heights, as this chapter shows, quickly found themselves beset with similar problems, which commonly oppress people struggling in the social hierarchy.

The first section of this chapter delivers a brief history of the settler colonial advance that led to settlement of stolen lands, their eventual purchase by the government and their subsequent reconfiguration into Lawrence Heights. The second and third sections give added context about how the development of Lawrence Heights was enabled, in large part, through the establishment of a metropolitan governance structure for Toronto and the advancement of a government-led agenda in the years after World War II to institute Keynesianism as the choice paradigm for policy development, stimulating employment, and redressing obstinate affordable housing shortages. From there, the chapter delves into the local political conflicts that arose in response to the proposal for building Lawrence Heights, which came primarily from neighbouring homeowners who opposed it entirely. Such opposition failed in the face of concerted government efforts to get Lawrence Heights built, a project that was advertised as a social good to house the less fortunate. The last section appraises the original structure and layout of Lawrence Heights in its form as a modernist public housing complex. As is discussed later in the book, Lawrence Heights was idealized as a "city on the hill" that would house those in need and *condition* them to avoid pathologies given to so-called slum dwellers.

Settler Colonialism

By the late eighteenth century, British settlers had secured significant territory, including that which would become Lawrence Heights, along the north shore of Lake Ontario from the Missisaugas through a series of land surrenders, including the 1787 Toronto Purchase (Freeman 2010, 24). At a rate of a mere 10 shillings per acre, British settlers soon bought up 250,830 acres of land while the Missisaugas received exclusive fishing rights in Etobicoke Creek. Negotiators withheld certain information from the Indigenous counterparties, including the provision that settlers would have exclusive use of the land in perpetuity, superseding Indigenous practices of communal use (Dehli 1990, 113).

When settler societies establish in rural and urban spaces, they attempt to convert property to maximize its exchange value; such colonial violence "targets Indigenous populations, their land, as well as those subjects — typically racialized, immigrant/refugee, and lower-income populations — who are not the idealized Western subject" (Crosby 2023, 174). In other words, rather than framing these events as discrete moments in history, they are better thought of as manifestations of an enduring drive by certain groups to control the resources of others and organize them into strict hierarchies. Indigenous Peoples were historically targeted by settlers, who expropriated their territories, lodging them in a precarious hierarchical position characterized by persisting social inequities, "deteriorating housing conditions and Indigenous homelessness" (Crosby 2023, 173).

Settler colonial relations are embodied within a host of government strategies predicated on the twin concepts of eugenics and euthenics. Eugenics refers to the applied pseudo-science "of controlling human reproduction in ways that eugenicists believed would improve the human race" whereas euthenics, relatedly, is "the science of better living, with the aim of improving the human race through controllable environment and hygiene" (Kelly et al. 2021, 13–14). By 1928, white settlers were categorizing Indigenous Peoples in Ontario as being mentally deficient according to the results of Euro-centric intelligence testing, leading these eugenicists to teach students about the virtues of eliminating so-called defectives through forced sterilization (19). Other social reformists claimed around the same time that euthenics was preferable to eugenics to resolve immorality and delinquency by "removing children from environments of poverty and placing them in conditions where they could be educated and reformed" (17). Euthenics informed policies in Canada intended to assimilate Indigenous Peoples into white settler society, including the forcible transfer of thousands of Indigenous children to church-operated residential schools (17). These policy strategies were made feasible only through the initial expropriation of Indigenous lands by white Europeans.

Graeme Wynn explains, to wit, that the British government began distributing land lots originally stolen from Indigenous Peoples to incoming settlers in Ontario, noting that by "1825, the total population was approximately 150,000; sixteen years later it was approaching 450,000" (1979, 51). The northern hinterland of York (before York became Toronto in 1834) comprises the land that now encompasses the municipality of North York. It was named North York after its incorporation into the County of York in 1922 and remained a sparsely populated farming community in central Ontario for decades. After World War II, the government committed to building new residences on this farmland as a partial response to the shortage of affordable housing in Toronto.

By zooming in on how these farmlands became settled and mined into sources of value, one can get a clearer sense for how this represents an ongoing and cyclical process. The lands that Lawrence Heights sits on were labelled Lots 6 and 7 (Concession 2) in North York by the British government in the nineteenth century. Each land plot was two hundred acres in size and was located north of Lawrence Avenue between Bathurst and Dufferin Streets. Both land plots were bought in 1812 by Henry Mulholland, a farmer and bricklayer who emigrated from the Ulster province of Clones, County Monaghan in Ireland to York's northern frontier in 1806. He had been one of the first city councillors for his home district, ingratiating himself by helping build a Methodist church and schoolhouse in his new community. Mulholland would fight on the side of the United Empire Loyalists as Captain in the Third York Militia against the Americans in the War of 1812 in the battles of York, Stoney

Creek, and Lundy's Lane. He was married to Jane Armstrong, and in 1814 they built a farm and settled with their ten children.

The need for the government to populate stolen lands with more settlers helped drive emigration out of parts of the United Kingdom that were beset with unemployment and famine during capitalism's formative years. English-speaking Canada was essentially the product of nineteenth-century mass emigration from England, Ireland, and Scotland that inundated a small eighteenth-century population base (Houston and Smyth 1990, 9). In "the three decades between the Peace of Waterloo and the onset of the Great Irish Famine in 1845," say Houston and Smyth (1990, 9), "half a million Irish traveled to British North America. They constituted 60 percent of the total inflow." Among the early settlers who made their way to Upper Canada, the Mulholland family were likely affluent enough to escape socioeconomic strife in Ireland. The influx of Irish farmers into these lands reflected a broader nation-building project. Protestantism was instituted as the nation-state's de-facto religion while Indigenous Peoples became signified as a lesser race who were without God.

Henry Mulholland exemplified the pioneer lifestyle, travelling to Ireland two or three times to convince Irish farmers in Ulster to emigrate to the colony, where they could settle and farm, bringing several friends and associates with each trip home. While travelling aboard a ship called *The Lady of the Lake* during a return trip from Ulster through the Strait of Belle Isle in 1833, Mulholland and other passengers drowned after the ship collided with an iceberg. Thomas Mulholland inherited his father's 400 acre estate on the west end of Bathurst Street and accumulated significant tracts of land in Innisfil, King, York Township (located southwest of what is now identified as North York and east of Etobicoke) and Toronto. Born in 1816, the younger Mulholland and his wife Mary Ann Conland had twelve children. He would go on to participate in the Rebellions of 1837 and 1838 on the side of the Loyalists. Thomas Mulholland took control of Lot 6 in the northern part of York (now North York) on Lawrence Avenue from in the year 1840.

Jane Mulholland, daughter of Henry Mulholland, married James Stewart, and they settled on a property that extended south to Lawrence East. Their daughter, Louisa Stewart, married George Stewart Henry, premier of Ontario between 1930 and 1934. After Henry died with little money, Stewart and her son took it upon themselves to build up their property into a successful farm and showplace. These formerly

Indigenous-owned land tracts, including the former Mulholland farmlands, were bought up by developers in the 1940s. In the 1950s, they became the lands that the Canadian government selected to build Lawrence Heights.

The Great Depression, Keynesianism, and Public Housing

When understanding why Lawrence Heights was built, it is important to recognize the role the government plays in mobilizing land into channels for investment and how major political-economic events and policy strategies become precursors for it. Adjusting our focus to the 1930s and early 1950s, several major events took place, including the Great Depression, WWII, and the postwar housing shortage in Toronto. Together, these became an effective mixture out of which a buildup of public housing would become possible.

The Great Depression, which began in 1929, poured gasoline onto an already creaky Canadian housing market. By the 1930s "virtually all aspects of the housing system had ceased to function normally" (Hulchanski 1986, 21). This fallout brewed interest in public housing among builders, social workers, architects, activists, and trade unions as a strategy to combat the Great Depression's effects. These groups viewed public housing as an ideal way to lower unemployment and fulfill the shelter needs of low-income individuals and families. Prior to the Depression, the federal government was wary of devoting more than minimal public resources towards helping people afford housing, as doing so might colour them as wasteful socialists.

Indeed, before the 1930s, any intervention by the government into the Canadian housing market was the exception rather than the rule. There was the "Better Housing Scheme" initiated by the federal government in 1919, but even that was minor in scope compared to what would come decades later. After the election of William Lyon McKenzie King in 1935, the government still kept itself on the fringes of the housing market since it maintained that the dire conditions brought on by the Depression would pass. The 1938 National Housing Act bolstered housing construction but did not make provisions and guidelines that would allow municipalities to build affordable rental housing. Fairly limited housing development was the norm in Canada through the 1920s, 30s, and early 40s because the Depression had slowed industry to a crawl.

After World War II, the government changed course when Keynesianism came into vogue. Stubborn housing shortages created a politically fraught situation for the federal government, with the real potential that many returning war veterans would join the legions of others who would not be able to find reasonably priced homes. Politicians, bureaucrats, and assorted experts had greater carte blanche to use public resources to stimulate growth. However, in Canada, the Keynesian program proved to be milder in scope than in, say, Great Britain or the United States. Canada's brand of Keynesianism was intended not to radically intervene in market affairs, says Neil Bradford (1999, 32), but to only "fine tune a mostly booming economy through tax cuts, investment incentives and automatic stabilizers," the last of which can be classified as welfare policies (for example, unemployment insurance, old age security, and child allowances). Fine tuning, in this way, was meant to keep people working, buying, spending, and investing in perpetuity, where the ebbs and flows of the business cycle get smoothed out to avoid future recessions, or worse, a Great Depression 2.0.

Canadian policymakers thus expressed their commitment to Keynesian-lite, staving off economic recessions by using counter-cyclical policies, such as public spending programs, to stimulate aggregate demand and smooth out fluctuations in the business cycle. Governance was to be conducted through ordered management, where technocratic experts took on greater responsibility for "managing" the economy and individuals' welfare, signalling a break from traditional liberalism, which had reigned in the years prior to the Great Depression and leaned towards something more proactive and interventionist. After the war, the housing development sector grew into a major presence within the Canadian business landscape. It was not just that public officials had been seduced by Keynesianism. Housing became a highly valuable commodity in a context where the middle class was burgeoning, many among them eager to take out a mortgage, work, and spend on new cars, stoves, fridges, and other appliances. Entrepreneurs saw the opportunity in investing in apartment and suburban housing. Toronto ramped up real-estate production accordingly, running parallel with brimming employment in an industrial sector characterized by rigidly organized Fordist production techniques that were popularized during the war. These factors combined to bring about higher population growth and fiscal revenues, lending added pressure to widen the city's fragile housing stock.

It was through the housing crisis and the completion of the war that the provincial government in Ontario saw the presence of low-income workers and families as the key ingredient to making public housing a source of new investment. At the time, struggling individuals and families were proliferating in industry-heavy cities. In 1944, the Final Report of the Subcommittee on Housing and Community Planning, otherwise known as the Curtis Report, "denounced the current state of Canadian housing and federal housing policy and called for a courageous federal housing policy that assured every Canadian family decent accommodation" (Brushett 2001, 75). The release of the subcommittee's report coincided with an increase in public demands from war veterans and activists (prominent names included Humphrey Carver and Albert Rose) that the government provide subsidized housing options to low-income families and the homeless. Public pressure for housing assistance for low-income families and otherwise vulnerable people got absorbed into the government's larger agenda to create more avenues for investment and better manage workers.

The government subsequently created a limited federally led social housing program with two primary delivery models for assisted living: limited dividend and public housing. The former was mostly reserved for seniors, with federal financing of it being eased via cost-sharing arrangements with the provinces. Social housing, meanwhile, consists of the whole stock of government-assisted housing, including public housing, not-for-profit and cooperative housing, rent supplement programs, and rural and Indigenous housing, which totalled 6.5 percent of Canada's total housing supply (roughly 650,000) units by the 1990s, which is when construction of it dried up (Smith 1995, 906). In the mid-century, social housing development in the form of non-profits, cooperatives, and public housing was a newfound strategy for the government to address difficulties that gained attention after WWII, namely unemployment, housing unaffordability, and homelessness. The federal government amended the National Housing Act in 1949 to create its public housing program. Accordingly, the CMHC created an architectural division that planned and supervised the construction in the 1950s of large public housing projects to address Toronto's housing shortage. These structures housed people and created work contracts for builders, engineers, architects, and public administrators, among others.

Despite the utility that public housing can provide, especially during calamitous recessions, it was surprising how little of it got built. Canada's public housing program was one social spending initiative among many. But even at Keynesianism's apex in the postwar age, the federal government's public housing program delivered small amounts of it compared to its mortgage insurance and direct lending programs, which catered more to people residing higher up in the social hierarchy. It was of such small scale that its impacts were little where it existed, and families receiving welfare already were generally ineligible to live in it. The 1944 National Housing Act and its subsequent amendments primarily benefited middle-class Canadians, who could feasibly afford a suburban home.

A 1964 report from the Ontario Association of Public Housing Authorities said that, after the federal government dissolved its emergency shelter program in 1948 and its veterans' rental housing construction plan in 1949, it put forward a relatively meagre public housing program, despite the severity of the postwar housing shortage, which persisted well into the mid-1950s. Between "1949 and 1963, only 12,000 public housing units were built (an average of 850 units a year)" (Hulchanski and Shapcott 2004, 2). Ultimately, the federal government manipulated its public housing program to afford itself maximal political advantage while doing as little as possible for people in lower-income brackets:

> The 1949 program was not successful in creating much accommodation; it was a masterful political stroke. Under the 1949 legislation, a complicated federal, provincial, municipal formula was devised. Consequently, public housing projects had to go through an estimated eighty steps before actually being constructed. This ensured that only where political demands were strongest would any public housing actually be constructed. (Bacher 1986, 8)

Public housing was instrumentalized by the government to placate interest groups pressuring legislators to assist people unable to afford to own or rent market-rate housing. Nearly half of the units built were situated in Ontario.

The public housing that was built at the time was managed locally by the Metropolitan Toronto Housing Authority (MTHA), the metropolitan arm of the OHC (Kipfer and Petrunia 2009, 116). A 1962 report in the *Toronto Daily Star* features excerpts of letters from frustrated public housing tenants:

We have to pay $65 a month for a three-room flat. Our three children a share a nine-by-nine bedroom. We have to share the bathroom with five other adults and three other children," says one letter. "My wife and I and two children live in one room," says another. "We share a kitchen and bathroom with four other adults and two children. We have no privacy what-soever. This costs us $25 a week. I gross $200 a month, and my wife earns another $120." (Cochrane 1962, 7)

The article says these letters are typical of the situation of the 1,200 low-income families that were listed on the MTHA's "active" waiting list, meaning they were approved for public housing but there were no available units to house them. They were part and parcel of the roughly 2,000 families who at the time had their names on Metro Toronto's housing waitlist with those applicants who had not yet received approval for placement, with only 150 having the remotest chance to get moved into a subsidized project, joining the more than 30,000 Metro residents who were in need of similarly assisted housing.

Of the limited public housing supply that did get built in Toronto, a portion of it became adapted to a longstanding objective of government policy, that is, to target and reshape urban spaces once they are deemed able to absorb significant labour and investment. In the early twentieth century, Victorian-esque slum dwellings were often torn down and public housing was erected as a substitute. The process became a two-pronged strategy of "slum clearance," followed by "renewal" of these same urban spaces. Concurrently, settler colonial relations became enmeshed in the treatment afforded to public housing tenants by the government, which was coloured by euthenics and eugenics alike.

A notorious case of a former "slum" becoming "renewed" happened in Cabbagetown. Located in the Old City of Toronto's east end, Cabbagetown was a nineteenth-century relic that derived its namesake from the Irish-born residents who were known for planting cabbages in their gardens. Comprised mainly of single-family row houses whose predominately Anglo-Saxon occupants often had boarders renting their upper stories, the houses in Cabbagetown became progressively dilapidated as land-lords declined to maintain them in the face of falling property values (Brushett 2001, 102). It would be the publishing of a landmark report in 1934 by a committee chaired by Lieutenant Governor Herbert Bruce that would change conditions for Cabbagetowners forever. The Bruce Report, as it was called, forwarded proposals for clearing and revamping several blocks east of Toronto's downtown, including Cabbagetown, described as ridden with structurally unsound and overcrowded buildings, rife with pollution, and lacking sanitation. The report's recommendation was for the city to raze these areas, which it called slums, and replace them with low-cost housing as a form of urban renewal.

In 1950, novelist and onetime Cabbagetowner Fred Garner wrote a well-known fictionalized (and probably semi-autobiographical) account of his old neighbourhood during the Great Depression that presented a more complex picture of Cabbagetown than the Bruce Report let on. At different points, Garner uses language evoking the image of the slum, writing that "the prevailing smell was one of decay, of old wet plaster and rotting wooden steps, the smell of a landlord's carelessness and neglect" (cited by Brushett 2001, 102). Taken as a whole, however, Garner's story of "the largest Anglo-Saxon slum in North America" depicts what Ryan James (2010, 71) argues is "a lively, complex and politically engaged community," which would fit with what Jane Jacobs described as a "type of 'slum' that possessed its own wisdoms and potential for regeneration but was condemned by 'paternalistic' planners who did not understand this."

Plans for slum clearance and urban renewal would get temporarily stalled by the war effort, but the influx of veterans coming back to Canada after the war helped worsen what was an already intractable affordable-housing shortage in cities like Toronto. In the postwar period, then, the agenda for urban regeneration gained renewed steam among local politicians and reformers. They believed they were killing two birds with one stone by replacing the blight of Cabbagetown with a self-contained public housing development called Regent Park in 1948. In the language of euthenists, Regent Park was designed to create an environment with limited thoroughfare and substantial courtyard surroundings that would shelter those with limited incomes and discourage them from indulging in abnormal behaviour characteristic of the so-called slum-dwelling poor.

At the time, Regent Park represented a novel form of urban renewal. Its design was influenced by Swiss-born French architect Charles-Édouard Jeanneret, better known by his alias Le Corbusier. Known for his commitment to modernist architecture, Le Corbusier sought to create "machines for modern living," homes that prioritized efficiency and rejected excessive ornamentation in favour of open floor plans to be filled with modern appliances and furniture. These ideas blended seamlessly with the techno-utopianism of the 1950s, when the industrial working class enjoyed higher standards of living and were expected to imbibe the docile middle-class "nuclear" two-parent family dynamic. Such docility was rooted, in part, in the adage that family breadwinners who carry a mortgage and other debts are less likely to go on strike at work. For this reason, among others, the business community should support a burgeoning middle class. Along this line, planners in Toronto also put their own spin on Le Corbusier, idealizing Regent Park as a "machine for democratic living," where husbands, wives, and their children performed their respective roles as equal partners in social reproduction (Brushett 2001, 218–19). A 69 acre complex by the time it was finished, Regent Park is bordered by River Street (east), Shuter Street (south), Gerrard Street (north), and Parliament Street (west). Its housing units, when viewed against the more numerous postmodern architecture that now envelops most of the city, do look like modernist artifacts that appear dropped into the landscape from another period.

Public Financing of Lawrence Heights

Lawrence Heights, meanwhile, was neither built in the inner city nor was it intended to become a fixture of urban renewal. But it was part of the same public housing program that gave rise to Regent Park, and both were designed with the intention of dissuading their occupants from indulging in the pathologies given to so-called slum dwellers. They would be part of a limited response by the government to tackle the shortage of affordable dwellings in Toronto and elsewhere. As the *Toronto Daily Star* remarked in 1961, Lawrence Heights was at that point the best and most affordable place to build public housing for large families in the suburbs.

A morass of fiscal and political challenges, however, gummed up what might otherwise have been more effective public housing service delivery. In 1961 the MTHA published a report that concluded that its public housing program had failed for three reasons: administrative relations between different orders of government had become tangled and uncooperative; a lack of coordination of resources for public housing programs; and suburban municipalities refused to accept projects in their midst.

A problem in the mid-century years was the lack of assistance available for lower middle-income families who could neither afford a mortgage nor wanted to live in subsidized housing. Due to limited supply, a metro-based family during this period would have no chance to occupy a fixed-rental dwelling if their income was over $4,150 since any subsidies would be eliminated if their income was at that level or more. These middle-income families found public housing doubly undesirable since there was no option to buy these homes. They were simultaneously ill-positioned to take on an expensive mortgage, let alone qualify for requisite home-ownership assistance. Feeling dejected, they projected resentment onto public housing dwellers, arguing that their tax dollars should not go to helping people when they cannot afford better housing either.

The social housing program involved coordination between the federal and provincial governments. The year when Toronto initiated the formation of metropolitan government, 1953, proved key. At this time, Toronto was set on overtaking Montreal as Canada's premier city, just as Ontario was committed to strengthening its urban-industrial base and provide massive funding for infrastructure (sewers, roads, electrical grids, etc.) to complement and support residential, commercial, and industrial urban and suburban development. Metropolitan government was a means to realize these goals in that Toronto was dealing with overcrowding and suburban flight due to migrations of people that had filled its wartime industries, in addition to the relaxation of immigration controls by a federal government committed to a postwar liberal order. Because the Greater Toronto Area was an assemblage of townships adjacent to the city, these jurisdictional boundaries made it difficult to coordinate and raise the necessary capital to finance the expansion of infrastructure to service Toronto's growing population.

Consolidating these areas permitted a collectivization of capital to be invested in them, allowing for an efficient and orderly expansion of suburban districts. Metropolitan Toronto became an umbrella of six local governments: Toronto, Scarborough, North York, Etobicoke, East York, and York. There was a territorial compromise of sorts; the metropolitan structure allowed the inner-city tax base to get milked for financing suburban infrastructure. It also permitted the spread of public transit and public housing into new suburban neighbourhoods — despite resistance from homeowners and local politicians. New suburban dwellers were afforded housing and transportation routes into and out of the inner city for commuting. Residential developments could be produced and serviced with the infrastructure in place, helping these townships flourish. Metro could borrow more cheaply than the single municipalities and townships could do on their own because it had a broad and affluent tax base and a solid credit rating. By issuing bonds, Metro paid the costs of building infrastructure in unserviced subdivisions. Its ability to borrow in the New York money market helped procure clean water supplies, resolve inadequate sewage disposal — restricting the dumping of human waste into Toronto's rivers — and get rid of thousands of unnecessary septic tanks.

With this metropolitan governance structure in place, the CMHC and Ontario built social housing on assemblies of serviced public land in the 1950s in Lawrence Heights in North York, Rexdale, Jane/Finch, Malvern, and elsewhere. Unlike nowadays, public housing had more voices promoting it after the war years. Its champions held that it possessed great potential to lure wealthy investors and would lower barriers to more expensive developments on inner-city properties by pushing lower-income people into subsidized housing elsewhere. These advocates insisted that public housing would top-up people's pocketbooks rather than siphon from them by enhancing Toronto's tax base, lowering social services costs for everyone in the long run.

The CMHC purchased the land for Lawrence Heights cheaply, "at $16,000 an acre and held it until the growth of Toronto caught up and surrounded the empty acres," after which Metro initiated the process of building the project using private sector contractors (Haggart 1958, 8). A statement from chair of the Council of Public Works from 1960 said Lawrence Heights

> was all made possible by the foresight and wisdom some ten or twelve years ago of the federal-provincial partnership in acquiring this very substantial block of land at a fraction of the price it would cost today. The Metropolitan Corporation's contribution to the project involved bringing metropolitan services such as sewers, water and storm drainage to the property at very substantial cost and entering into of the original agreement that the Metropolitan Corporation would contribute, under the old formula, to the difference between $25 per unit of taxes and normal taxes to the local municipality. (Yardhouse 1960, 2)

The CMHC's land purchase was coveted, but development had to wait until the appropriate infrastructure was in place. The *Globe and Mail* reported in July of 1955 that the "scarcity of serviced land in Metropolitan Toronto pushed land prices to prohibitive heights for such projects" ("Way Cleared for Start" 1955, 5). The government chose to build Lawrence Heights on these North York farmlands in part because it was cheaper to do so than in the inner city. Politicians and planners opposed building more public housing on expensive inner-city land, which they wanted to keep reserved for more profitable enterprises.

An article from December 10, 1954 in the *Globe and Mail* acknowledges the dual importance of implementing planning strategies in the inner city as well as in the outskirts in North York, as expressed by Mayor Nathan Phillips ("Cart Before the Horse" 1954, 6). However, the article says of Lawrence Heights that it was unwise for the government to invest major sums in new municipal services, such as sewage disposal, water treatment, public transportation, electricity, schools, roads, and firefighting in outlying subdivisions when the same services are already available in the inner city that are being underused despite its greater density. The article posits that so-called "run-down" inner-city areas should be redeveloped instead of putting resources towards public housing in the suburbs, under the pretence that it would capture more municipal tax revenues, place public housing tenants closer to work and other attractions.

In hindsight, the writer of this *Globe and Mail* piece from 1954 may not have appreciated the extent to which the building of Lawrence Heights represented the extension of capital and people into what had been to that point only sparsely populated suburbs, a de rigueur move by urban planners in the post–WWII context. That the municipal governance structure permitted the building of infrastructure in North York was an action meant to stimulate an influx of two-parent families into these outskirts, where they could proceed buying appliances, cars, and other amenities while commuting into the city through what were major public works projects like the Allen Expressway. It would be in later decades, well after the suburbs had been built up, that the government would turn its sights on *redeveloping* sites like Lawrence Heights that by now are considered "rundown" in the public conciousness.

Born in Conflict

When it comes to understanding how Lawrence Heights became so common a target for stigmatization and public resentment, it helps to document some warning signs that haunted it from its beginnings. There was, for instance, significant opposition mounted against the proposed construction of Lawrence Heights by people living in abutting Lawrence Manor, a subdivision of privately owned detached homes. Lawrence Manor Ratepayers' Association members were advancing various stigmatizing *images* of what they considered Lawrence Heights to represent and who would be living there. Lawrence Manor is bounded north by the Highway 401, Lawrence Avenue to the south, the Allen Expressway to the west, and Bathurst Street along its eastern frontier. A letter from November 7, 1980, addressed to the head of Development Control for North York by the chair of the association described Lawrence Manor as being comprised of two distinct residential groups: young families living mostly in starter homes alongside low-income families and pensioners renting low-rise apartments along Lawrence Avenue and Bathurst Street.

While Lawrence Manor had a diverse demographic profile in terms of income and class, the relationship between its politically active members and the public housing tenants living next to them has long been fraught. When Lawrence Heights was announced as a new project, it was met with loud protests from surrounding residents of the "swank Bathurst-Lawrence area" who felt the development would devalue their homes ("Happy with Lawrence Heights" 1958, 8). They put together a petition of six hundred names protesting the development and repeatedly tore into officials during meetings of the North York Planning Board and Council.

On July 28, 1954, the Lawrence Manor Ratepayers' Association marshalled three hundred angry homeowners from the area of Lawrence and Bathurst Streets to rally in opposition to Lawrence Heights during a committee hearing in North York. One city councillor excoriated the contingent for being selfish, saying "it is because people don't want them in their area that thousands of other people haven't decent accommodation today," and he was promptly booed into silence (Haggart 1958, 7). A lawyer hired by the Ratepayers Association appeared at the Ontario Municipal Board (OMB) to oppose the project, and he too was chastised when the OMB chair responded: "You want to keep 'foreigners' out of your subdivision, I take it" (Haggart 1958, 7).

The opposition to Lawrence Heights did fail in its objective to get the project either withdrawn from consideration, stalled, or built elsewhere. After losing the fight to stop construction, Lawrence Manor homeowners demanded the area "be fenced off to contain its tenants" (Jones 1970, 26). A fence was eventually established and was to become a lasting symbol of the strife and opposition levelled against the original project.

There is evidence that the approval of Lawrence Heights was met less through the work of public officials committed to assisting the under-housed and more through prudential relegation of resources — namely land, labour, and money — towards creating subsidized housing in ways that complemented the imperatives of the business class and loudly disavowed any association with socialism. Take the example of Fred Gardiner, who was the first chair of the Metropolitan Toronto Council, from 1953 to 1961. Nicknamed "Big Daddy," Gardiner became the namesake of the Gardiner Expressway, fitting his profile as an advocate of capital-intensive public works projects. In 1954, Gardiner had been informed surreptitiously by Robert Winters, the federal minister responsible for housing, that Prime Minister Louis St. Laurent was seriously considering vetoing Lawrence Heights on account of it representing preferential treatment given to Toronto. Gardiner coaxed Winters into helping write a letter to St. Laurent, which succeeded at neutralizing the threat of the veto (Colton 1980, 133).

A foremost spokesperson for Lawrence Heights, Gardiner became embroiled in a dispute with local organizers who were dead set on stopping Lawrence Heights. In a last-gasp move to halt its construction, a three-man delegation travelled to Ottawa with an eight-page brief intended for the public works minister, claiming that the height of the proposed buildings posed a safety risk due to their proximity to aircraft taking off and landing at nearby Downsview Airport. Gardiner replied that neither the Department of Transport nor the Royal Canadian Airforce objected to the size of the buildings or their proposed location, but that the government would consider re-scaling them down to a three-storey maximum height. North York residents, furthermore, would benefit from the storm drainage sewers that Metro installed near the edge of the site for Lawrence Heights and that it would also pay dividends for Lawrence Manor explicitly by ensuring "their water courses would be piped, and the area would no longer drain into open ditches in the area" ("Housing Project Urged On" 1955, 35). As Gardiner put it:

Metro is vitally interested in this project, which would enable it to discharge one of its responsibilities: to provide housing for the people in the Metropolitan area. I don't think it's improper or asking too much to ask the area municipalities to help us out with our problems. ("Housing Project Urged On" 1955, 35)

Gardiner's words echo those voiced by other city councillors quoted above who made the proposal for Lawrence Heights sound like a matter of social justice, especially when confronted by hostile Lawrence Manor residents. In such instances, these public officials make the case that housing access must be extended to those in need and doing so may require convincing those opposing it of the need for compassion (in terms of living closer to people in a lower-income class) and, in Gardiner's case, to inform such parties that the project, in fact, offers them material benefits as well.

Further public statements made years later by Gardiner, however, are reminders that public housing, as a policy agenda, was driven less by principle and considerations for social justice and more by politically prudent investment decisions. The *Globe and Mail* described the selection of North York for Lawrence Heights as a cynical ploy by the government — via the persuasive power of Fred Gardiner — to generate "a public display of action on housing, regardless of other considerations" ("Cart Before the Horse" 1954, 6). Indeed, on January 8, 1960, the *Toronto Daily Star* conducted an interview with Gardiner, where he is repeatedly asked why the government cannot build more public housing and the questioner proposes different strategies to him that could achieve this end. In his replies, Gardiner dismissed such calls as being predicated on a naïve belief that money grows on trees and that they fail to appreciate how public financing of public housing depends on a careful navigation of competing interests, saving money, and making canny investment choices.

Specifically, Gardiner claimed that building expansive public housing projects would throw the federal government's budget out of whack. Neither, he said, could the government generate money for public housing by taking land that they bought at a low price and selling it for a higher price to private developers because that would be unfair to those who originally sold their land holdings to public authorities. Metro could not issue its own bonds to finance public housing either, said Gardiner, because bond buyers would perceive it as an overly dangerous investment. Neither can you build scattered subsidized housing supplies in private subdivisions because doing so, as Gardiner puts it, would compel people to reject such programs altogether. Finally, Gardiner surmised that the government could not use its capital works program to prioritize public housing because it cannot be disaggregated from other infrastructure costs.

So long as you say public housing cannot be any more a priority than schools, sewer systems, and roads, you can help ensure it *never* becomes a priority by burying it under everything else. In other words, the government in 1960 found ever more complicated reasons to refrain from building substantial public housing. Just one year after Lawrence Heights was opened, the *Toronto Daily Star* reported that not a single unit of new subsidized public housing was to be built in 1960 ("How Metro Fails" 1960, 2). Thirty-eight housing units were added to Lawrence Heights in 1961, far beneath the thousand per year that Metropolitan Toronto Council promised. The council did its best to pass the buck, blaming the shortfall on lacking fiscal support for these developments from Ontario and the federal government. At the municipal, provincial, and federal level, public housing appeared to get superseded by other budgetary considerations.

Apart from being vigorously protested by members of the Lawrence Manor subdivision, the initiation of Lawrence Heights also required significant negotiation between multiple parties. Let us again cite the chair of Metropolitan Council to the minister of public works, who said of Lawrence Heights in 1960:

> This project, being of the magnitude which it is, encountered very substantial resistance from residents living in a pretty wide area adjacent to it. The Metropolitan Corporation in conjunction with Central Mortgage and Housing Corporation and the Department of Planning and Development carried on extensive negotiations extending over about two years with a number of ratepayers' associations, the Planning Board of the Township of North York and the Municipality of North York before the local municipality would approve the rezoning incidental to the project. (Yardhouse 1960, 2)

After it opened in 1959, Lawrence Heights was, as we have seen, populated by a tenant base of predominately low-income Western

Europeans, most of whom came from the United Kingdom. Lawrence Heights provided 1,081 units to low-income families chosen through an application process. The entirety of the project cost $13 million to build, with the CMHC covering 75 percent of the costs, Ontario paying 17.5 percent and Metropolitan Toronto paying the remaining 7.5 percent. Upon opening, rents varied between $60 and $90 monthly, depending on the size of the unit and the tenant's total income.

Design and Layout of Lawrence Heights

The design choices applied to Lawrence Heights reflected conflicting notions held by public officials. On the one hand, its layout was meant to incubate within the tenant base attitudes of self-reliance and middle-class docility, typified by heteronormative nuclear families. The housing was built to be close-knit, with ample green space. Such designs accorded with planning ideas from people like Ebenezer Howard, Lewis Mumford, and Catherine Bauer Wurster, which had achieved conventional status by the postwar years. Their thinking, as Jane Jacobs (1961, 20) puts it, was that "the street is bad as an environment for humans; houses should be turned away from it and faced inward, toward sheltered greens. Frequent streets are wasteful, of advantage only to real estate speculators who measure value by the front foot." People could be pushed to adopt the healthy behaviours characteristic of the middle class so long as their environment was structured to make that possible. On the other hand, such beliefs were tempered by expectations that the same tenants could not, in fact, be reformed at all and would have to be closely monitored by government authorities and walled off from outsiders, who had to be protected from them.

These criteria, for instance, mirror the prescriptions for slum clearance and urban renewal in the 1934 Bruce Report. Slums were to be substituted by public housing sites that would involve

> construction of a varying mixture of single-family dwellings, duplexes and apartments. All of the dwellings were to be built on the periphery leaving the central area free as green space and playgrounds for children. In addition to reducing land coverage occupied by buildings, there were to be no through roads in the interior of the project. (Brushett 2001, 113)

While making a toast during a gala luncheon, Herbert Bruce expressed how slum dwellers can be *rehabilitated* by placing them in a new environment:

It seems to me that the only availing remedy in Toronto is a planned decentralization which will take the outmoded factory away from our congested central areas and substitute for it on the outskirts a new modern building. That would permit workers to establish their homes convenient to their work in surroundings where their children would learn by experience that grass is a green, living and loving carpet, and that there are really and truly other and livelier flowers than those of the lithographed calendar that hangs on the cracked, crumbling and soiled wall of a murky room into which the sun's rays have never penetrated. (Brushett 2001, 104)

Thus, public housing officials indicated that slum conditions produced immoral and troubled inhabitants who could be reformed by putting them in newer, healthier environments. However, the fortress-like designs of the public housing structures and intensive surveillance of their inhabitants suggested government officials doubted whether the "environment or individual morality" was responsible for generating slums (Brushett 2001, 185).

These conflicting attitudes permeated the design and layout of Lawrence Heights and had major impacts on the people living there. CMHC architect George Wrigglesworth originally wanted Lawrence Heights to include "twelve-story cruciform buildings in the Le Corbusier style" intended to counteract the crowdedness, dirtiness, and pervasive immorality that was considered endemic in industrial inner-city spaces

Apartment housing and courtyard in Lawrence Heights (photo credit: Ryan Kelpin)

Row housing in Lawrence Heights (photo credit: Ryan Kelpin)

(Sewell 1993, 103). Le Corbusier, who like Ebenezer Howard saw "city streets as unfit for human beings," envisioned an ideal city of towering high-density skyscrapers, lifting people off the ground level, which would be reserved for parklands and the occasional cultural centre (Jacobs 1961, 342).

The complexes that were built had a density of "ten units per acre, and even though that density could easily be built as detached houses on thirty-foot lots, many units are located in three-story walk-up structures. Others are in row houses, set in blocks of six or eight units, and still others in four-story apartment buildings" (Sewell 1993, 103). A set of semi-detached and single houses comprise the rest of the units, altogether sheltering approximately 4,600 people ("Limit on Income" 1966, 8).

In *Life in the Heights,* W.R. Delagran describes Lawrence Heights in functionalist terms:

> It has only limited access from the north, east and south. The western approach passes through a well-established middle-income area and is sealed off to road traffic at the border between public and private homes. There is nothing here that is calculated to arouse the interest of anyone travelling the main traffic arteries. A cursory examination of a

map, however, shows it to be an anomaly in the suburbs. This is confirmed by the visitor, not because of unpaved streets, shoddy homes or absence of landscaping. These features so often associated with low-income housing are conspicuously absent, in fact the apartments and homes have been arranged with more imagination and more concern for their occupants than the average suburban tract. (1966, 1-2)

The real difference, as Delagran sees it, is that the buildings reflect a settlement pattern not exclusively dictated by the value of the local real estate.

Houses and courts are interspersed with open space. The roads are winding and wider than the average street so that visibility is good and traffic accidents are few. First impressions make it easy to classify these dwellings with their painted panels, coloured walls and remarkable sameness as "barracks living," but this is a superficial view, for the buildings are not structurally different from any other. (Delagran 1966, 2)

But by the early 1960s, the tone had already started to shift from enthusiasm to disparagement. One report says Lawrence Heights and Regent Park now represent "the old look in public housing," a "huge project that is a community in itself and unto itself, tending to shut in people who live there and to shut out the people who don't" ("New Look in Low-Rent Housing" 1961, 7).

Public policy not only managed to isolate Lawrence Heights tenants from outsiders, but it also harmed the capacity for people living there to have close access to needed services. A major problem was the bisection of Lawrence Heights into a western and eastern side by the Allen Expressway to link automobile traffic between North York and inner-city Toronto. According to one observer, because Lawrence Heights was split in two by the expressway, roadway access was further limited, hampering the neighbourhood's "ability to develop as a cohesive borough … The school board deepened the fissure, says [former city councillor Howard Moscoe], by bussing kids from Lawrence Heights to schools remote from the area while closer facilities went wanting for students" (Pratt 2004, B3).

This bussing policy, too, reflects the eugenicist mindset of governments officials as regards their treatment of low-income public housing tenants, mirroring their similar treatment of Indigenous Peoples. In their view, if children from so-called defective tenant families are overly clustered in the classroom, schools will not work effectively. Such policies, which date back to the early 1960s, had lasting damage on facilities in Lawrence Heights like the Bathurst Heights Secondary School, which closed in June 2001 due to lacking enrolment, with Moscoe suggesting "the less official reason was to eliminate the school's bad reputation" (Pratt 2004, B3). In a sense, eugenics got refracted into the content of the bussing policy.

The Allen Expressway was also wound into plans for the Spadina Expressway in the 1940s and 1950s, where enthusiasm for the latter gathered steam by 1959 (the same year Lawrence Heights was opened) and was

> to be a roughly ten-kilometer stretch of controlled-access highway connecting the new northern and north-western suburbs with the city core. Its northern terminus would be at Highway 401, an inter-city expressway built by the provincial government in the early 1950s across the entire metropolitan area, so the Spadina was intended to serve intercity travelers going in and out of Toronto as well as metropolitan commuters coming in and out of downtown. (White 2014, 33)

Members of the Lawrence Manor Ratepayers' Association loudly supported this plan. The group spearheaded a movement to get other ratepayer groups join in an all-out fight for its approval. Saul Cowan, chair of the association, was quoted by the *Toronto Daily Star* as saying that without the expressway, North York would be a perpetual dormitory suburb that would never grow and flourish on its own, remaining a place only where people travel through to get to Toronto ("Plan Fight for Spadina" 1962, 8).

Concurrently, a campaign called Stop the Spadina was being mounted by a group of Torontonians who pressured the government to halt the building of the Spadina Expressway. The trajectory of this campaign revealed a parochial streak among some prominent voices within its membership. Of the voices that comprised the Stop the Spadina campaign, Toronto resident Jane Jacobs was one of the loudest. Jacobs joined other academics and professionals to oppose the Spadina Expressway on the grounds that it would have "dumped a great deal of traffic into the heart of many Toronto residential neighbourhoods," including Jacob's own neighbourhood, the Annex (Wellman 2006, 219). In *The Death and*

Life of Great American Cities, Jacobs writes:

> Theoretically, city expressways are always presented as means for taking cars off of other streets, and thereby relieving city streets of traffic. In real life, this works only if and when the expressways are well under capacity use; left unconsidered is the eventual destination, off the expressway, of that increased flow of vehicles. Instead of serving as bypassers, expressways in cities serve too frequently as dumpers. (1961, 366)

The Stop the Spadina campaign helped persuade Ontario "Red Tory" premier William Davis to kill the expressway planning by June 3, 1971. He is quoted as saying:

> If we are building a transportation system to serve the automobile, the Spadina Expressway would be a good place to start. But if we are building a transportation system to serve the people, the Spadina Expressway would be a good place to stop. (Wellman 2006, 219)

But for all the concerns that major voices like Jacobs had for keeping vehicular traffic and pollution low in residential neighbourhoods in the downtown, she and others involved in the Stop the Spadina movement seemed to have little to say about what the Allen Expressway did to people living in less advantaged districts like Lawrence Heights.

For that matter, the only completed section of the Spadina Expressway is what became the Allen Expressway. Chronically congested with moving vehicles, the expressway "slices through the Lawrence Heights neighbourhood like a traffic-heavy maw" (Mehler-Paperny 2010). Writing in *The Local*, a Toronto-based magazine, Shawn Micallef (2020) says the divide formed by the Allen Expressway created its own mythology, with the west side called "America" because it had no resources and underserved housing and the east side called "Canada" because it had a relatively greater number of public schools, as well as a health centre, a recreation centre, and other amenities. The fact that the area was bisected, says Micallef, hindered the mobility of residents, who had to travel north and south as opposed to east and west. A city planning report says bluntly that "Lawrence Heights has never overcome the physical barrier presented by Allen Road's trench" (City of Toronto 2017a, 2).

Lawrence Heights tenants were forced to live with the negative impacts of urban and suburban sprawl which precipitated expressway construction, in part because there was a limited amount of non-market housing in the postwar years that could be made available for struggling families. Comparatively, the construction of market-rate housing was ramped up significantly in the inner suburbs in places like North York. This was a development borne out of structural advancements over the 1970s and 1980s that positioned Toronto as the country's primary business and financial centre, a move that corresponded with Ontario superseding Quebec as Canada's most economically dynamic province. Jon Caulfield (1994, 42) describes metropolitan growth in Toronto as consisting of a plethora of high-rise developments, rising office towers, and expressway construction in the inner city, with concurrent and rapid urbanization of the outskirts, where "farm fields became subdivisions, shopping and industrial malls replaced pastures and woodlots, and highways sliced through once-drowsy ravines as apartment towers rose beside them." Caulfield then zooms outward, identifying larger aggregate forces dating back to the nineteenth century that helped precipitate these local events:

- A rise of entrepreneurial Toronto banks
- Development of northern Ontario resource industry and shift in foreign investment flows away from Europe into the United States with Toronto as head-office and primary Canadian outpost
- In the late twentieth century, Toronto becomes the Canadian headquarters for corporate administration, international finance, and commercialism
- Major fiscal investments in public and private investments in housing construction Ontario funded public works to strengthen urban-industrial economic base and municipal authorities used zoning and planning instruments to stimulate growth. (1994, 42-43)

These ingredients made Toronto's metropolitan growth a national magnet for capital and labour. Suburban sprawl, expressway construction, and even public housing became newfound reservoirs of value.

As for Lawrence Heights, it was soon derided in bureaucratic reports as representing failed ideals. A 1967 report for Metro titled *A Proposal for the Introduction of Social Services into Low-Income Neighbourhoods with Specific Reference to Public Housing Projects* says the following:

Recent research in Lawrence Heights has made it abundantly clear that the social aspects of public housing have been seriously neglected. Although there were very few complaints about the accommodation or actual physical layout, the respondents' expressed considerable apathy towards the general quality of the population living here. A more careful selection of people admitted to public housing would no doubt go a long way towards correcting this situation, but it leaves the needs of the most desperate unmet …

Selection control has its place but an adequately staffed Social Services Unit would increase a projects capacity to contain and help those who require it, i.e., those who need more than adequate shelter to cope with their problems … There are many who will argue that such a specialized service is unnecessary — all it would really succeed in doing would be to set a project population apart and make them different. The subscribers to this view give lip service to the myth of equality.

"Actually," the report adds,

the argument is designed to maintain the status-quo and keep them in a situation offering limited opportunities. It's ridiculous to argue that low-income populations have the same job opportunities, that they are as well-fed, clothed and provided for medically. The children cannot hope to enjoy the same educational, cultural and recreational chances of their more affluent counterparts in the middle-income homes. Giving these families the opportunities available for the middle income should therefore be our long-term goal. (Delagran 1967, 1)

As reported in the *Globe and Mail*, in 1969 Lawrence Heights was targeted for a pilot project in social action meant to "improve" its image and *its people* through social programming, painting and judo classes, science clubs, and the like. These enterprises were organized through collaborations between social service agencies, tenants, "boards of education, the National Council of Jewish Women, Lawrence Heights Family and Recreation, Big Brothers of Metro, North York Public Library, Seneca

College of Applied Arts and Technology, Girl Guides, Brownies, Boy Scouts, Venturers, Visiting Homemakers Association, other schools and manufacturers outside Lawrence Heights" (Carson 1969, W1). The same story refers to "the toolmakers, truck drivers, married university students and single-parent families of Lawrence Heights" and their timidity about feeling the "glare of publicity," and who expressed shame about living in a neighbourhood "rated low on the social scale" that they were forced into on account of being unable to afford market-rate housing. A member of the Lawrence Heights Judo Club was quoted as saying that judo classes are "important for the community that has to overcome the attitude that people in subsidized housing lack skills because they can't afford higher rents."

Journalist Ron Haggart (1964, 7) wrote an editorial in the *Toronto Daily Star* claiming that the stigma attached to public housing tenants is rooted in a misunderstanding held by people who mis-associate Toronto-based public housing as being "welfare-housing," of the kind he associates with "ghettoes of the south side of Chicago and the east side of Manhattan" rather than being occupied by working-class wage-earners who cannot afford shelter without assistance. Another important point, though, is that people associate *welfare* with social assistance that is purely for low-income people. Tax breaks for the affluent are a form of welfare, as are housing subsidies for homeowners. Once a person is perceived as a welfare recipient, they are easily construed as having failed to measure up and conform with middle-class expectations. Overcoming these stigmas proves challenging, to say the least, where narratives like these from decades ago could appear in a newspaper today.

Interviews conducted with early Lawrence Heights residents in 1966 by Delagran for *Life in the Heights* share the views of some who feel appreciated because of being provided better shelter than they had before. Others describe feeling alienated and developing an inferiority complex:

> About 75 percent of the respondents who "migrated" like it better than where they lived before mainly because of the superior accommodation … Some desire to live a quieter and less public life than is permitted here; others see the area predominately populated by alcoholics, mismatched couples, ill-suited parents and loud, rough-tongued children and teenagers who do not seem to be attached to anyone. (1966, 13)

Delagran says that for some of these tenants, the move to Lawrence Heights involved being separated from friends and relatives and isolation from facilities they have grown to accept as part of a community, e.g., hospital clinics, cheap shopping, movies, and good economical transportation. Lawrence Heights "made them aware of being set apart; being different from those who live on an ordinary street. Encounters with 'outsiders' often confirmed their fear of living in a 'camp' or 'jungle' where an inferior breed of person lives" (12).

These emotions were not rooted in paranoia or conspiratorial thinking. In 1960, Deputy Police Chief John Murray spoke during a meeting of the League of Frightened Mothers, a gathering to protest speeding and "hot-rodding" around Lawrence Heights. During the gathering, Murray critiqued the parenting skills of public housing tenants in the area, saying they let their children race around like bunny rabbits without any supervision ("Kids Run Free Like Bunnies" 1960, 1). One member of a delegation attending a conference on social welfare in 1970 remarked to the *Globe and Mail* about Lawrence Heights, after having toured it, saying she doesn't "know how anybody could live in this, I'd go batty" ("How Could Anybody Live Here" 1970, W4).

Another story from 1972 centred on participants in a dressmaking workshop conducted in the Lawrence Heights Community Centre, with one student pushing back on negative images of the area, saying "it's so lovely and clean here" (Carter 1972, W3). Everyone in the class agreed, however, about the pervasive loneliness plaguing Lawrence Heights, with one saying there should be sewing classes available to tenants "in every (OHC) project. There are too many people around here who spend too much time alone. They'd be better here doing something than spending 10 days in 999." The number "999" is a reference to the former Ontario Hospital at 999 Queen Street West in Toronto, designed to treat patients struggling with mental illness. At its opening in 1850, it was called the Provincial Lunatic Asylum, before being re-named several times. In 1871, it became the Asylum for the Insane and then the Hospital for the Insane in 1905, before becoming the Ontario Hospital in 1919.

Collectively, these testimonies from early Lawrence Heights tenants speak to a shared commitment to persevere and live well despite the obstacles posed against them. They lived largely isolated from outside communities in an environment that officials designed under the conflicting assumptions that it could rehabilitate them into self-reliant persons while also keeping them under close government supervision. These actions by the government are emblematic of prevailing settler colonial relations. As with the treatment that settlers inflicted upon Indigenous Peoples, where the latter got coercively fitted into a social hierarchy that would help keep them on the margins of society, public housing tenants occupying Lawrence Heights were similarly living under oppressive government control.

CHAPTER TWO

Race, Oppression, and Struggle

They treat you like you don't exist in society when you are on the outside. But on the inside, you are home.
— Lawrence Heights resident (Pratt 2004, B03)

Mid-century public housing developments like Lawrence Heights reflected what was, at the time, the apex of modernism and the techno-utopian ideas associated with it. Defined by efficient straight-line design principles, as opposed to classical ornateness and extravagance, high modernist architecture gained popularity in parallel with the rise of Fordism[2] and related strategies for mass production predicated on scientifically organizing the labour process to render workers into better functioning machines. Correlatively, the form and function of the home was to complement the modernist structuring of the working day, where efficient design facilitates the daily social reproduction of (generally male) workers with every other family member playing their defined role. This idea of the home as a "machine for democratic living" influenced the design of public housing, and planners, using environmentally deterministic reasoning, thought that low-income families would conform to a middle-class ideal defined by whiteness, patriarchy, materialism, and affluence.

When these ideals associated with modernist architecture got applied to public housing districts like Lawrence Heights, they became infused with similarly hierarchical notions suggesting that the occupants must be perpetually warehoused, socially programmed, and deemed incapable of rising out of their low status in the social hierarchy. Such planning and administrative practices are, furthermore, underpinned

---

2   A common definition of Fordism "is a system of mass production combining the new technological innovations of the early twentieth century which accelerated the pace of manufacture, particularly the assembly line, with a managerial ethos encouraging greater efficiency in the organisation of work" (Watson 2019, 145).

by settler colonial relations, which are set on stripping away Indigenous land rights, replacing them with white European property rights and capitalist social relations, and barricading the associated hierarchical order from whatever threatens it.

As with Indigenous Peoples, early occupants of the public housing units in Lawrence Heights similarly found themselves pressed to the margins of society. Despite the common perception of the postwar years in Canada as being a high point for redistributive public policy, the government's priorities remained centred on delivering assistance to those capable of affording privately owned detached homes, improving their access to insured mortgage loans and zoning lands to create new subdivisions. Given their de-commodified status, public housing programs were marginalized from their beginnings, and, as explained below, any notion of expanding them further would be quickly negated.

People residing in the existing public housing supply, including Lawrence Heights, found themselves living in oppressive conditions. As this chapter documents, once Canada's immigration policy widened, people from more ethnically diverse backgrounds with limited resources began emigrating to Toronto and found themselves with narrow options for affordable housing. Those who were shuttled into an already stigmatized Lawrence Heights dealt the problem of struggling to make ends meet while being simultaneously pressed into a precarious societal position on account of being racialized. Racialization is defined by Robert Miles (1989, 75) as a "process of categorization through which social relations between people [are] structured by the signification of human biological characteristics in such a way as to define and construct different social collectivities" (cited by Owusu-Bempah 2014, 39). The casting of non-white, low-income public housing tenants into racialized groupings has inextricable links to racist colonial imaginaries and pseudo-race sciences that affix "immutable" characteristics onto Indigenous and (primarily) Black and Brown people, such as predisposition to criminality and possessing low intelligence.

This chapter connects a series of historical threads to bring us later in the book to a fully fledged explanation of how Lawrence Heights became a revitalization target. These threads include the degradation of Canada's public housing program, the parallel widening of immigration patterns in Toronto, the subsequent racialization of the tenant base in Lawrence Heights, and the increasingly oppressive living conditions experienced by tenants. The news media has helped shape a mostly degradative image of this neighbourhood, defining it by drug dealing, crime, and poverty. Rather than being given access to necessary public resources, the predominately racialized tenants in Lawrence Heights have instead contended with a well-funded police force. The more privileged segments of the city, meanwhile, see a negatively skewed image of a neighbourhood that they already shun and avoid. These are manifestations of what Robyn Maynard (2017, 3) defines as anti-Blackness, referring to government funded violence applied towards the "erasure of the Black experience." Underlying these temporal events is the same tension introduced in the previous chapter — government policies and social programming rooted in euthenics.

These issues are fleshed out in four sections, the first of which gives a brief accounting of the troubled state of Canada's public housing program, touching on legislative changes that helped stall what was an already meagre initiative. In the second section we explore key political developments in the late twentieth century that stimulated wider demographics of migrants into Canadian cities, including Toronto, where those possessed with fewer resources became progressively overrepresented in public housing districts like Lawrence Heights. We investigate the precarious situation facing newly racialized public housing tenants to struggle to find well-paying jobs in places like Toronto at a time when post-industrialism began taking hold. The third section presents sources documenting mistrust and mistreatment expressed towards the tenant base in Lawrence Heights by local authorities and what appears to be disproportionate support lent by officials towards neighbouring homeowners in Lawrence Manor. Relatedly, the fourth and final section looks at how an increasingly racialized tenant base in Lawrence Heights has been intensely stigmatized by the news media, the police, and resentful public authorities who blame these same tenants for not transitioning into the middle class like supporters of public housing envisioned. It is the fomentation of these conditions that helped render Lawrence Heights into an ideal target for "revitalization."

Canadian Public Housing Under Fire

Several developments that happened in the spectrum of Canadian public housing policy at the turn of the 1960s help explain how the community in Lawrence Heights became undermined and progressively more stigmatized by the wider public sphere. In 1969, the federally commissioned Hellyer Task Force critiqued "the physical adequacy and quality of life" in large public housing projects (CMHC 1987, 10), concluding that public housing was poorly designed and isolated from surrounding communities that wanted little to do with it. Despite more federal aid for increasing the public housing stock, "the number of low-income families, individuals, and elderly people in need of assistance remained high. There were increasing social problems being experienced in large-scale projects, prompting a sustained anti–public housing reaction from the public" (10). Subsequently, the government withdrew from expanding its public housing program, instead prioritizing non-profit and cooperative housing, which made better use of private funds.

National Housing Act amendments in 1973 permitted the federal government to directly fund, without provincial involvement, the building of third-sector housing, which is taken up by non-profit housing corporations. The preferred method of providing housing for low-income families was reformed through these amendments, which ushered in a wave of social housing construction with a focus on smaller non-profit-based housing. Where did this leave the public housing program? Following an evaluation between 1969 and 1974, the National Housing Act was revised in 1974, decreeing that the existing public housing stock would continue to be managed by provincial authorities.

Just as the federal government decided to not support the expansion of public housing programs any further, the Ontario government was met with public consternation from wealthier neighbourhoods, such as Lawrence Manor, in Metropolitan Toronto when it proposed to expand its own public housing supply. Suburban homeowners protested about "projects being built near them, and councils have grumbled about swelling welfare rolls, burgeoning school population and demands for social services for what have always been considered city problems" ("Public Housing at Whose Expense" 1966, 7). The OHC began gradually steering away from building public housing after 1976, largely due to the public's negative perception of existing housing projects. Such stigmatizing views of public housing would, as well, get progressively welded onto similarly prejudicial assumptions about racialized communities where residents are politically and economically disadvantaged. Residents of Lawrence Heights would come to experience these prejudices viscerally.

Lawrence Heights in Focus

Looking at the course of events by which Toronto became a so-called "global city" in the later decades of the twentieth century helps us see how Lawrence Heights' changing demographics became reflective (over time) of bigger tectonic shifts in immigration patterns and policy, capital flows, labour market trends, and barriers to housing affordability. To start with, two major periods of mass immigration shook up the demographic profile of Canadian cities. The first, as we saw earlier, was a wave of European migrant farmers attracted to the offer of land by the federal government in the early 1900s, which opened the western half of the country. The second wave of migrants flowed into Canada from the 1950s onwards, beginning with Europeans until barriers were lowered to people from Asia, Africa, Latin America, the Middle East, the Caribbean, and beyond.

The barriers were a product of Canadian immigration policy having "overtly distinguished between preferred and non-preferred races from 1876 until the 1960s" (Thobani 2000a, 16). This discriminatory hierarchy categorized "preferred races (initially British and French, and later, other European nationalities) and non-preferred races (from Asia, the Caribbean and Africa)," which limited access to citizenship until the 1960s and 1970s (Thobani 2000b, 36). Canadian immigration policy switched in the late 1960s "from a preference for 'white' immigrants to a points system based on criteria such as educational qualifications, occupational skills, and language ability. [The 1967 Immigration Act] allowed people from all countries of the world to apply for entry to Canada, regardless of ethnic or racial background" (Murdie 2008, 3).

Similarly, the passage of the 1971 Multiculturalism Act was intended to encourage and facilitate full participation in Canadian society by "cultural minority groups" (Dewing 2009, 3). Beyond its officially stated purposes, this turn in Canadian immigration policy towards multiculturalism was supercharged by the "increased demand for both high- and low-skilled employees in the emerging service sector, more emphasis on family reunification and humanitarian migrants, and reduced immigration from Europe" following the region's post–WWII economic recovery (Murdie 2008, 5-6). Sunera Thobani (2000a, 18) refers to how

> the discourse of "cultural" difference has come to encode "racial" difference, and to signify membership in the national/

racial community … The [Immigration Act] expressed a reorganization of processes of racialization in a period when increased immigration from the third world had become critical to providing the "cheap" labour needed for economic expansion. The category "immigrant," meaning literally a geographical "outsider" in the first instance, continued to be ideologically defined by the [Immigration Act] as a "social" and "cultural" outsider to the nation: the racialized category immigrant drew upon the historical status of non-preferred races as outsiders, and re-codified it as immigrants who were to remain "outsiders."

The Immigration and Multiculturalism Acts helped advance a racial hierarchy that became naturalized through the officialdom of government legislation. In this vein, migrants from preferred and non-preferred parts of the world could be put through a process to obtain citizenship in exchange for providing surplus labour for capital.

The effects of these broader changes in immigration policy and labour market trends became pronounced in Toronto, which by the 1960s was undergoing a transition from a former industrial hub to the "global city" that it is now. This watershed moment saw the city undergo a post-industrial makeover and become increasingly gentrified. The labour market gradually catered more to white-collar professionals than to blue-collar workers, moving away from providing industrial warehousing and wholesaling employment towards retail and finance, insurance, and real estate–based services. Major banking centres and retail got built up in the downtown core, with greater employment and demand for central-city dwellings pushing up land values and stimulating the de-conversion of what was formerly plentiful multi- and single-occupancy homes into condominiums. Industry subsequently migrated out of the core towards inner suburban municipalities like North York that were no longer defined by agricultural production and farming.

Immigration patterns fluctuated too. In the early twentieth century, Jewish, Italian, Portuguese, and Chinese migrants tended to settle in Toronto's inner city, with places like "the Ward" near the Old City Hall being a once bustling hub for Jewish and Chinese merchants (Murdie and Teixeira 2003). Beginning in the late 1940s, the Ward became reshaped by private development with a slice of publicly owned lands set aside for new civic spaces. Construction began on the New City Hall and

Nathan Philips Square in 1955, gradually erasing the Ward from existence, effectively streamlining the resettlement of Jewish migrants away from the inner city into segregated suburban enclaves and stimulating the relatively more forceful displacement of Chinese families further north near Queen and Spadina, which became the new Chinatown by the year 1970. These events became a facsimile of the proliferation of condominiums throughout Toronto's downtown and reflected a trend of gentrifiers coming to favour neighbourhoods that were former areas of rapid growth for Asian and European migrants. The population living in the downtown core, for instance, doubled by 200,000 residents between 1976 and 2016 (Ross 2017, 302-303).

Migration and settlement patterns among predominately low-income individuals and families also changed, with such new entrants tending to settle in Toronto's inner suburbs and on the city's outskirts rather than in the inner city. There is a multi-sided explanation for what was a dramatic change in the spatial distribution of migrants. Beginning in 1971, a gradual dispersal of lower-waged employment opportunities moved from the inner city to the suburbs, coinciding with the gentrification of inner-city neighbourhoods, which made affordable housing in adequately serviced areas no longer an option for most newcomers. Looking at the Yonge Street Corridor, which refers to property located on or in close proximity to Yonge Street, the "longest street in the world," there was by the late 2010s a proposed sixteen hundred stories of (mostly) luxury condominiums as brownfield investments were planned for that area, raising the concern of Toronto's chief planner, who wondered aloud if redevelopment in the area needed to be paused (Ross 2017, 202–3).

There is variance in terms of migrants' access to housing, especially among Asians, including lower-income refugees from Vietnam and Sri Lanka, relatively well-educated entrants from India and mainland China, and wealthy Chinese from Hong Kong and Taiwan, who more easily become homeowners in suburban districts compared to these other groups (Murdie and Teixeira 2003, 152-153). Relatedly, there has also been a historical tendency for migrant groups settling in Toronto, particularly "European Jews, Italians, Portuguese, and Greeks," to become spatially clustered "where most of their cultural and religious institutions, businesses, and services" tend to be located (Murdie and Teixeira 2003, 148). Between 1971 and 2006, groups of lower-income migrants from different parts of Africa, Central and South America, Asia, and the Caribbean also became spatially concentrated in the cheaper-to-rent high-rise apartments and public housing districts in Scarborough, North York, northern Etobicoke, and in inner city Toronto.

Migrants in this situation sought cultural and socioeconomic proximity to each other and to escape racial discrimination, particularly from inner-city gentrifiers who were hostile to the ethnic diversity that Canada's multicultural turn was intended to celebrate (Hulchanski 2010, 21). Stefan Kipfer and Jason Petrunia (2009, 119) note that by 2000, 80 percent of Regent Park residents were persons of colour, with people living there since the 1970s having to cope with the worst effects of

> economic restructuring (the loss of unionized manufacturing jobs, the growth of low-wage, casualized service, and sweat-shop jobs), unaffordable housing markets (caused gentrication and land rent inflation), and neoliberalizing shifts in public policy (including shrinking housing subsidies and inreasingly stringent criteria to calculate RGI eligibility). As a result, in 2000, most Regent Park residents belonged to low-income, underemployed or welfare-dependent families, a significant portion of whom were led by single women.

With modernist public housing construction stalling after publication of the 1969 Hellyer Report, Torontonians possessed of limited means would find themselves facing compounding housing affordability problems. The private sector essentially abandoned rental housing construction beginning in the 1980s, though some multi-family cooperative and non-profit housing continued to be erected with federal assistance (August and Walks 2018, 126). Toronto underwent a major recession in the early 1990s, "and by the end of the decade rental construction was not enough to keep pace with the loss of units from demolition, and condominium conversion" (126). Many low-income racialized migrants, eager to settle and start new lives in a wealthy city like Toronto thus found themselves confronted with new internally erected barriers in the form of unffordable housing.

Ostensibly positive immigration policy initiatives exacerbated precarious working and living conditions faced by low-income migrants, particularly Caribbean women, settling in Toronto. The federal government initiated three successive policy programs: the Caribbean Domestic Scheme (1955–1967), the Foreign Domestic Workers Program

(1981), and the Live-In-Caregiver Program (1992), a revised version of the Foreign Domestic Workers Program, which began in 1973 (Darden 2006, 153). Such programs function as recruitment devices for migrant labourers to live and work in Canada but also restrict Black men from the Caribbean in favour of single Black women, requiring them to disconnect from familial roles as caregivers in their own families and become "resources that nurtured white Canadian families" (161–62). Caribbean migrant women became a readily exploitable source of labour relegated to these spheres of work, helping fuel the production and circulation of capital. Simultaneously, their presence as members of domestic labour programs gets wound into the fiction of Canada as a bastion of liberal multiculturalism that is hospitable to Global South workers that it invites into its borders.

Lawrence Heights experienced a migratory flow that mirrored the broader immigration patterns accelerated in the city. Table 2.1 shows changes in the ethnic origins of Lawrence Heights tenants between 1971 and 2011. The data shows answers from respondents in the corresponding census tract (5250286) for Lawrence Heights. Although census tract 5250286 does not fit strictly within the boundaries of Lawrence Heights, it does give us a rough picture of the area's demographics. Census respondents from the British Isles are put in a single category as they encompassed a dominant proportion of people in this tract, as revealed in the numbers from 1971, before steeply dropping over the following decades until 2011. The ethnic category "Black" was no longer present in the statistics from 2006 onwards, which helps explain the boosted numbers in the "African" and "Caribbean" categories.

Like in other public housing neighbourhoods in Metropolitan Toronto, the ethnic origins of Lawrence Heights tenants became increasingly diversified between the 1970s and 1990s. Before the passage of the 1967 Immigration Act and 1971 Multiculturalism Act, immigration policy was driven by the principle of "ethnic suitability," which established a hierarchy of migrants, with those higher up the chain gaining entry over those below them, starting with British and Americans, Northern Europeans, Southern and Eastern Europeans, and an effective restriction of people from Asia and Africa (Ralston 1999, 34). The number of Europeans in Lawrence Heights remains high relative to the other groups, but people from the Caribbean, Latin America, Africa, and Asia begin climbing from 1996 onwards.

Table 2.1 Changing Demographics in Lawrence Heights (1971–2011)

Demographic Category	1971	1986	1996	2006	2011
British Isles	1795	680	200	415	315
European	1895	1720	1620	1920	1830
Indigenous	5		10	10	95
*Black	35	210	690	370	355
Caribbean			60	290	505
Latin, Central, and South American	30		115	110	230
African			230	695	490
Arab and West Asian			45	20	120
South Asian			80	45	215
East and Southeast Asian			130	290	380
Total	3730	2610	3180	4165	4535

Note: Numbers drawn from archived census data. Percentages calculated by author. Data from Computing in the Humanities and Social Sciences.

The flux in immigration policy, real estate developments and economic growth helped precipitate greater ethnic diversity among people living in North York. Before the end of WWII, North York had a measure of cultural and racial homogeneity in that it was made up almost entirely of Methodists, with the British being the largest population. Thousands of newcomers poured in after the war, including "Italians, Germans, Poles, French, Dutch and Belgians, Russians, Ukrainians, Scandinavians, Asians, and other Europeans," spurring greater diversification along ethnic and religious lines (Hart 1968, 274). Moreover, the Yorkdale Shopping Centre's opening in 1964 prompted more immigration into towns like North York, which was, as explained earlier, commonly described before the war as a refuge for white Protestant farmers.

Rising numbers of African-Caribbean tenants in Lawrence Heights became a cheap source of exploitable labour for the industry and service sectors in Toronto who also tended to lack "the resources to buy a house or move into private rental housing" (Murdie et al. 2006, 16). The lack of financial resources narrowed these groups' range of choices and ability to pay for affordable housing. The problem was worsened by structural changes that made Toronto into a "global city," affecting the phasing out of manufacturing and industry, and phasing in of services, tourism, and rising gentrification pressures in the inner city. The flow of low-income African-Caribbean families into Toronto became a fixture in the relationship between visible minorities, immigrants, and multiple forms of deprivation experienced in emergent pockets of poverty and distress in the inner suburbs "populated principally by these groups," with public housing complexes in North York and Scarborough being prominent examples (Ley and Smith 2000, 42).

Public housing districts controlled by the OHC, which the MTHA ran as the administrative body at the local level, saw Black households become considerably overrepresented between 1971 and 1986 compared to the rest of the Census Metropolitan Area (Murdie 2002, 445). This outcome relates

> to the relative recency of black Caribbean immigration to Toronto, the disproportionate number of female-headed single-parent families within Toronto's black population and supply, cost and discriminatory constraints within Toronto's rental market. The most likely explanation for the observed concentration of Afro-Caribbeans in suburban MTHA housing is a form of "constrained choice" that emerged in the 1970s when newly built public housing units in the suburbs corresponded with a demand from recently arrived Caribbean immigrants for low-cost rental housing. (Murdie 2002, 445–46)

With constrained choice, those most desperate for housing are encouraged to accept the first offer for affordable housing. Those who are more financially secure, meanwhile, can wait longer and obtain better housing. Such trends increase "the odds of poor visible minorities of each group ending up in the lowest-cost, least-desirable neighborhoods from which they cannot afford to escape, including in social housing in the inner suburbs" (Walks and Bourne 2006, 274). Toronto, meanwhile, adopted the slogan "Diversity Is Our Strength" in the late 1990s. This message promoted the growth model for a "global city" that requires vast numbers of low-wage workers commuting from inner suburban housing to do jobs throughout the six administrative districts that together constitute Toronto post-amalgamation. By this point, Toronto's inner suburbs became the "ports of entry for new waves of non-European immigration" (Keil 2002, 592). These workers were seen as integral sources of surplus labour and were overrepresented by visible minorities, who tend to struggle to move out of lower-cost neighbourhoods.

Political Struggles in Lawrence Heights

The Canadian government adjusted policy in the 1960s and 1970s to safeguard and fasten shifts in the relations of production through widening migration flows. A reactive effect was to help change inner-city spaces into magnets for tourism, services, and real estate capital, with an accordant re-distribution of lower-cost housing and settlement of disadvantaged workers to the outskirts of the burgeoning "global city" version of Toronto. Simultaneously, treatment of the tenant base in Lawrence Heights by government officials became steadily more repressive.

Over the 1970s and into the 1990s, Lawrence Heights' tenant base was drawn from diverse regions, including the Caribbean, Latin America, West and East Africa, across Asia, and Europe. While global in this sense, the neighbourhood nevertheless remained geographically isolated, thanks to a design scheme, to borrow the language of euthenics, intended to fashion its residents into model citizens. These design choices included segregating the populace and minimizing the chaotic hustle and bustle of street life in inner-city slums, as people like Le Corbusier envisioned.

The housing structures that comprise Lawrence Heights sit in courtyards that possess the only entry and exit points onto Varna Drive, which serves as a twisting distributor road (Beradi 2018, 27). The layout of Lawrence Heights exacerbates its separateness from the outside:

> Unlike the grid pattern that is used across the rest of the city,
> the roadways in Lawrence Heights are a labyrinth of twists

and turns, dead end-streets, and cul-de-sacs, giving way to the moniker "Jungle" or "Jungle City." The neighbourhood is designed around a series of open spaces and parkettes, which are linked together by footpaths that diminish pedestrian contact with public streets. (Beradi 2018, 27)

Despite being geographically isolated, Lawrence Heights residents have persistently fostered a shared sense of community and institutions of self-governance amongst themselves. The area came to be equipped with a community centre, food bank, health centre, public schools, churches, and parks. Such amenities, however, were only developed through significant social struggle. Over a decade had passed since Lawrence Heights was opened in 1959, for instance, and its tenants still lacked access to doctors and adequate medical care (Hollobon 1970, 12).

Out of desperation, tenants formed a committee in 1970 to investigate ways to get a medical clinic opened in the neighbourhood. The committee's chair, a long-time Lawrence Heights tenant, struggled to get her husband immediate help after he suffered a heart attack at 4:30 one morning. People living in Lawrence Heights during this period often took their children to Sick Kids and adults to inner-city Toronto hospitals, a problem complicated further by the fact that their homes rested in a two-fare transit zone, where a trip downtown and back cost extra money, and they had to rely on buses that stopped running at 6 pm weekdays and never ran on weekends. They could otherwise go to Northwestern General, with North York Branson and North York General Hospitals sitting at roughly the same distance, but since none of these are teaching hospitals, they suffered staffing shortages and prolonged wait times (Holloban 1970, 12). The committee began consulting with doctors, social workers, nurses, and union leaders to try and carve out space for an approved clinic to be set up, following examples of community clinics in Saskatchewan and Sault Ste. Marie, which had been established by the United Steelworkers of America. After a two-year span of committee meetings, the putting forward of policy briefs, and seeking development space, the Lawrence Heights clinic opened in July 1972 in the health room of Flemington Road Public School.

Political organizing among people in Lawrence Heights was a feature of daily life from the get-go. In 1959, for instance, the first tenants moving into Lawrence Heights were suddenly faced with soaring heating bills. The bills were disastrously expensive for these low-income families. Many tenants failed to pay, and the Consumers' Gas Company promptly cut their supply. One family described shivering in their home, illnesses plaguing them throughout the winter, and doing the laundry by boiling water on the electric stove in a saucepan after the washing machine broke down and not having the money to pay for the repairs ("Tempers Rise with Gas Bills" 1959, 8).

The Lawrence Heights Tenants' Association (LHTA) was formed during this time, with one of their first actions being the submission of a brief to the oil and gas provider, helping their neighbours get their power supply reinstated and affording them breathing space to settle their debts. The MTHA told the *Globe and Mail* that it withheld from intervening on the heating bill issue out of concern that it would sap tenants' initiative and create dangerous precedents. By 1959, the LHTA's membership provided caregiving to ailing tenants and organized recreational activities for adults and children in the area. An undated document from the Toronto Municipal Archives describes the constitution for the LHTA:

> To carry on activities designed to assist the welfare of its members ... To carry on social activities to extend the friendship and acquaintances of the members ... To establish connection or relationship with other groups or organizations interested in the welfare of our association ... To eliminate juvenile delinquency in Toronto by providing good healthy entertainment ... To acquire and maintain a Community Centre ... To function solely as a non-political, non-partisan, non-sectarian association ... General membership may be accorded to any person who is a tenant of the Lawrence Heights Project ... To see that existing membership is satisfied ... To visit the sick, and assist to dispense good cheer ... To be responsible for seeing that recreational facilities and activities are provided for the children of Lawrence Heights ... Promote and report all favourable happenings to the newspapers, periodicals, etc. (LHTA n.d.)

Beyond these responsibilities, the LHTA was also set up to liaise with neighbours in surrounding privately owned subdivisions, such as Lawrence Manor, whose own ratepayers' association had so vociferously argued against the building of public housing in their vicinity. At first,

LHTA members were sharing space with similar groups at Flemington Road Public School but found themselves burdened with high fees charged by the local board of education. Eventually, the MTHA figured that Lawrence Heights deserved a community centre that would be comparable to other centres commonly found in other housing developments of the same type. The new community centre was built with support split between the provincial and federal governments and was to be administered by the MTHA.

These archived stories might give the impression that a holistic relationship arose between tenant-led organizations and the government that worked akin to a well-oiled machine. A social service consultant with the North York Board of Education was interviewed by the *Globe and Mail* in 1970, describing the relationship between public agencies and Lawrence Heights tenants in positive terms, saying that the agencies are "not going around doing things for people but working with them to make things possible" ("How Could Anybody Live Here?" 1970, W4). One may be inclined to think that social reformists did, in fact, believe that public housing tenants could be reformed, that they could ward off the pathologies given to slum dwellers and join the middle class. In this vein, Lawrence Heights tenants embrace a similar profile as homeowners in Lawrence Manor, who fit the bill as so-called responsible citizens.

Other archived sources, though, paint a more complicated picture of the dynamics between the government and tenant-led efforts to create arrangements for self-governance. In 1970, a resident of Lawrence Heights and member of the Ontario Federation of Citizens' Associations advocated that the OHC take steps to turn management of public housing projects over to tenants but said that the OHC was "offering only powerless positions on housing advisory boards" (Allen 1970, 15). Political officials in Scarborough and Toronto said they "distrust many tenant and neighbourhood associations" (15). Similarly, the Metro Housing and Social Services Committee chair concluded that "most local associations have no legitimate claim to speak for people they say they represent" (15). A coordinator for Lawrence Heights Family and Child Services spoke up during a Senate poverty committee hearing at Flemington Public School on March 10, 1970, attended by clergy, politicians, counsellors, and police officers, pressing the government to "supply needed capital — no strings attached — to community activist groups, to people who want to tackle their problems their own way" (Szende 1970, 8). Denouncing the government further, the speaker decried their endless consults "with the poor," where they limited their time and attention for those tenant representatives who made it onto the boards of agencies. These examples reveal how advocates for self-governance in Lawrence Heights during this period ran up against a government that insisted they required paternalistic treatment.

When Lawrence Heights tenants challenged the authority of the government, they risked being threatened with eviction. In 1970, the *Toronto Daily Star* documented a public complaint by tenant representatives in Lawrence Heights and five other public housing projects in Metro that the OHC was pressuring them into signing new leases with no room for negotiations ("Public Housing Tenants Protest Harassment" 1970, B3). Objecting tenants drafted their own lease, says the report, which would prevent eviction without reason and allow them to hire contractors to do home repairs when the OHC refused.

Some government officials were sympathetic to the concerns of tenants in OHC-controlled public housing districts during this period. A 1979 letter by three elected members of North York City Council, including the familiar Howard Moscoe, sent the following to the minister of housing:

> We are writing to protest the procedures that have recently been introduced by the Ontario Housing Corporation wherein OHC residents are subjected to a degrading process of verifying their total monthly income. Under these regulations, if copies of cheques are not provided, this can result in an automatic termination of their tenancy. The source of income form that OHC is providing for its tenants is reprehensible. Its content would appear to suggest that all OHC tenants are neglecting to declare their entire income. The onus of proof is being transferred from OHC to the tenant. It is as if all tenants are assumed guilty until they prove that they are indeed innocent. Surely, the Ontario Housing Corporation can come up with a more humane way of dealing with tenants, without impinging on their personal freedom and human dignity. (Moscoe, O'Neill, and Foster 1979)

Many low-income families were forced to apply for a limited number of public housing units. Those fortunate to pass the application had to rely on the government for shelter and were then treated punitively as wards and not just as receivers of short-term help. This situation worsened as tenants were progressively drawn more from diverse regions outside Europe, compelling them to struggle also against racism.

People in Lawrence Manor who exercised their political rights to participate collectively in civic matters were treated markedly differently. They were not repressed or dismissed in the same fashion as their counterparts in Lawrence Heights. The social concerns that most animated these ratepayers' association members tended to revolve around proposed real estate developments. Their objectives were to mobilize their resources and authority as *respectable* citizens, homeowners, and taxpayers to keep out any developments that compromised their perceived interests.

In late 1979, the North York City Council and Ontario Municipal Board both approved amendments to a bylaw that was intended to remove restrictions on group homes for people living with addiction and ex-prisoners, including parolees and probationers, which had not previously been permitted operate in North York. The Joint Housing Committee of the Metro Toronto Branch of the Canadian Mental Health Association (CMHA) and the Community Resources Consultants (CRC) of Toronto gave a presentation to a hearing of OMB on October 17, 1979, praising the City of Toronto for its support of the bylaw amendment and Metro Council's commitment to "to permit the adequate provision of all residential care facilities through as-of-right zoning in all areas permitting residential uses" (CMHA/CRC 1979, 3). Implementing the bylaw was intended to ensure that people living in North York should be able to access rehabilitation and parole programs, as well as group home placement in their own community.

The Lawrence Manor Ratepayers' Association was having none of it. In December 19, 1980, their secretary, Judith Fine, and the group's leadership sent a letter to the clerk's office for North York, linking their fears of group homes with their rejection of Lawrence Heights, referred to below with the eponym of "Ontario's largest housing complex":

> Regardless of the merits of the Group Homes themselves, we would note that our area is already carrying more than its full share of institutional buildings, from general public services to Senior Citizens Developments to the *largest Ontario Housing*

complex in the Province. This housing complex has given our community a great deal of trouble with vandalism, robberies, abuse of children, etc., and we are in constant contact with the police over some such matter (sic). We feel it would be unfair to further burden our area with additional problems, which Group Homes invariably create. (Fine 1980, emphasis mine).

These ratepayers had long insisted that their objections to real estate developments, including those intended to assist struggling persons and families, are rooted in concerns over higher density and damaged property values. But they have proven to be just as opposed to sharing space with anything or anyone that represents the familiar spectre of urban disorder, and any appearance of tenement living, crime, and disease.

Archived letters dating back to the early 1980s, as well, detail acrimonious exchanges between the leadership of the Lawrence Manor Ratepayers' Association and Howard Moscoe, who was at that time the councillor of Ward 4 in North York. The source of their disagreement lay in a development proposal put forward in 1981 by the Tridel Corporation to build an apartment building for seniors at the southwest corner of Bathurst Street and Prince Charles Drive, otherwise referred to as the Saranac Neighbourhood. Moscoe (1983) wrote to the Lawrence Manor Ratepayers' Association executive, noting their concern about not being involved enough in deliberating the proposal and iterating to them that he intended to fully involve them in these discussions. In a reply to Moscoe dated June 13, 1983, Eleanor Rosen, president of the ratepayers' association, decried Moscoe for forcing the development proposal down their throats while demanding to "know when we wiped our asses." Rosen remarked that it is unnatural for a politician associated with the New Democratic Party to favour the developer's interests over "the people" and concluded by demanding that Moscoe cease negotiating with Tridel and suggesting he "get professional help" (Rosen 1983, 1).

Other archived files speak to the insular attitude shared by politically active ratepayers in Lawrence Manor. Possessed with the status of being organized property owners who pay taxes, these ratepayer association members pressed the local government repeatedly to heed their recommendations when making decisions about development that would affect their surroundings. The Lawrence Manor Ratepayers' Association's Redevelopment Sub-Committee presented a report to the

North York Planning Board dated March 17, 1981, discussing proposed high-density housing for the Saranac Neighbourhood by a company called Rayel Construction Ltd. The report details potentially negative impacts on dwellers in Lawrence Manor. Its authors warn that submitting to developer-led pressures to redevelop lands with low-density apartments into higher density housing could result in the inner city losing needed rental housing stock by building it in the suburbs and negative impacts on the living standards of adjacent single-family homes.

In this same report, the ratepayers present two scenarios for what the area will look like by the year 1990, with Scenario A based on North York facilitating "managed change" and Scenario B based on "rapid fragmentation." Scenario A draws a sunny picture of Lawrence Manor a decade into the future, with no high-rise buildings "walling-in" the district and little conflict between generations — with change being mostly confined to additions made to the existing housing stock. Scenario B is dystopic. It describes a "canyon of high rises" plaguing Lawrence Manor, bad-blood between the "high-risers" and the "single-detached," roiling parking space conflicts, vandalism, property damage, worsening traffic, and recurrent battles raging between condominium developers and owners of single-family homes, who resent the disruptive change, leading more people to "quit the area."

The ratepayers conclude their report by asking officials to follow the planning staff recommendation that the application put forward by Rayel Construction get deferred until the North York Planning Board could properly assess the area's composition, lest they invite Scenario B to take shape. For these ratepayers, Scenario B would be like the plot of the 1979 movie *The Warriors,* where every gang in New York descends on a single turf. Only in the ratepayers' imagined storyline, the "gangs" are high-rise developers and marauding condominium dwellers collapsing onto a sleepy suburb.

A subsequent North York Planning Board meeting, held on April 8, 1981, was attended by numerous officials and area residents supporting the Lawrence Manor Ratepayers' Association's goals. During that meeting, a unanimous decision was made to receive and refer to staff the ratepayers' own report. Afterwards, a motion was moved and carried unanimously to affirm the request by Rayel Construction to close out their development application. The successful endeavour by people in Lawrence Manor to get Rayel's application stopped was, in its principle and intent, a repeat of the failed opposition plan they mounted against Lawrence Heights. They simply wanted to avoid being neighbours with another class of dwellers and to hinder whatever they felt might damage their property values. When the government denied the demands from Lawrence Manor ratepayers to quell the building of Lawrence Heights, it was not as if these people took the decision in good faith and were courteous to the newcomers. The literal fence closing off their subdivision from any contact with Lawrence Heights would be a microcosm of the broader stigmas that came to stick on residents of the "jungle."

Oppression and Stigmatization

Institutions outside the government contributed to the stigmatization of Lawrence Heights tenants. The media is worth spotlighting. While the media generally may serve the public good by reporting on events of the day, it has routinely framed Lawrence Heights selectively, influencing how the public understands an area architecturally structured to be cut off from others. Reporters, even inadvertently, can privilege outsiders "over insiders, with the neighbourhood constituted as a problematic space and its residents as passive victims. The effect is to further the stigmatization of an already marginalized neighbourhood , and to accentuate the disempowerment of its residents" (Liu and Blomley 2013, 119).

A review of articles from the *Toronto Daily Star*, the *Globe and Mail*, and the *Toronto Star* between 1970 and 2004 reveal some interesting patterns (see Table 2.2). In my review, the presence of specific themes was recorded when they appeared within articles — in their titles, abstracts, and full text — but the themes were only counted once when appearing multiple times to avoid skewing the results. Several stories, for instance, discussed public policy and government action (and inaction) regarding improving the quality of social services in the area, such as providing subsidized daycare, adequate public education, and anti–drug abuse and crime prevention programs for at-risk youth. Others elaborated on the violation of tenants' rights by authorities, including the police, MTHA, OHC, and Canada Mortgage and Housing Corporation (CMHC). These articles cited members of the community and organizations like the Lawrence Heights Residents' Association and the Federation of Metro Tenants' Association.

A single story explicitly touched on the problems of stigmatization that Lawrence Heights must fight against, especially when surrounding residents have fenced themselves off from it. Although, perhaps

Table 2.2 Themes Discussed in News Articles on Lawrence Heights (1970–2004)

Recurring Themes	No. of Occurrences	Percentage of Total
Gun violence, murder, fear, security	48	19%
Police involvement, raids, sweeps	34	13%
Crime, assaults and robberies, drugs, etc.	34	13%
Government action and policy issues	30	12%
Discussions of race	21	8%
Community meetings	20	8%
Police brutality	10	4%
Troubled neighbourhood	9	4%
Mentions of "jungle"	7	3%
Anger	8	3%
Tenants' rights being violated	6	2%
Safety	6	2%
Low-income families	6	2%
Positive view of the neighbourhood	4	2%
Single-parent families	4	2%
Eviction	3	1%
Lacking social services	2	1%
Two-parent families	1	0%
Stigmatization	1	0%
Total	254	100%

unsurprisingly, media attention tended to fixate on sensational events involving violence and drug use, one report mentioned tenants who were happy to make Lawrence Heights home:

> Just the same, some who make their homes inside the Lawrence Heights fence aren't convinced it's a bad place to be. Aba Alamin, a mother of six in her mid-40s, has lived in the housing project since 1992. Even as she casts an eye across her front yard, strewn as it is with crushed bleach bottles and Tim Horton's cups, she's generous with her praise. "It's a very, very

beautiful area," she says ... "The people of Lawrence Heights are very kind," she says. "You don't see yourself living in government housing when you're here; you see yourself living in a mansion." (Pratt 2004, B03)

More often, stories published between 1970 and 2004 projected an image of Lawrence Heights as a hostile and disordered place.

Black scholars have long documented links between anti-Blackness and the criminalization of racialized persons living in Toronto as well as elsewhere. Criminologist Akwasi Owusu-Bempah explains that as Canada's immigration reforms took shape in the late 1960s, an influx of Black migrants settled in Toronto. Tensions grew between police and Toronto's Black communities after several police shootings involving Black men happened in the late 1970s (Owusu-Bempah 2014, 2). Following an uptick of social unrest in response to these killings, the Ontario government formed the Task Force on Race Relations and Policing, whose 1989 report concluded that racialized Ontarians felt they were unfairly policed and that diminishing public confidence was making policing more challenging (4). Despite the issue of anti-Blackness having been forced onto the Ontario government's agenda, the years 1992–2003 witnessed the average homicide victimization rate among Black people in Toronto at a level five times higher than the overall city homicide rate (6).

It is no accident that such crime rates increased in the late decades of the twentieth century, precisely when neoliberalism came into vogue as a vehicle for capital to wrest greater control over working people in the aftermath of the postwar Keynesian years. In that mid-century period, relatively robust welfare policies and stronger labour rights had temporarily redistributed a modicum of greater wealth and political power towards workers and what was then a bustling middle class. A 2008 study by Rinaldo Walcott and other researchers credited neoliberal public policies as exacerbating conditions of desperation and alienation that ignite violence in Black communities, including "the elimination of employment equity, termination of after-school programs, the closing of recreational facilities, and cuts to social assistance and social housing programs" (cited by Owusu-Bempah 2014, 5–6). Neoliberalism provided policymakers with tools to privatize public assets, reduce social supports, and compel workers to rely more on private sources of credit and service provision to fill the vacuum. While these trends have affected affluent and low-income communities alike, they have axiomatically impacted the latter more intensely.

Anti-Black racism feeds on virulent stereotypes about Black people and criminality, which then get propagated by the mass media and other institutions. Such "stereotypes can consciously or unconsciously shape behaviours, actions and attitudes towards people of African descent" (Mullings, Morgan and Quelleng 2016, 24). Paul Gilroy (1987, 76) notes further that as "Black crime becomes an increasing focus of police activity," it is the media that "become willing partners in fostering the racialization of crime" (cited by Benjamin 2003, 16). The media knows that people tend to be more interested in news that stirs up anxieties, fears, voyeuristic tendencies, and resentments. The more the media focuses on coverage of negativity and tragedy, the more it becomes biased as a medium of the negative where it embraces "abnormality, negativity, crime, or conflict" (Fleras 2011, 13). But this is not a fatalistic situation. Media companies can (and sometimes do) strive to produce more balanced and holistic coverage of complex social issues and to explore reasons for why some communities are more disadvantaged than others, especially those with higher concentrations of low-income, racialized families.

It is important to remember that members of oppressed Black communities share a long history of resisting anti-Black racism, white supremacy, and the material institutions that support their constitutive social hierarchies, whether it be the slave trade, corporate empires, or the police and criminal justice system to name a few. Historian Afua Cooper (2007, 13) writes about Black people resisting slave-trade practices in Upper Canada between 1793 and 1803 by escaping to places in the Old Northwest Territories, such as Michigan, Ohio, and parts of Wisconsin. American writer and civil rights activist James Baldwin (1961, 65) writes that oppressive treatment of Black people by police is performed out a knowing fear of civil resistance to the hierarchies that keep white supremacy functioning:

> The only way to police the ghetto is to be oppressive ...
> They represent the force of the white world, and that world's
> criminal profit and ease, to keep the black man corralled up
> here, in his place. The badge, the gun in the holster, and the

swinging club make vivid what will happen should his rebellion become overt. (cited by Corman 1969, 579)

Years ago, the North York Community House began publishing
a series of digital stories, which included tales from police officers
about the fear they experienced coming into Lawrence Heights. They
envisioned people grabbing them, throwing them down, and taking
their guns. One can see how this fear translates into hyper-vigilance and
resentment, fuelling anti-Black racism on the part of officers seeking to
keep the status quo of police–tenant relations in place.

These considerations reverberate in archived stories about Lawrence
Heights and similarly oriented public housing districts in the 1980s and
1990s. Some of these articles speak of police contact with tenants and
town hall meetings between residents speaking out about police brutality, mistreatment by the government in its position as an obtrusive
landlord, and the need to address what media consumers are encouraged to assume is rampant drug use and illegality. The Lawrence Heights
Community Centre became a venue for tenants and other interested
parties to debate and discuss solutions to these problems.

Part of the increase in stories centring gun violence had to do with
the continuous coverage of a high-profile murder at a bakery in downtown Toronto in 1994 by four suspects who were Lawrence Heights
tenants. The news media justifies coverage of such events because they

*Exterior of Lawrence Heights Community Centre. The mural references the Limitless
Heights Scholarship Program, an initiative that received funding from Heights Development (photo credit: Ryan Kelpin)*

inform readers on matters relating to public safety. But the disproportionate attention paid to such incidents, and their connection to Lawrence Heights, can encourage readers to absorb a one-dimensional view of the community that is characteristic of anti-Black racism. Susan Bennett (2000, 272) says media, government, and academic discourses "have long associated public housing with 'negative archetypal symbols' of . . . high rises, gangs, and garbage" (cited by August 2014, 1163). While images of Lawrence Heights as "disordered" were repeatedly conveyed through news coverage, former Toronto Mayor John Sewell felt compelled to answer for its *failings* — and that we should see it as such:

> What's more, says Sewell, Lawrence Heights was flawed by the good intentions that spawned it. The project was designed to provide starter housing, with the idea that people would stay until they got on their feet, and then move on. "But as we found out," says Sewell, "people don't move on. Particularly if they're poor, they don't have any opportunities to move on. No one (realized) that, in society, there are a lot of people, who, for structural reasons, weren't going to make it into the middle class." (Pratt 2004, B03)

Sewell is right to identify the importance of structural causes as helping prolong the residency of many Lawrence Heights tenants. His assessment that it failed on account of "good intentions," however, deserves further interrogation as to what is meant by the word *good*.

A central intent of mid-century public housing complexes was to provide needed shelter to those who could not afford to buy or rent housing in the private market, which many people would see as being a public good. As John Sewell puts it, such assistance was intended to give recipients a measure of temporary comfort and relief so that they could work towards improving their living situation to a point where they could afford private market housing. What became bound up with this ostensibly "good" intent were a great many prejudicial and paternalistic assumptions expressed by public housing authorities about the people receiving this assistance. Essentially, public housing tenants became — according to Jane Jacobs (1961, 324) — proverbial guinea pigs to be experimented on by utopian minded planners. The experiment became creating a segregated environment that would allow public housing authorities to remould their occupants into successful entrants into the middle class, leading to a full-fledged embrace of euthenics minded planning that would likely fail to meet many people's conception of good intentions.

As to how planners came to embrace segregated public housing and euthenics as well-intentioned policy, Jacobs (1961, 324) sees the answer lying in a commonly held faith among planners in misguided ortho-doxy. Planners, says Jacobs, believed that people who cannot afford to be sheltered by private enterprise must, unlike anyone else, be socially segregated in government-controlled housing based on one statistic: their lacking income. While governments do not normally insist on assuming ownership and management duties for airports, museums, or other enterprises that it subsidizes, public housing is a unique outlier (324). The bureaucracies that construct and oversee public housing com-plexes came to occupy two poles, the first being a heightened fear (and Pavlovian reaction) to any expressed frustration by "their capricious masters, the taxpayers" whenever these constituent members of the middle class find fault in public housing tenants' "housekeeping, morals or standards of amenity" (325). At the other pole, these same bureau-cracies convey arrogance about how they treat public housing tenants, deeming they be segregated and made to live in peculiar conditions that the requisite authorities believe will rectify any presence of slum dwell-ing pathology (325).

Jacobs might have appraised the situation in Lawrence Heights in much the same way. It is a segregated public housing complex that has been owned and managed by public authorities in ways that reveal a similarly arrogant attitude in terms of their treatment of the tenant base over time. "Well-intentioned" public authorities did not opt to merely provide subsidies for people unable to afford private housing but designed government owned and operated structures like Lawrence Heights to warehouse these same people to help them join the middle class. All the while, they isolated and closely managed the tenant base, assuring taxpayers in Lawrence Manor and elsewhere that Lawrence Heights and other segregated public housing districts would remain at a sufficient remove from them.

Sewell's remarks could be amended to say that the government's approach to building, owning, and managing mid-century style public housing was in many ways a failure on account of good intentions being subsumed by bureaucratic arrogance and ignorance. "Because we lack any ideology that puts government as the landlord and owner of public housing in context with the rest of our national life," writes Jacobs (1961, 325), "we have no sense about how to contend with such a thing." Archived letters document frustration voiced by public officials, who discuss their role in Lawrence Heights as akin to being managers of social despair. In 1984, city councillor Howard Moscoe (1984, 2) wrote to the chief of police, Jack Marks, demanding a clean-up of the drug trade in a building in Lawrence Heights, noting that "Ontario Housing has largely washed their hands of the matter, their attitude being that this is a police matter." In a reply, a police staffer says tenants complained about drug trafficking in the neighbourhood and that the situation is "constantly monitored by the Uniform Officers in that specific zone and the plainclothesmen" (Crawford 1984). One can understand how Lawrence Heights, given its isolated status, would become deeply stigmatized as being crime-ridden.

Over time, public officials projected a view of Lawrence Heights as a policy failure, which eventually helped rouse support for those who wanted to tear it down and replace it with new socially mixed real estate via "revitalization." When subsidized housing becomes "revitalized" through public-private partnerships, capital seizes the opportunity to invest in the re-creation of districts that have become widely perceived as dysfunctional and unsafe. Enough people must first believe such an image to be true so that officials can press forward. The more a place *becomes* unsafe in the wider public consciousness, the more willing they are to avoid it, and prejudice and ignorance fill the gaps. The negative image of Lawrence Heights has been rendered through this feedback loop, with the media amplifying its intensity.

Material objectives that fuel anti-Black racism, namely the safeguarding of white supremacy through domination, get masked by the government as policy measures intended to preserve urban security. To this end, Toronto has labelled certain districts as being priorities:

> Following numerous incidences of gun violence, policy officials became concerned with the growing spatial concentration of poverty and the links between poverty and crime. As a result, they designated a number of neighborhoods "at-risk" or "priority" neighborhoods and began targeting these areas for strategic interventions. (Leslie and Hunt 2013, 1172)

The decision to designate thirteen Toronto neighbourhoods as "at risk" was complemented further by a landmark report published in 2004 by the United Way, a major international network of local non-profit groups. This report found that "poverty in Toronto has become concentrated by neighborhood areas more so than was the case 20 years ago," with "high rates of poverty and diversity" noted as indicators (Sriskandarajah 2020, 2). Toronto's inner suburbs in Scarborough, western North York, and northern Etobicoke were perfect containers for low-income people to migrate to as many census tracts include two contrasting urban forms, namely cheaper-to-rent "high-rise apartments on the major arterial roads and single-family, more traditional suburban housing on quieter residential streets" (Hulchanski 2010, 21).

The well-publicized 2005 Boxing Day shooting of Jane Creba became a tragic event that was instrumentalized by the Ontario government to lend added policing support to its urban security agenda when it subsequently put forward over $50 million to combat gang violence. Desmond Cole (2022, 39) writes that in

> Canadian mythology, police exist as a force for good in our communities. But when the media publicizes an act of police brutality, especially if the target is Black, the story changes slightly. We begin to speak more of the necessity of cops. Police apologists remind us what a hard job policing is, and that despite its harms, an armed police force with the discretion to kill is still essential for "peace" and "order."

The neighbourhoods of Jamestown-Rexdale, Jane-Finch, and Weston-Mt. Dennis were identified by officials as ideal areas for a gang intervention program, meant to steer youths away from wayward activities (Owusu-Bempah 2014, 116). The fourth named priority neighbourhood was Lawrence Heights. It was deemed as matching the others with comparable levels of poverty, lacking economic opportunities for young people, and youth criminal activity.

There remains a presence of euthenics as an idea and practice that outside forces have projected onto people living in Lawrence Heights, which can be interpreted as an underlying motivator for public policy decisions. The eugenicist-minded belief that so-called slum dwellers are inherently given to pathological behaviours helped catalyze the push by reform-minded officials to rid Toronto of their presence. But it was euthenics that became the preferred method by which the government was to try and achieve this goal, and building modernist public housing sites like Lawrence Heights were an instrument for doing so. As described in Chapter 1, reformers expressed a duality of perspectives. They felt that poor (pathologized) people *could* be remoulded in public housing that was designed as proper machines for democratic living, and at the same time, they also believed they *could not* be reformed and would need perpetual public management of an intensive and oppressive kind.

When its tenant base became racialized, Lawrence Heights became associated with the familiar stereotypes attributed to housing projects that we hear in countless venues in the public sphere — in the media, in townhalls, and in casual conversations. As these negative stereotypes proliferate, they make anti-Black racist attitudes "commonsensical," buttressing the aims of legislation, policies, and programs that are to have major effects on the futures of people in Lawrence Heights. Statements from public officials and from op-ed columnists declare Lawrence Heights to be a failed enterprise that it is crime-ridden, ill-functioning, and in need of revamping. In 1997, the Community Quality of Life Project was completed through a partnership between the Lawrence Heights and South Riverdale Community Health Centres, and the University of Toronto (see Raphael et al. 1999). The people involved surveyed groups of Lawrence Heights tenants, with numerous youth, adults, and seniors taking part. Their responses are summarized as follows:

- Interactions with neighbours were alternately positive and negative.
- Lack of access to quality social services is a problem.
- Parkland, local schools, and libraries are viewed positively.
- There are concerns about deteriorating housing conditions.
- Racial tensions are present in the neighbourhood and in local schools.
- There are worries about public safety.

These findings may reflect civic issues that are common to many low-income districts, but apart from sounding familiar, they do reflect tenants' frustrations with the direction that Lawrence Heights has taken. To this point, they give us a clearer sense for why tenants are often the loudest voices desiring revitalization, despite their awareness of the challenges it poses in terms of upsetting their daily lives.

Politicians and other decision makers have freely admited that modernist public housing constituted a failure in public policy terms by having segregated low-income people, producing pockets of concentrated poverty. It formally declared a new path forward. The idea now was not to develop housing purely for low-income tenants, fashioning them into machines for democratic living, where occupants would be, figuratively speaking, reassembled into members of the middle class. Instead, the aim of this new redevelopment model was to transplant the middle class alongside the proverbial slum dwellers, placing them both in similarly new and expensive mixed-use developments. In so doing, the government encourages the middle class to colonize Lawrence Heights as auxiliaries for the police and social services. Their role is to act as informal moral authorities to simultaneously *reform* their less advantaged neighbours, while also being the "eyes on the street," as Jane Jacobs says, keeping their co-inhabitants *in line* in a less explicitly coercive manner than do the police — even though they may well interact very little with one another, if at all.

In this scenario, the predominately racialized tenants of Lawrence Heights have indeed been confronted with powerful forces: anti-Black racism, stigmatization, and a government intent on refashioning their neighbourhood in tandem with its private developer partners. As the next chapter shows, the Canadian government's embrace of neoliberalism in the late twentieth century, and its accordant heightened prioritization of social spending cutbacks, privatization of public assets, and the administrative devolution of responsibility over social housing management by the province of Ontario onto its municipalities were to become major drivers for revitalization planning.

CHAPTER THREE

Neoliberalism and Revitalization in Lawrence Heights

Despite the fact of all the things that are fading away around us, the material things that are fading away around us, the anchor is us. We have friends that we've lost but we are here, and we are left here on this earth for a purpose. Because we are the anchors.
— Spoken during a commemoration of the
pre-"revitalization" Regent Park

Social forces and events entwined to help render Lawrence Heights into a "revitalization" target. To start with, the Regent Park revitalization, which began in the 1990s, was publicized as a success story where publicly owned housing became shiny and new through the magic of a public-private partnership. Its achievements could be seen as a victory for those who celebrate the lasting influence of neoliberalism on public policy. While it can generate economic growth, neoliberalism has likewise inflicted damaging impacts upon society. Working people have seen capital absorb greater shares of their incomes, and technology continues displacing workers wherever possible to bring down costs, hammering labour into precarity in an age long coloured by persistent outsourcing, sub-contracting, and suppression of collective bargaining power. In the case of Lawrence Heights, which is comprised of struggling individuals and families, these effects are felt intensely and have been entwined with the destructive impacts of anti-Black racism and other damaging measures taken by governments and capital to hold inequitable social hierarchies together.

This chapter looks at the revitalization plan that was put into action, with euthenics-based reforms and intensive surveillance strategies for the predominately racialized Lawrence Heights tenants repackaged into a mixture that aligned with the precepts of neoliberalism, multiculturalism, and new urbanism, which have amassed an enduring popularity in policymaking and planning circles in recent decades.

Private developer partners armed with masses of capital have joined with revitalization planners in the public sector to destroy modernist postwar public housing and replace it with socially mixed developments. The new structures tend to eschew the inward facing and efficiency-based designs of old. Their appearance mimics the typically expensive developments around inner-city Toronto, with little distinction between the condominiums and townhouses built for TCHC renters and their new market-rate-paying neighbours. Gone is the Le Corbusier–inspired street layout, its original intention to avoid permitting much vehicular and foot traffic from outside the neighbourhood, which was meant to clamp down on the chaotic street-level activity characteristic of the inner-city "slum." Instead, new urbanist-inspired multi-street networks and bike lanes are being built, allowing for higher density, walkability, and smoother flowing traffic in and out of the new housing, commercial businesses, abundant green spaces, and cultural amenities. New developments and enhanced freedom of movement, in turn, help attract the middle class into these formerly segregated areas.

As a set of ideals for environmentally conscious urban planning, new urbanism has cohered with the theory of social mixing to form what has become a formidable paradigm. In late 1980s America, academic fervour for poverty deconcentration became influential in planning circles, its proponents arguing that when disadvantaged people live clustered together with poor quality services and spatially distanced from job networks, dangerous "neighbourhood effects" get produced, with isolation from "middle class role models" and "mainstream patterns of behaviour" leading to the "spread of so-called 'underclass behaviours' via peer influence or 'contagion effects'" (August 2014, 1161). This premise reveals the persisting duality of moral environmentalism, where reformers veer back and forth between attributing so-called underclass behaviours to the structural shortcomings of environments and otherwise to "individual character defects and moral laxity" (1162).

In the United States, the popularity of the neighbourhood-effects thesis helped precipitate the creation of the HOPE VI program, which was meant to deconcentrate poverty through the replacement of public housing sites with mixed-income developments. Such programs arose in the early 1990s, at a time when neoliberalism was enjoying maximal strength in its influence over policy decisions, with governments opting where possible to scale back social programs to combat social problems. Instead of governments, individuals living in concentrated poverty would themselves get mobilized to effect change in their own communities through participation in planning activities. While liberatory sounding, such participation is rigidly controlled by these same governments. The involvement of disadvantaged persons in such activities is typically limited to offering input (e.g., through surveys) on decisions outside their control, administering small local programs, and doing community outreach to bring more people on board with poverty deconcentration initiatives, often to leverage cooperation by the private sector in lieu of more public resources.

The makeup of the Lawrence Heights revitalization is clearly influenced by the neighbourhood-effects thesis. As this chapter shows, after responsibility for social housing was downloaded by the Ontario government onto its municipalities, the TCHC found itself lacking resources to service its public housing supply in neighbourhoods like Lawrence Heights. Thus, the TCHC had a financial incentive to partner with the private sector to rebuild the housing in these areas.

Following the neighbourhood-effects thesis, a major tenet of revitalization planning is to foster tenant participation. In practice, such tenant involvement is directed towards fulfilling bureaucratic functions in service to the local government, including devising and administering local programs (i.e., job training, administering community arts programs, interviewing other tenants). The language of revitalization planning, like that of slum clearance and urban renewal, is similarly configured as delivering benefits to the low-income people it targets. Whereas public housing sites were originally idealized as machines for democratic living that would rehabilitate their low-income occupants, now they are commonly derided as segregated pockets of concentrated poverty. With poverty deconcentration, suddenly socially mixed developments are considered inclusive, healthy, and prosperous. Tenants are allowed to participate in revitalization planning to the extent that they comport themselves to helping deliver on the objectives of the government and its private developer partners, whose aim, broadly speaking, is to better align the neighbourhood with white middle-class tastes and sensibilities.

Relatedly, contemporary urban planning ideals tend to simulate the larger political and cultural climate in diverse multicultural cities like Toronto. In its supposed "global city" formation, Toronto has transformed in response to the loosening of immigration restrictions in the late 1960s, transitioning away from export-focused industry towards a heavily service-based economy that augments the finance, insurance, and real estate sectors. It has become reliant on service workers, many of whom are migrants, who tend to struggle with low wages, limited benefits, and scarce job protections. In this milieu, urban planners tend to push forward appeals to multicultural awareness and the rhetorical need for communities to be inclusive, healthy, green, and planned in a socially equitable fashion. By this measure, public housing sites like Lawrence Heights are being paid newfound attention by the government and capital to the extent that they can be redeveloped with new residential and commercial real estate.

This policy-focused chapter unfolds in four parts. First, it briefly describes the impact of neoliberalism on the direction of policies governing social housing in the context of Ontario and Toronto. Doing so illuminates how certain policy changes, such as the downloading of former provincial oversight of social housing onto cities in Ontario, led social housing providers like the TCHC to pick up the slack and assist Lawrence Heights tenants, only with fewer resources to do so. The second section shows how revitalization emerged as the commonsensical policy strategy for Lawrence Heights and that neoliberalism was an inextricable component of its makeup. The third and fourth sections get us into the nuts and bolts of policies that determined the rebuilding of housing and the physical and social infrastructure in Lawrence Heights, which includes everything from roads to community programs.

Neoliberalism and Social Housing

To make sense of why the Lawrence Heights revitalization plan looks the way it does, it helps to briefly trace the influence that neoliberalism had on the direction of policy that determined which level of government manages Ontario's social housing supply. The 1990s was a critical period in this regard. Policy changes affected Ontario's public housing administration, and these effects reverberated in Toronto. Canada's neoliberal turn became typified by Ontario's governing strategies between 1995 and 2003 under the Mike Harris–led Progressive Conservative Party, which held sway with what it termed a "Common Sense Revolution."

During an interview with Steve Paikin, Mike Harris spelled out his goal for Ontario with the Common Sense Revolution, which among other things, involved getting the government out of the way of the business community:

> In a situation where you're the highest taxed, most heavily regulated, where our private sector job creators and investors are saying, "Ontario is not a good place to do business," you better fix that just as quick as you can. (Paikin 1994)

Though Harris preferred shelter subsidies over public housing, the subsidies themselves dried up after the Ontario government instituted cuts across the board in 1995, despite a steep climb in rents. Milton Friedman, a poster child for neoliberalism, wrote critically of public housing and rental subsidies alike, arguing that they contribute to the paternalization of the relationship between governments and people receiving social assistance rather than encouraging the market to develop more housing where enhanced supply could put downward pressure on rental costs (Friedman and Friedman 1990, 109). But neoliberalism (as a set of policy prescriptions) is processual, unfolding unevenly and differing in content depending on where and when it occurs.

Going forward with the Common Sense Revolution in the mid-1990s, Harris reconfigured the local political infrastructure to make it amenable to the objectives of austerity and intensified the privatization of affordable housing production. In practice, the Harris-led government enabled the shrinking and streamlining of the public sector, including a 21 percent cut in municipal welfare benefits in 1995, hundreds of local governments amalgamated, a reduction of 21,000 full-time provincial social service jobs, and the legalization of sixty-hour workweeks (predicated on an unwillingness to listen to public and private sector union demands) (Keil 2002, 589). These moves followed in step with cuts to "affordable housing income supplements, employment programs, youth recreation service and settlement programs for new immigrants" (Viswanathan 2010, 263). By 1998, the Harris-led government had amalgamated Toronto despite significant public opposition to it. Toronto got implicitly targeted under the pretence that the provincial budget needing balancing (with funding support for big cities being a costly expense) and that provincial income taxes needed to be lowered by 30 percent (Boudreau 1999, 771).

Amalgamation was a strategy ostensibly aimed at cost savings by reducing service overlap in Toronto and surrounding municipalities. J.A. Boudreau (1999, 772) says:

> The rationale was that amalgamation of Metropolitan Toronto would save money by eliminating duplication of services in the former two-tiered municipal structure; it would eliminate competition between existing municipalities and thus free the way for economic growth; and it would disentangle the complex two-tiered structure, thus increasing accountability to taxpayers.

The backdrop that informed the passage of the City of Toronto Act, 1997, into law was characterized by strife and competition between two opposing models for local governance, with the big city on one side and suburban North York on the other. Toronto intended to drive up growth by increasing density requirements for residential developments, enlarging its public transit system, and using property taxes to finance numerous social services, while the suburbs of North York embodied fiscal conservatism. They prioritized car use and wanted services delivered through the market rather than by the government.

Initially, conflict over the City of Toronto Act was intense. Supporters maintained it would attract foreign investment and would reduce service "duplication and red tape," while opposers, like spokespeople for the Citizens for Local Democracy, said that despite the province's authority to alter municipal structures, "it lost its legitimacy because it was rushed through the legislature without prior public consultations" (Boudreau 1999, 774). But the forces supporting amalgamation and the suburban model for urban governance would carry the day, culminating in the 1998 mayoral election victory of neoliberal-friendly candidate Mel Lastman, who swept into office in Toronto after already having been mayor of North York between 1973 and 1997. Ontario subsequently passed the City of Toronto Act (Bill 103) in 1997, facilitating the Metro Toronto–based amalgamation by 1998 and dissolving the federation of Metropolitan Toronto with its six constituent municipalities: City of Toronto, North York, East York, Scarborough, York, Etobicoke, into a single-tier City of Toronto.

The consolidation of these municipalities into the so-called "mega-city" helped precipitate what is now happening in Lawrence Heights.

Amalgamation was fundamentally about disciplining Toronto, which Conservatives painted as a fiscal mess possessed with lengthening welfare rolls, high unemployment, and a real estate market characterized by backroom deals between local officials and developers (Keil 2000, 768). These issues had been exacerbated by preceding events that hit Toronto, like the collapse of its real estate market in 1989, followed by a deep recession in the early 1990s, setting off fiscal crises in all the municipalities that comprised the old metropolitan system.

As told by Roger Keil (2000, 765), the former territorial compromise that underpinned the metropolitan system beginning in 1953, where inner-city taxpayers financed the growth of the suburbs, was reversed following amalgamation in 1998. With the new system, Ontario refused to integrate urban, suburban, and exurban districts into an effective regional governance system, allowing wealthier tax bases (whom the Conservatives did not want to antagonize) in the exurbs to wall themselves off from inner-city concerns (Kipfer and Keil 2002, 241). Concurrently, the province made cuts to its transfer payments on top of downloading costs for social housing, public transit, and other programs onto municipalities, adding more stress to their property tax bases. The Conservatives were laying the foundation for neoliberal policy regimes by rendering the local government less capable of managing its obligations.

Amalgamation did much to further de-democratize the planning process in Toronto. It replaced the former official planning processes that characterized the Old City of Toronto, which was characterized by chaotic public consultations that could stonewall, or at least render it harder for local officials and technocrats to institute change fluidly. What amalgamation did was make it more difficult for everyday citizens to impact the government's agenda. Indeed, under the veneer of removing red tape, amalgamation led to the new Official Community Plan. This saw *select* decision makers — politicians, bureaucrats, developers, business interests, etc. — present a vision for a future "competitive city," which included identifying "priority areas for development," and set "priorities for capital expenditures," culminating in a report titled *The Vision for Toronto* in the summer of 2000 (Kipfer and Keil 2000, 32).

In its megacity form, Toronto became purposed to better attract affluent workers and investors by adopting a "global city" multiculturalist orientation where it could compete with other so-called global cities to attract tourists, fiscal revenues, and the business class. Toronto City

Council fully endorsed the executive decision maker–approved Official Community Plan, which was "required to deal with global economic competition, new municipal responsibilities, and the changing social fabric" and was characterized by "economic development policies, purely symbolic multiculturalism, and revanchist law-and-order policies" (Kipfer and Keil 2000, 28). These policy directions fed the government's appetite for gentrifying inner-city spaces by redeveloping those whose occupants are made to struggle most in the social hierarchy. Jeff Crump (2003, 185) wrote of HOPE VI in the United States that redeveloping under-served racialized communities amounts to recolonizing them by "bringing middle-class European-Americans back to the inner-city," which they fled during post-industrial periods of white flight. Similar practices have spread to Canadian cities like Toronto, where redevelopment strategies are themselves advancing out of the inner city into the inner suburbs. In Lawrence Heights, the middle class is being ushered into an area it has long ignored, likely making it whiter and more affluent. Amalgamating North York and the other six administrative districts into one Toronto became a facilitative tool to make this happen.

At the level of public administration and policymaking, amalgamation was indeed smoke and mirrors. It was formally about making cities larger, more robust, and more autonomous, with the province downloading jurisdictional control over formerly provincial concerns onto these same cities. But amalgamated cities like Toronto did not necessarily have the requisite money to handle new jurisdictional responsibilities. When Toronto began struggling to pay for services, such as public housing, in its post-amalgamation context, opportunities opened for private partners to help while also realizing the aims of the Official Community Plan.

Look at what happened when Toronto assumed responsibility for social housing that was formerly controlled by the Ontario government. The CMHC devolved control over social housing onto provinces in 1996 under the auspices of deficit-obsessed finance minister Paul Martin. Then Ontario passed the Social Housing Reform Act in 2001, putting it under control of municipalities. But even after being made larger through amalgamation, with a streamlined service provision system, Toronto was left with a limited revenue base to pay for these services. A city revenue fact sheet published on the City of Toronto's website in 2016 details the sources of its budget of $11.8 billion, the main one being property taxes, followed by user fees, the Municipal Land Transfer Tax, the Third Party/Billboard Sign Tax and provincial and federal transfers. Cities cannot legally run budget deficits, putting further pressure on them to cut spending.

In the absence of a large revenue base and increased transfers from senior governments, Toronto struggled to support the existing social housing supply after downloading took place, much less build more of it. After its election, the Harris administration cancelled an additional 17,000 units. Minutes from a Toronto City Council meeting from 1999 reveal the city's struggles to finance social housing expenses without provincial support, noting that "the worst predictions of amalgamation are unfolding at this present time, namely the provincial government downloading significant new responsibilities to the City of Toronto without any additional funding" (Toronto City Council 1999, 50). Consequently, local governments have prioritized cost-cutting rather than enhancing publicly funded services. These events are summarized in the following timeline:

- Liberal Finance Minister Paul Martin announces that "housing for the poor" is no longer a responsibility of the federal government.
- Mike Harris–led Ontario passed the Social Housing Reform Act, 2000 (SHRA), formalizing the downloading of public housing management onto newly created 47 local service districts that overtook control from the province.
- Most Ontario-based housing providers are affiliated with municipal governments that lack the taxing authority to create revenues to finance expenditures associated with maintaining the housing supply.
- The SHRA stipulated that local service districts invest part of their funds in the provincial-level Social Housing Services Corporation, which was set up to provide legal advice and management support, stripping resources that could otherwise go towards servicing public housing tenants.
- The TCHC, the largest and most entrepreneurial of these service providers, began selling portions of its public housing portfolio to provide rental space for commercial tenants and transfer parcels of its supply to private developers to build market-rate housing and condominiums (Hackworth and Moriah 2006, 515–16; 520; 522).

What this timeline describes is a process of gridlock, referring to a gradual drying up of public money that should be devoted to servicing public housing. Once public money goes away, private interests can swoop in.

The more service providers feel the squeeze, austerity tends to get prioritized to ease the pressure. Devaluing an existing built environment via gridlock becomes an effective precursor for new waves of investment. As David Harvey might put it, whenever capital gets invested in the building up of a given space or landscape, whether it be public housing, storefronts, a mall, or otherwise, at some point over time that same space must get devalued, with the existing assets becoming depreciated and outmoded enough to make way for a new round of investment, so that more money can be made. Gridlock was evident after the passage of the SHRA by the Harris-led Ontario government. In so doing, Ontario withdrew funds for social housing expenses without any measures in place for local providers to raise more money. "Fiscal and administrative devolution of many areas of regulation and social policy," writes political scientist Greg Albo (2018, 10), "has typically occurred without the transfer of adequate fiscal resources in the federal transfer regime, with the express intent of stepping up market disciplines and social austerity." Provincial transfer cuts made Toronto more cash-strapped, made worse by demands from people wanting infrastructure improvements, particularly for housing and transit (Albo and Fanelli 2019, 271).

Other legislative moves contributed to gridlock. In 2001, Toronto invoked the Ontario Business Corporations Act to establish the TCHC, which operates as an arms-length institution with the local government as its sole shareholder. Under the city's auspices, neoliberalism became the mantra by which the TCHC would manage the public housing that comprises a portion of its overall social housing supply. The TCHC witnessed its growing maintenance backlog and saw devolution and Toronto's amalgamation as a window "to create cost and service delivery efficiencies," "reinvent public housing," and "re-examine the possibility of redevelopment and regeneration" (Lehrer, Keil and Kipfer 2010, 86). Without more tools to raise revenues, development projects become a means to "generate charges and to widen the tax base. Provincial states aided this process by deregulating municipal planning controls" and keeping regional planning bodies unobtrusive (Albo and Fanelli 2019, 271–72).

Michael Prue, former New Democratic Party member and representative of the Beaches–East York riding in Toronto, made a statement in the

Ontario legislature in 2008 decrying the Conservative Party's moves to download social housing responsibility onto local providers, triggering more rapid degradation of the city's social housing stock via gridlock:

> You have to remember that this was a downloaded service of the Harris government that the McGuinty government has had for five years and has done virtually nothing with. The state of repair has decayed over each and every one of those five years to where it is now in an atrocious and abominable state. I challenge any of the members to go into those housing places, to go into Jane-Finch, to go into Regent Park, to go into all of those places where people live — Lawrence Heights — and look at the state of the infrastructure. (Prue 2008, 791)

Prue's account represents the usual jockeying between different party members. The NDP lambasts the Conservative Party, the Liberals double down on these critiques, and the typical defence and counterattacks come when Conservative members take the floor.

Looking at the larger trajectory of these debates about social housing management over a longer timespan, we can discern a gradual affirmation between these political representatives (regardless of party affiliation) on the merits of revitalization, which gridlock helped make possible. Take this quote from former Liberal Party member Peter Milczyn (2018, 6808), who remarked in the Ontario legislature in 2018 that the government must zero in on areas with high concentrations of social housing and

> reinvest in them, to take the old housing stock and, in some cases, refurbish and retrofit what exists, and, in many cases, take the amount of land that is there and create new housing, replace the old housing stock and add more housing to build up those communities.

When the quality of the housing degrades enough, tenants are more likely to welcome the major influx of capital that revitalization brings. An official involved with Pathways to Education describes visiting homes in Lawrence Heights:

> When you go into some of these buildings — and let's say it's thirty degrees plus — and they're trying to keep some windows

open. Some people have their front door open. They're sitting in their apartments in shorts and no shirts. There might be a couple fans going and you begin to see the un-livable conditions in some of these communities. When you hear people tell you stories about how whenever it rains their basement floods. People talk about mould issues within their properties and how long it takes to get those issues rectified. I went into one family's home — and to be completely honest here — one of the things I noticed when I got in the front door, there was it seemed like there were dozens of cockroaches. (Personal communication, October 21, 2020)

Such neglect makes it easier for the government to convince TCHC tenants that tearing down and rebuilding their neighbourhoods from scratch is the common-sensical path forward.

Those pointing to gridlock as a worthy impetus to "reinvent public housing" were further emboldened by escalating discourses in the early 2000s identifying so-called priority neighbourhoods in Toronto. The United Way of Greater Toronto published a report called *Poverty by Postal Code* in 2004 "highlighting a widening gap between Toronto's rich and poor over the previous two decades, and an increasing spatial concentration of poverty" (cited by Leslie and Hunt 2013, 1175). The government started marshalling significant institutional power in 2005:

> The Strong Neighbourhood Taskforce (composed of United Way and the City of Toronto, with the support of the Government of Canada, the Province of Ontario and the private sector) put forward the first and most explicit call for "targeted intervention in specific neighbourhoods" to de-concentrate poverty. (Saberi 2017, 55)

During this same period, in 2005, the news media devoted intense coverage to what it called the Year of the Gun, when stories on gun violence identified participants and victims as tending to live in neighbourhoods of spatially concentrated poverty, juicing up support for government intervention in these areas. Deconcentrating poverty, then, involved officials insisting that they can make low-income, racialized communities healthier through social mixing. The other side of the coin was also about emboldening the white middle class to seize these areas.

These discourses create a type of subjective inversion where vulnerable people *become* threatening people in the wider public sphere, with police intervention being the commonly accepted solvent. Following the events of 2004 and 2005, Toronto officially listed thirteen priority neighbourhoods — areas that the state associates with spatially concentrated poverty — which were targeted for "revitalization" through public-private partnerships between the TCHC and private development firms. The TCHC-led redevelopment of public sites like Regent Park took shape as the blueprint for similar initiatives in the other priority areas.

Settler colonial relations no less undergird the policy strategies for priority neighbourhoods as they do in other avenues. European settlers descended on Indigenous Peoples with the stated intention of "civilizing them," seizing control over their territories, and simultaneously establishing a racial hierarchy. Desmond Cole (2022, 8) writes:

> White supremacy is a hierarchy, with whiteness at the top. Indigenous peoples of the Americas, whose lands have been colonized by white settlers, occupy a low place on this hierarchy — white supremacy is trying to replace them. But Black people, whom British and French colonizers brought to this land in chains four centuries ago, are at the bottom of the ladder.

As a policy strategy, revitalization is as much about reasserting white middle-class dominance over racialized persons, who get blamed for a community's failings, as it is about generating social supports. Public officials and developers will always descend on these disadvantaged areas under a halo of good intentions. Witness this statement from the city about its Strong Neighbourhoods Strategy, which gained approval from Toronto City Council in August 2009:

> In some cases, past decisions to build large public housing communities with limited services and infrastructure have contributed to the marginalization of low-income families and individuals in social housing buildings. Much of this social housing can be found within high needs neighbourhoods where there is a concentration of poverty, coupled with a lack of community infrastructure. Toronto's Strong Neighbourhoods Strategy seeks to strengthen the most disadvantaged neighbourhoods through an integrated,

place-based partnership that connects the three orders of government with local stakeholders to better target community resources. (City of Toronto 2009, 27)

Such declarations are tactful because they envelop the Strong Neighbourhoods Strategy within the logic of social services, where it becomes less about creating a high-profile opportunity for investment — akin to tearing down and rebuilding a home or building — and more about lending a hand to people in need. It gains affirmation from people and organizations who have solid reputations as charitable organizations. Directly beside the above quote is a statement from a social service agency, the St. Stephen's Community House:

People want family-friendly public housing spread across the city in quiet, safe neighbourhoods. Most want to live near conveniences like shopping, good TTC, excellent schools and parks and services such as community centres and libraries. (City of Toronto 2009, 27)

The St. Stephen's Community House is attesting to the viability of the city's plans for revitalization and the intentions and beliefs that underpin social mixing. Here is a charitable organization saying that public housing will be quiet, safe, and family friendly provided it gets relatively dispersed across Toronto. By this measure, people holding negative preconceptions about existing public housing complexes are right to think that way — that these areas, where people are numerous and living too close together, are noisy, unsafe, and ill-suited for family living. Thus, non-profits link up with developers, the media, and officials to gild the plan in Lawrence Heights, shielding it from significant dissent.

"Urban Revitalization" and Neoliberalism

This supportive structure for urban revitalization got neatly wedded to the aims of competitive city governance. To this end, policy developments also arose at the provincial level with respect to altering jurisdictional control over social housing and initiating Toronto's amalgamation. However, these provincial policy moves were complemented by local dynamics that helped thrust the urban revitalization agenda forward. Beginning in the 1990s, and continuing through the 2000s, a scandalous and dysfunctional picture of Toronto's housing market arose that was furnished in part by an urban development machine that eventually was so impugned by local leadership that they were forced to revise it. The reforms called into question the machinery of local government and bureaucracy as the source of the troubles and sought to reconfigure it into a leaner and professionalized system that would efficiently partner with entrepreneurially minded planners, consultants, architects, and developers, while insisting it would be cleaner, more transparently democratic, and cater to a wider cadre of interests than simply their tax base, the homeowners, ratepayers associations, and the business class.

Traditionally, urban development politics in Toronto mirrored what is commonly found in municipalities across Canada. Broadly speaking, at the local level one finds "non-partisan, business friendly politics, weak local socialism, and an orientation towards property and homeowners' interests" (Kipfer and Keil 2002, 231). Toronto's development politics has long had the reputation of being a corrupt sphere of wheeling and dealing. In *The Developers*, James Lorimer (1978, ix) describes Toronto-based developers as being "ruthless in pursuing their business interests" and using tactics "more reminiscent of organized crime than anything else, particularly the developers involved in the rough world of high-rise apartments." Constructing these projects, as Lorimer puts it, saw "fine buildings knocked down, homeowners harassed to sell the houses they lived in for years, tenants used as political hostages, [and] politicians and planners paid off when necessary" (x). During the tenure of Toronto mayor Art Eggleton, in power from 1980 to 1991, city planners remained "preoccupied with 'making deals' with developers and extracting density exactions from the downtown office boom" (Kipfer and Keil 2002, 239).

Rapid residential and commercial development culminated in the real estate market collapse of 1989. A recession followed, creating higher unemployment, stretching social services to their limit, and placing expensive social housing in the crosshairs of politicians and believers in the sanctity and universal benefits of free markets. Once fiscal crises struck the six municipalities that formed Metro Toronto, a window opened up for Tory Mike Harris to get elected as premier of Ontario, setting the Common Sense Revolution in motion by 1995 and stirring a move towards aggressive neoliberalism (Desfor, Keil, and Wekerle 2006, 136).

The fervour for neoliberal revolution at the provincial level filtered into changes in urban governance, as personified by the results of the 1997 mayoral race, when a freshly amalgamated Toronto was called on to choose its new leader. In competition with one another was the liberal incumbent Barbara Hall against fiery conservative Mel Lastman, who had formerly been mayor of North York for over two decades. The *Toronto Star* had described the campaign as being fought over the question of who could fix the city's socioeconomic troubles, including slowing growth, languishing unused industrial landscapes, crime, and shrinking tax revenues. Lastman won handily on a right-wing, suburban-friendly platform, arguing that the road to recovery must not damage homeowners and overburdened taxpayers, while also removing from the city the homeless and other vulnerable groups, who became the targets onto which angry people could direct their resentments about what they saw as a failing city.

Lastman's victory conformed nicely with the aims of Mike Harris, who came into office promising to bring the public deficit down to zero and reduce income taxes by 30 percent. These aims translated into Ontario making aggressive social services cuts, shifting the burden of welfare provisioning onto cities (who relied on newly shrinking provincial transfer payments and property tax revenues), making cuts to education and the healthcare system, stalling further social housing construction, and eventually proceeding with amalgamation. Advocates for amalgamation promised to bring the Toronto real estate business out of the back room and eliminate the corruption. It became the animating event behind the construction of the new Official Plan, which was purposed towards winning a bid to host the 2008 Olympics and redeveloping Toronto's waterfront. The Official Plan was meant to crystallize Toronto's transition to engendering smart growth through redeveloping targeted areas, particularly those with concentrated units of social housing, via a seemingly democratic "visioning" process undertaken by a combination of bureaucrats, developers, planners, business leaders, newspaper executives, union presidents, and non-profit representatives (Kipfer and Keil 2002, 247).

By the latter part of the 1990s, Toronto had re-emerged from the deep real estate slump of 1989, with gentrification creeping towards Regent Park at its north, south, and east sides via encroaching factory conversions, townhouse developments, and condominiums (Lehrer, Keil, and Kipfer 2010, 86). Recognizing the challenges of funding and managing a deteriorating public housing stock amidst these proliferating developments, the TCHC conjured a model to fit Toronto's newfound competitive city paradigm.

In the 2000s, neoliberalism in Ontario shifted from a hard-edged blunt tool into a more technocratic, expertise-driven, and superficially inclusionary process that helped it conform better with the multicultural posture that Toronto had gradually adopted. The Harris Conservatives gave way to the Dalton McGuinty Liberal administration after its 2003 election victory. But it was hardly a blow to the existing order. Inclusionary neoliberalism amounted to Liberals selectively halting "irresponsible tax cuts for a few" while decisively locking in the Harris-era cuts to Ontario's public sector (Albo 2018, 23). In 2005, the Liberals formed the Ministry of Public Infrastructure Renewal to target public assets to undergo privatization.

These trends bled into Toronto, with its priority neighbourhoods becoming prime development targets. Alternatives to the Regent Park "revitalization" were suppressed by the media, NDP city councillors, grassroots organizations, and politicians, including Toronto mayor David Miller (Kipfer and Petrunia 2009, 129). In 2010, Miller provided similar support for reinvestment in Lawrence Heights, and planning for the "revitalization" began gaining traction locally. As a strategic initiative, it benefited from amalgamation and provincial downloading, further hardwiring a commitment to austerity and privatization into City Hall.

The inclination of housing reformers to move low-income families around to wherever new money can be made is expedited by the disrepair in existing housing structures. Harris-led Conservatives won re-election in 1999 and "made more funding cuts to Ontario municipalities for social housing, public transit, and other areas for which cities had shared responsibility with the province" (Maley 2019, 507–08). After the amalgamation and downloading of social housing responsibility, the TCHC was forced to work with less money. A 2008 TCHC report noted that "tenants have complained for years about the woeful state of their units. Since the province 'downloaded' responsibility for social housing to the city in 2001, TCHC has lacked the money to keep up repairs" (Vincent 2008, A8). The TCHC said that the cost of repairs and housing maintenance would rise exponentially if steps were not taken to close the gap between available funding and the level of needed investments.

During one forum in 2011, a TCHC representative spoke to financing challenges associated with resolving the massive capital and repair backlog which threatened to speed up the deterioration of the TCHC's housing stock. According to the TCHC rep, "Every year, despite significant investment, new needs arise, meaning the funding gap will continue to grow unless we find new sources of funding" (2011a). Considering its funding gap, the TCHC instituted the Housing Works Real Estate Investment Strategy, centred on "Repair, Replace, Retrofit and Revitalize." The TCHC planned to apply this strategy to its thirteen priority communities, each of which consisted of townhouses and low-rise units in a "poor state of repair" and all having "intensification potential." Intensification refers to the redevelopment of Toronto's priority public housing districts to add more people and traffic. These forums assist in making "repair, replace, retrofit and revitalize" appear as the viable alternatives to what would otherwise remain a hopeless situation.

The Lawrence Heights plan had three central components: tearing down existing housing and building a new housing supply; upgrading what planners call hard infrastructure (e.g., roads, sewers); and creating social infrastructure, like parks, schools, and community centres. These features became selling points, where not only the housing gets replaced, but a *new social environment* is offered up. In its original form, Lawrence Heights was itself designed to be a *healthy* new environment, a peculiarly enclosed one that would reform its low-income inhabitants, rather than be like other inner-city neighbourhoods, which could devolve into slums. One city report from October 5, 2020, describes the revitalization as lending everyone involved a chance to "create a *healthy* and vibrant mixed-use and mixed-income community where residents have access to quality housing, services and facilities" (City of Toronto 2020, 4, emphasis mine). Creating a healthy environment in Lawrence Heights now involves a reversal, in part because the TCHC's private developer partners want quality returns on their investments.

Putting the Lawrence Heights plan into action involved undertaking multiple phases of study, discussion, and decision making between the TCHC and tenants, local institutions, the Toronto School Board, and other non-profits, with final revision and approval coming from municipal legislative bodies. The first phase of planning saw the TCHC engaging in discussion with the community between 2008 and 2010, culminating in the finishing of a secondary plan in 2011, which was eventually approved, first by North York City Council and then by Toronto City Council.

As to how tenants living in Lawrence Heights feel about the revitalization, a good number of opinions have been captured in the press.

Indeed, the Lawrence Heights revitalization has enjoyed intermittent attention from major media companies. In an article in the *Toronto Star* journalist Donovan Vincent (2007a) cites a recording artist who has lived in Lawrence Heights all their life: "Prime real estate. That's what this is all about." Another article from the same author cites other voices on the subject, one claiming that Lawrence Heights only needs its problems fixed, not a wholesale redevelopment, others expressing fear about developers coming in and taking over, feeling despondent about a plan that they say was approved regardless of how they felt about it (Vincent 2007b). Years later, the *Star* published a piece citing a youth leader from Lawrence Heights: "What I've seen is that there are a lot of residents actually wanting (income diversity) to come into Lawrence Heights" (Kane 2013). While only a sample, such stories give us a flavour of what people in Lawrence Heights have had to say about this project.

Local politicians, too, engaged with the Lawrence Heights plan on behalf of their constituents, channelling it into a campaign issue in some cases. When former councillor Howard Moscoe retired in 2010 from representing Ward 15, Eglinton-Lawrence (the riding that includes Lawrence Heights), a two-member race emerged between Liberal Josh Colle and Progressive Conservative Rob Davis. Colle voiced concerns about the plan but said it would be impossible to stop, having received overwhelming support in Toronto City Council with a vote of 41–3. Davis, meanwhile, claimed the project was so flawed that he would try to reopen the motion for approval if elected (Poisson 2010, GT.4).

Shortly after North York Council unanimously backed the revitalization, councillor Maria Augimeri attended an emotionally charged townhall meeting and accused detractors of the project as racists who did not want to see the lives of Lawrence Heights tenants improve. The detractors, who were part of a group called Save Our Streets, insisted that their objections were rooted in fears that the multi-million-dollar plan would attract thousands more people to the area, jamming traffic flows and overwhelming the infrastructure (Grant 2010, A14). The late Rob Ford, who at the time was running for mayor in Toronto, attended a Save Our Streets rally at one point, vowing to kill the revitalization once in office. Eventually, the now notorious Ford would win the mayorship, but the plan for Lawrence Heights kept pressing forward.

At the planning level, the secondary plan that was eventually approved stipulated major changes to policies governing land use, including housing, utilities (e.g., lighting, sewer systems), and transportation. Lawrence Heights was itself folded into a larger plan for reconstructing the entire area bordered by Lawrence Avenue and sitting on both sides of the Allen Expressway. The Lawrence-Allen Study area comprises several communities; there are sections marked as Lawrence Heights TCHC properties (1208 replacement homes), school sites, Lawrence Square (now called the Lawrence Allen Shopping Centre), avenues, and apartment neighbourhoods. There are also several parks, major retail centres, and public buildings included in the designs.

The scale of this secondary planning area has created openings for expensive private consultants to get involved with the local government to render the area more commercially profitable. Urban Strategies, a global urban design and planning consultancy firm, says on its website that it has "worked with the City of Toronto's Parks, Forestry and Recreation department and Scott Torrance Landscape Architects to complete the Lawrence-Allen Public Realm Master Plan." This master plan for the entire Lawrence-Allen area includes upgrades for road and above grade (above the surface of the ground) infrastructure, water and wastewater and below grade (underground) infrastructure, parks and greenway, and community recreation facilities.

Creating a Vision for "Revitalization"

Beyond the formal planning processes that have shaped the Lawrence Heights "revitalization," a key source of advertising the plan to city planning experts, the real estate sector, and the wider public has been the media. News media, trade publications, and entertainment magazines are routinely instrumentalized to promote government policies and their projects in addition to the usual advertising of commodities and services. Table 3.1 analyzes the content of forty-four news and magazine articles on Lawrence Heights published between 2004 and 2020. The year 2004 marks the beginning of discussions on the Lawrence Heights revitalization in press circles. Recurring themes were identified while reviewing the articles, and each piece was coded whenever its content reflected one or more of these themes. Each code was used once per article to avoid skewing the results.

Several articles raise concerns that added density may put too much weight on infrastructure and could upset the community's social fabric. But just as many articles underscore the diminishing quality

Table 3.1 Analysis of News Articles on Lawrence Heights Revitalization (2008–2020)

Recurring Themes	No. of Occurrences	Percentage of Total
Crime/drug use/mentions of "jungle"	28	63.64%
Positive view of the revitalization	15	34.09%
Officials promoting revitalization	12	27.27%
History of Lawrence Heights	11	25.00%
Concerns about infrastructure stress	11	25.00%
Poor quality of housing	9	20.50%
Negative view of the revitalization	7	15.91%
Residents favouring revitalization	5	11.36%
Residents opposing revitalization	5	11.36%
Total	44	100%

of housing in Lawrence Heights. An even more significant number of articles talked about the neighbourhood's reputation as being dysfunctional, with the implication being that a makeover is warranted (63.64 percent).

It is true that the government has mismanaged its social housing supply in Lawrence Heights, and altering this situation is a needed imperative to realize a better future. And it is true that the government has positioned itself as both the source and solution to the problem — strangling these social housing sites of money for capital repairs and upkeep — and now pushing forward with a socially mixed redevelopment project. It is also a perfect truism to say that disadvantaged people want and deserve more job opportunities and greater access to vibrant businesses, amenities, and improved infrastructure. The government claims that common sense requires that it accomplishes this task using its preferred policy toolkit, bulldozing the existing homes to re-render them palatable for middle-class tastes, enhancing the presence of affluent residents to exert moral authority, and amplifying gentrification pressures. Surely, these are elements of the Lawrence Heights plan that the long-disadvantaged people living there would object to if they had the political power to do so.

"Revitalizing" the Housing Supply

With significant promotional ammunition behind it, the Lawrence Heights Development Plan became absorbed into the bigger Lawrence Allen Revitalization Study, with housing construction as its fulcrum. The entirety of the housing side of this plan is scheduled to take shape over twenty years through the course of four phases of construction, with the centrepiece being the replacement of 1,208 existing RGI homes for the more than 3,500 residents, along with the construction of "an additional 4,092 market condominium and townhouse units" (Heights Development 2015, 4). At the heart of the plan is the idea that the existing public housing supply in Lawrence Heights is to be replaced but not expanded. To expand the supply, so says the TCHC, would be to enhance the same stigmas that have afflicted people living in the original structures.

Phases 1 through 4 of the Lawrence Heights plan involves building a "mix of TCHC and market buildings and townhouses," with Phases 2 and 4 being on the east side of the Allen Expressway, while Phase 3 is on the west side (City of Toronto 2019, 13). Phase 1 construction began in 2015, to be completed over seven to ten years: "The Yorkdale Condominiums, and Yorkdale Condominiums 2 will be the first two buildings constructed in Phase 1. The next components of Phase 1 include 175 market and 57 TCHC rental townhouses as well as a new public Park" (Heights Development 2015, 4). The TCHC's website says planning for phases 2 and 3 is still underway.

Public housing residents are being re-located into new RGI units sitting adjacent to the new market-rate condominiums, but it is misleading to suggest that public housing tenants and newcomers are fully integrated as the market-rate buildings are to be separated from the TCHC units via a common green space or mews. An official with Unison Health and Community Services in Lawrence Heights says that when TCHC residents were made aware of this new living arrangement, they feared being ostracized by those coming in to populate the market-rate units beside them. Social mixing may exacerbate the same kind of isolation experienced by Lawrence Heights residents from Lawrence Manor and other neighbourhoods — the difference being their isolation will be within the community rather than outside it.

Design choices that separate original Lawrence Heights tenants from affluent newcomers conflict with the idea of social mixing, which has been a big selling point of the Regent Park model. Social mixing, further-more, is not a panacea. What social-mixing advocates say is roughly the same thing that urban planners were saying in England in the 1930s, which was that "slum" areas "condemned their inhabitants to 'a travesty of existence'" (Garside 1988, 35). In 1930, a professor of hygiene and public health at the University of Birmingham remarked that "slums produce something more than bad health — they make bad citizens" (35). While planners today shy away from such caustic language, the verbiage of social mixing is still paternalistic and cloaked in environmental determinism, where so-called bad citizens can be re-molded to fit a "healthier" image provided they are made to live closer to the middle class.

In the Lawrence Heights case, each construction phase involves the existing public housing structures being torn down, requiring temporary relocation of residents from each neighbourhood section, depending on what portions of the housing are being rebuilt in each phase. This same policy was applied in Regent Park under the name of "right of return." Right of return proved in some respects to be a bait-and-switch, with some tenants excluded from returning. TCHC staff revised the policy after Phase 1 of the Regent Park plan got underway, stipulating that tenants "had to be in 'good standing' to be able to return with varying definitions of what that meant (can't be in arrears, can't be dealing drugs, can't have 'anti-social behaviour')" (Metcalf Foundation 2021, 16). Some Regent Park tenants undergoing temporary displacement complained that they ended up being moved to far-flung neighbourhoods during construction. A report published in the *Guardian* notes that temporary relocation often stretched on for years, with some Regent Park tenants choosing not to suffer through another move and deciding to stay in their new surroundings instead (Hayes 2016). By the summer of 2021, 375 households had either waived their right of return, moved out of TCHC public housing, or died while being temporarily displaced.

In moves intended by planners to redress the problems of the right-of-return policy between the TCHC and Lawrence Heights tenants, the decision was made to temporarily displace residents to an outside dis-trict or into vacant homes in other parts of the community. The TCHC declared that it will give five months' notice of requirement to move and cover moving costs and that tenants have the right to return to their new units so long as they remain in good standing with no increase in their monthly rental costs. Giving Lawrence Heights tenants the option to stay in vacant units within the same neighbourhood was a sticking point in early discussions between planners, tenants and other stakeholders between 2008 and 2010. Reserving empty units for temporarily displaced Lawrence Heights tenants meant that people already on waitlists for TCHC housing would be forced to wait longer for vacancies.

For persons denied placement in Lawrence Heights units during the construction phases of the "revitalization," it does not help that social housing construction has dried up for decades in Ontario, much less Toronto, leaving a major supply shortage. On its website, the Ontario Coalition Against Poverty says the local government should buy and re-zone lands to build more social housing given that the supply of it has not expanded since the 1990s and that in 2021 waitlists had reached upwards of twelve years or more. De-commodified housing is simply less of a concern for the government and the business community when lands can otherwise be used for more expensive market-rate housing. What makes "revitalizations" so attractive is you have governments willing to sell parts of lands under public control over to private entities, with both sides partnering up to create new housing that is intended to create more growth than the publicly owned assets that were on the land previously.

The process of strangling Lawrence Heights of additional funding helped clear a path for initiating a complex financing scheme that made previous "revitalization" campaigns possible in Regent Park and Rivertowne in East End Toronto (Vincent 2010, A1). One might ask why the TCHC would not just renovate the existing homes rather than demolish them? Officials would likely counter that the money for mass renovations is not available and that the funding and repair backlog is too large. It was former TCHC chief executive officer Derek Ballantyne who said about Regent Park that to simply leave too much social housing concentrated in one place entrenches the same lasting stigmas (Daly 2005, B01).

During the 2011 forum, TCHC staff said that renovation of existing units would not accomplish its overriding goal of correcting lacking integration between public housing tenants and outsiders. Flattening the housing and rebuilding identical looking public and privately owned units, says the TCHC, renders a "mixed community, [improves] connectivity, and avoids creating isolated neighbourhoods" (TCHC 2011b). In 2011, the policy strategy and financing plan for Lawrence Heights came together for review and approval by the city. After the Lawrence Heights plan was folded into the more significant Lawrence-Allen Secondary Plan designs, both of which required approval from the city, official justifications for it by the TCHC were even more bolstered given the money and the interested parties involved.

A significant portion of the money for construction in Lawrence Heights comes from the private developers that form the other side of the partnership with the government. The TCHC put out a call seeking real estate developers, and in 2013 it selected Context and Metropia (now Heights Development) to engage in Phase 1 of the reconstruction. Once Heights Development came aboard, financing the replacement RGI housing units (1,208 total) became possible through "revitalization revenue" since the TCHC's funding gap left it with less money to invest in construction. It would be, says the City of Toronto, the "revenues from private market sales and leveraging long-term financing" that would front the "costs of replacing the social housing units, given that there is currently no existing federal/provincial funding program to support replacement housing capital costs" (City of Toronto 2011, 8). The provincial and federal governments aided this public-private partnership by withholding public resources from social housing providers like the TCHC.

Rather than rely on the city for financial assistance to fund the roughly $350 million for constructing the RGI housing, the TCHC intends to build its replacement RGI housing units using money it

Ongoing housing construction in Lawrence Heights (photo credit: Ryan Kelpin)

New housing developments in Lawrence Heights (photo credit: Ryan Kelpin)

accrues from selling and leasing portions of its lands to its developer partners over the multiple phases of the revitalization. Private market units can then, in turn, get built by developers on the properties they purchase. TCHC-controlled lands are interwoven with tracts owned by the Toronto District School Board and the City of Toronto, which forms a total of sixty-five hectares of publicly owned land within the district comprising Lawrence Heights.

Context and Metropia bring their reputation and building expertise to their partnership with the government, along with significant resources. Metropia's website advertises its team of experienced real estate and investment professionals, its multiple awards, and its involvement in several upscale developments in Yorkville and Pickering, in addition to Lawrence Heights. Context, meanwhile, is a successful firm as well with high-profile projects on its portfolio, including the Library District Condominiums, which overlook Fort York, another mixed-use development called the Market Wharf, located south of St. Lawrence Market in Toronto, and a restoration of the historic Loretto, located farther west in the leafy well-to-do Annex neighbourhood. Context's pedigree is boosted, as well, through its association with Waterloo Capital, a private investment fund with access to capital from selected accredited investors. Howard Cohen, one of the founders of Context, was quoted in the *Toronto Star* as having high confidence that condo buyers would be attracted to the "fantastic location" that is Lawrence Heights, with its proximity to Yorkdale Mall and Lawrence West subway station (Kane 2013).

Comparatively, social housing providers like the TCHC have continued operating with fewer resources since the late 1990s. Without extensive public funding, the TCHC issued a call for proposals so that certain developers — in this case Metropia and Context — could be selected and brought on board to offer their resources in lieu of those that might otherwise come from the public purse, which would be distributed and accounted for by democratic institutions. Heights Development, with its dual-firm structure, does indeed bring significant expertise and money, but this comes with the condition that the new Lawrence Heights is made into a lucrative investment. These developers have extensive investment portfolios, teams of executives, consultants, and other staff who need to be paid and an imperative to generate growth and compete.

Compared to public institutions, Heights Development is mostly sealed off from public accountability structures, which makes sense given that they are corporate businesses and not an extension of the government. Unlike a local city council or non-profit, for instance, little public information about Metropia and Context is readily available. A Google search of either firm yields few results beyond links to their respective websites. Public scrutiny and oversight over the Lawrence Heights plan tend to fall more so onto institutions like the TCHC rather than its private sector partners.

David Harvey (2015, 12:10) argues that one of the problems with making areas more urban is that since the 1970s they have been inclined towards appearing more homogenous, whether you happen to be looking at new residential and commercial landmarks in Sao Paulo, Santiago, Mexico City, New York, or Istanbul. The sleek architectural styles that are being applied to new housing designs for Lawrence Heights resemble similar-looking developments popping up all over downtown Toronto. A few examples include the Canary District and Corktown, King-Parliament, and the enhancing densification of St. Jamestown. Those in charge of the new designs for Lawrence Heights have strategic intentions to make the area mirror inner-city Toronto. Attracting more affluent people by building more expensive housing, retail, landmarks, and amenities is expected to meet the needs of the developers to make this project profitable.

For that matter, Lawrence Heights has long been deprived of necessary services, like grocery stores and banks. Once it gained traction as a "revitalization" target, Lawrence Heights was suddenly talked about by people like Toronto city councillor Josh Colle as having major potential as an under-used space with a strong community. The language of social mixing, as communicated by Colle and others, paints a vision of Lawrence Heights as a healthier and safer neighbourhood that has stronger connections to people living around it. Affluent residents move in, whipping up commercial activity and simultaneously exerting moral authority over social housing occupants, displacing threats to the sanctity of a middle-class lifestyle.

Infrastructure and Financing

The government and its private partners have channelled a lot of resources and planning towards "reshaping" both the hard and social infrastructure within Lawrence Heights. It happens that the area was first built to be a superblock with looping principal streets and cul-de-sacs that were designed to filter people easily into a central park and elementary school. Through traffic was discouraged on these pathways, and a separate web of green spaces and pedestrian walkways were put in place to let children walk to school without crossing a major road. While beneficial for pedestrian safety, the streetscape designs contributed to the isolated feeling of the space. With the revitalization, roadways are to be upgraded to accommodate added density, permitting vehicles to enter and exit more freely. Additional through streets are said to be the necessary solvent.

City councillor Josh Colle wrote a letter in 2018 to the North York Community Council asking for Lawrence Heights to have streetscapes that that allow for better vehicular access in and through the district, but which also allow for enhanced walkability and bike usage. and to make room for landscapes that can support community gardens and greenhouses. Such initiatives are all meant to promote human-scaled urban design, and their incorporation into the revitalization planning speaks to how progressivism and environmentalism have become melded to the agendas of big business and real-estate developers to the extent they can be profitable. TCHC staff members have voiced their commitment to progressive causes, such as developing more green space and cycling lanes in Lawrence Heights to help combat climate change.

In 2010, planners delivered a report to the North York Community Council detailing a public infrastructure plan totalling $240 million for libraries, childcare, and sewers, along with roadway reconstruction, which, when combined with the cost of replacing the RGI housing units ($350 million), amounted to a price tag of $590 million for the entire revitalization, excluding the private market units to be built on the same lands. The TCHC formed its master plan for infrastructure building for all four phases and went about securing funding to complete it. A City of Toronto report from 2010 notes that the TCHC's financial strategy addresses only how to finance the cost of replacing the TCHC-controlled housing in Lawrence Heights, with its price tag of $350 million. The TCHC is to finance replacement of the housing from the sale of the publicly owned lands in the area to their private partners in combination with profit sharing reaped from the sale of new housing. Devising this arrangement with private developers is crucial, says the TCHC, since there was no existing federal or provincial funding programs that would support replacement housing capital costs.

When it comes to financing the new infrastructure costs, though, the TCHC's agenda is murkier. With the Regent Park plan, Toronto assumed the whole cost of social infrastructure, including the building of parks and community facilities, and entered into a cost-sharing agreement with the TCHC to cover hard infrastructure rebuilding (roads, etc.) since the high land values (they sold portions to their private partners) and intensification opportunities permitted the TCHC to foot 40 percent of the bill. To build Lawrence Heights in its original form, the government benefited from purchasing the lands in North York at a bargain compared to more expensive land costs found south in the inner city. But its location in the inner suburbs presented a financing problem that went in the reverse direction when it came to the revitalization. Lawrence Heights is more expansive than Regent Park, which is in the inner city, and has had multiple public and private landowners. The value of the land itself is lower and offers lesser opportunity for intensification as regards redevelopment potential. Until recently, these lands were separate tracts owned by the TCHC, the City of Toronto, the Toronto District School Board, and RioCan, a real-estate investment trust.

An added issue with social infrastructure is that it affects the entire Lawrence-Allen area, which has led to complications over brokering plans for infrastructure building. Who will pay for it when the TCHC's lands cannot be sold to private interests for as much money? With jurisdiction split among multiple landholders, settling negotiations is difficult. The school properties — Baycrest Public School, Sir Sandford Fleming Academy, Flemington Public School and Bathurst Heights Secondary School — are all owned by the Toronto District School Board. The remainder of the lands are owned by private entities, including the Baycrest Centre for Geriatric Care and neighbouring shopping plazas, like the Yorkdale Shopping Centre, the Lawrence Square Mall, and Lawrence Plaza. The school board agreed to coordinate with planners for a long-term vision centred on turning Bathurst Heights lands into a mixed-use site divided between residential units, a new secondary school, an aquarium, and childcare centre. Negotiating jurisdictional challenges with the financing of the infrastructure development is a problem that the city government is dealing with in order that its partnership with the private sector is a fruitful one.

The TCHC agreed with the city to get infrastructure funding, including for new road construction, for Phase 1. Still, each subsequent phase requires negotiation and approval. Toronto City Council decided that the TCHC should submit business plans to public finance officials before each successive phase of the revitalization to determine what is feasible. Announcing these plans launched a wave of public criticism, predominately from homeowners living in the wider Lawrence-Allen area, who complained that their surroundings were ill-prepared to handle the increased density.

Another important aspect of the social infrastructure modules in the Lawrence Heights plan is the development of community support, job training, scholarships, and public arts and culture programs. The developer agreement made between the TCHC and Heights Development for Phase 1 of the revitalization set aside a minimum of $3.5 million for community benefits in the form of scholarships, training, and employment opportunities for Lawrence Heights tenants. At the centre of this element of the planning for Phase 1 has been creating and implementing the SDP, another ingredient adapted from the Regent Park model. Toronto City Council directed public administrators to work in tandem with the TCHC, "Lawrence Heights Inter-Organizational Network (LHION), community partners, residents, and other City Divisions including Toronto Employment and Social Services (TESS), and Economic Development and Culture" to create an SDP for Lawrence Heights (City of Toronto 2010b, 3). The TCHC identifies social development as the requisite key by which tenants will overcome their isolation and social exclusion, predicated often on unfair stereotypes and misconceptions about the neighbourhood.

Initiatives like the SDP stress inclusivity, with residents becoming part of a mobilization of resources and expertise. It is seen as the solution for what gets understood as a plagued group of people who need proper affixing to middle-class ideals through the vehicle of social mixing. The influence of the neighbourhood-effects thesis is evident here as well. Recall that proponents of neighbourhood effects insist that the well-being of people living in concentrated poverty is impacted by environmental-structural factors, such as a withdrawal of social services, but also by the activities of social networks, which can be mobilized to effect positive change. From the vantage point of people who favour neoliberalism as a driver of public policy development, central planning is never the answer as it is incapable of allocating resources to address complex social issues that are best left to impersonal and self-correcting market systems. Social networks comprised of people living in concentrated poverty, say the proponents of neighbourhood-effects theory, can best address their local issues on their own terms rather than having publicly funded social services do it for them. However, their energies get no less controlled by the agenda of the TCHC, its private partners, and the city government, which are principally directed to empowering markets.

Consider the language in the 2012 primary report on the SDP, which was produced in collaboration between the TCHC, the City of Toronto, the Social Development Plan Steering Committee, and other community groups. The SDP, says the report, is an example of planning with "the people," with tenants having been invited to help identify priorities that need addressing (City of Toronto, TCHC and SDP Steering Committee 2012, 3). Beyond ensuring that important grievances receive attention, tenant involvement creates a holistic sounding plan that is said to empower "the people" rather than making it look as if the government is directing how the revitalization will proceed. Take note of the wording in the SDP report, where a *healthy* Lawrence Heights is socially mixed and possessed of mixed land uses and thriving new businesses. The report says to "build a *healthy* community that offers all residents *equal* opportunity, *respect*, and *empowerment*" (iv, emphasis in original). It goes further, saying Lawrence Heights is to become

> a *Healthy* and welcoming community that is supportive to
> all residents, with a sustainable environment and a thriving

economy; *Equal* opportunities to benefit from community assets and services, free from discrimination and oppression; *Respect* for all community members by community members; and *Empowerment*, so that all members are able to participate in our community's decision making. (iv, emphasis in original)

The report offers more specifics along three metrics — improved housing, infrastructure, and employment opportunities:

Revitalization brings us an opportunity to improve Toronto Community Housing's rent-geared-to-income (RGI) housing. It is a chance to create a healthy and vibrant mixed-use and mixed-income community where our residents have access to quality housing, services, and facilities. We envision a neighbourhood where everyone feels like they belong … Green space includes parks, sidewalks, landscaping and green roots. Many green spaces and good physical infrastructure are vital elements for a healthy community. We therefore need to plan to maximize the positive physical and environmental impact from revitalization in Lawrence Heights … Employment is a key aspect of this Social Development Plan. Some of our residents find it difficult to prepare for and access job opportunities. Combined with our Employment Strategy, the Toronto and Social Services' "An Employment Service Plan for the Revitalization of Lawrence-Allen" will provide our residents with services and support to better prepare them for job opportunities. (vi)

With these statements, the SDP implicitly equates Lawrence Heights with concentrated poverty, as being segregated, ill-functioning, and unhealthy. With the revitalization, the tenants living in TCHC-controlled housing will no longer be *sickened* but empowered to work and live well. The ethos of new urbanism and multiculturalism are enshrined in the references to walkability, green spaces, and inclusivity, where mixed-income communities are newly desirable features of formerly segregated public housing sites.

As for its policy dimensions, the broad strokes of the SDP focus on delivering "education/school programs and initiatives, community supports and services for newcomers, health care programs, food security initiatives, accessible legal support, and services that are youth, senior, and gender-oriented" (13). Assisting Lawrence Heights residents with employment opportunities is of prime importance to the SDP's architects. Partnering with TESS, SDP organizers intend to connect

> residents to available jobs and employment services through various forms of communication, including the internet, TESS offices, and local agencies. 2. Offer specific training and education in areas that have consistent job opportunities (for example: customer service, carpentry, electrical). 3. Ensure literacy, language (ESL), basic education, life skills training, and work experience programs are available to whoever needs them. (44)

Looking at the Lawrence Heights SDP strictly in terms of its strategic benefits for officials and decision makers, there is a connective tissue between it and the ideas of neoliberal thinkers like Milton Friedman. In their 1979 book *Free to Choose*, Milton and Rose Friedman argue that public welfare provision is a corrupt enterprise. It compels people to depend on the state as if it were a parent. They lose their desire to work as self-determined individuals and to make a living through cooperative market relations. The idea is to convince people in Lawrence Heights to live up to how the middle class envisions itself. An enforced order of professionalism is required, leading to the appearance of a free society, which in fact requires a good deal of enforced conformity. For developers, the objective is to finish the plan and reap the yields on their investment, and the expense of providing social infrastructure programs and community engagement is a worthwhile cost.

This chapter has fleshed out the policies, political pressures, and activities that have formally set the Lawrence Heights plan in motion. For the most part, its focus has been on detailing involvement in this plan by politicians, bureaucrats, private developer partners, and other official agents who are working to remake this public housing neighbourhood in the image preferred by the government, the business community, and the middle class. In the next chapter, our attention zeroes in on the work being done by Lawrence Heights tenants, non-profit organizations, and various community organizers in the terrain of revitalization planning. We will see how tenant participation gets effectively channelled into doing what the local government requires of them. To a not insignificant extent, the efforts by community members, volunteers, and non-profits gets filtered by the dictates of existing local bureaucratic proceduralism, neoliberal-infused policy regimes, and the interests of the government more generally. At the same time, these tenants reveal a shared commitment to fending off the forces that continue to stigmatize them. They are determined to better their lives and those of their neighbours in the course of their work in the revitalization planning, despite getting heavily assimilated into the machinery that is overturning their neighbourhood.

CHAPTER FOUR

A Community Wrestles with Change

*People are at a cautious point. They're going to be skeptical …
Do they really care about us?*
> — Lawrence Heights resident

Lawrence Heights is a community people don't want to leave.
> — Youth leader, social justice advocate, musician, and
> Lawrence Heights resident (born and raised)

In February 2021, Betsy Powell of the *Toronto Star* wrote a story about recurrent harms being inflicted on Lawrence Heights tenants by social media users, following the posting on YouTube of a music video disrespecting several Toronto-based neighbourhoods and gangs — prompting fears that it might lead to real-world retaliatory violence. One month prior to Powell's account being published, Toronto City Council had requested a report on potential actions that public institutions and the government could take to mitigate threats "of violence, intimidation and hate on social media that target marginalized communities" (Powell 2021). Powell's story refers to the arrest in the fall of 2020 of one Rowan Atkins, who allegedly directed their 3,000 Instagram followers to shoot everyone living in Regent Park.

No reference is made to the revitalization in Powell's article, but its presence looms in the background. When Lawrence Heights is described by Toronto City Council as a marginalized community, that is no doubt a truism. The label, though, also serves an instrumental purpose by signalling that the people living there need the help that revitalization provides. In this instance, we could replace the sympathetic sounding "marginalized" with a more vitriolic word like "dysfunctional," which the government would not use publicly, but the same meaning gets communicated to the *Toronto Star* audience: that this place is newsworthy when connected to violent events or when the plans for revitalization get discussed, often with talk of its controversy as an invasive plan and an implication that something needs to be done to save the neighbourhood from itself.

That people outside Lawrence Heights have a stigmatizing view of the area is not lost on many who live there. It can even foster stronger bonds and a sense of togetherness. LHION, for instance, was one of several entities involved in an event hosted by Labour Community Services back on September 25, 2019, called We All Belong: Labour's Commitment to Refugees, which spotlighted stories told through spoken word and panel presentations from numerous refugees settled in neighbourhoods like Regent Park and Lawrence Heights. Since its inception in 2005, LHION has become a large local network of social service organizations with a membership base of forty-plus agencies, tenants, and grassroots organizations. Formally, LHION is described as follows:

> Made up of various city divisions and community agencies, the Lawrence Heights Inter-Organizational Network (LHION) was established to enhance and increase local employment planning, service coordination, provision, and access to local services. It strengthens the partnerships in the Lawrence Heights neighbourhood among our service providers. The workgroup has sponsored various events, such as the Youth Opportunity Fairs, Youth in Policing Initiatives, Community Awareness Fair, and more. (City of Toronto, TCHC and SDP Steering Committee 2012, 47)

During a morning meeting at the Lawrence Heights Community Centre, LHION organizers encouraged everyone present to attend We All Belong later that evening, in part to combat the one-sided views of public housing tenants, often struggling migrant families, that are propagated by the news media.

We All Belong was put on at the Daniels Spectrum Cultural Centre in Regent Park. Opened in 2012, the Daniels Spectrum is a joint venture between Artscape, a group of charitable non-profit organizations, Toronto Community Housing, and the Daniels Corporation, which provided a lead gift to facilitate its construction in the Regent Park community. The Daniels Corporation partnered with the TCHC to re-build Regent Park's 1,350 social housing units at "an average cost of $450,000 per unit (excluding the cost of land) and has added 1,769 market units (rental and ownership)" (Tsenkova 2022, 779). To help make the partnership lucrative enough for its private partner, the City of Toronto waived development and property taxes on the new social housing, and it "absorbed the infrastructure costs with $1.61 million assistance from senior governments" (779). Front-loading the Regent Park plan in its first phase led to more of its higher density market units being built with the expectation of luring enough middle-class residents to create a properly mixed neighbourhood.

Sasha Tsenkova (2022, 779–80) lists the contributions made to Regent Park through the nexus of the TCHC, the Daniels Corporation, and various non-profits, which included an "aquatic centre, a community centre [read: Daniels Spectrum], and an athletic field," which got combined with fashionably designed new residences to bring a "new vibe to the neighbourhood, new businesses, new residents, and *new memories*" (emphasis mine). The term "new memories" connotes both psychological erasure and reconstruction. It operates psychically in conjunction with the rebuilding of the physical housing structures, where stigma-ridden memories can be wiped away and replaced with newer and cleaner memories in a neighbourhood that has the appropriate vibes. Among the new public streets being constructed during

Housing on newly constructed Turtle Island Road (photo credit: Ryan Kelpin)

Streetscape mural hidden behind a fence on the new Turtle Island Road (photo credit: Ryan Kelpin)

Phase 1 of the Lawrence Heights revitalization is Turtle Island Road, which derives its name from an Indigenous story about Earth's creation. In Canada, a society where settler colonialism is baked into its functioning, Indigenous stories and images are raw material that can be blended into newly profitable real estate developments on what remain stolen territories. Names like Turtle Island Road are then presented as multiculturally friendly and tasteful representations of contemporary planning ideals revolving around social equity and inclusion.

There is a tension between the pressures for change that urban revitalization brings and the efforts by disadvantaged tenants in places like Regent Park and Lawrence Heights to hold on to their shared bonds, memories, and experiences. In the refined-looking performance space in Daniels Spectrum, tenants and guests spoke candidly during We All Belong. They lent insights into the challenges of coming to Toronto as refugees, reflecting on their desires to make new lives—finding new careers, starting families, and struggling against prejudices towards those of them living in public housing in a city where affordable housing is increasingly difficult to find.

Communal storytelling, the sharing of personal testimony, can be interpreted as activism. It can be seen as resistance to miscarriages of justice and to the uneven societal distribution of public and private goods. When people come together in forums like We All Belong, they can find solace and solidarity in the sharing of lived experiences. Friendships can be formed, with these new bonds potentially translating into action against injustice.

A broad and mutable understanding of activism helps inform us about how tenants in Lawrence Heights have engaged in the revitalization. A good deal of tenant participation has been filtered into LHION, this network being a conduit through which tenants' voices get heard. LHION, meanwhile, operates as an extension of the local government with its emphasis on coordinating public resources into job training for Lawrence Heights tenants and giving them priority as hires for new employment opportunities. Its efforts are then publicly advertised by the city as helping realize demands made upon revitalization planners by Lawrence Heights tenants.

Looking at the activist side of the Lawrence Heights plan reveals intersections between it and other involved sectors, including private sector developers. In 2021, an organization called the Brownsville Partnership posted a YouTube video documenting a Lawrence Heights Revitalization Learning Session, intended to inform its audience about ongoing investment activities in the Brownsville public housing district in Brooklyn, New York. In the video, speakers describe Heights Development's composite firms as performing the role of a surrogate government body, negotiating arrangements with organizers, tenants, and the TCHC to provide grants and financial literacy training to Lawrence Heights tenants who desire opportunities for homeownership and employment opportunities associated with the demolition of existing units and the cleaning and setting up of vacant ones to house temporarily displaced persons and families (Brownsville Partnership 2021, 56:40).

A representative from the TCHC takes a moment in the video to inadvertently suggest that its private partners are not to be trusted:

> When working with developer partners, make sure you use very transparent language on contributions and stuff like that. Here's an example. We negotiated a financial contribution from a developer partner that they would invest into the community. Then you get down the road, and you discover you have one understanding of the agreement and they have

a different understanding. And that's an administrative thing,
but it's also something that speaks to community members as
well. (58:38)

Those who argue for a stripped-down public sector, lower taxes, and
less democratic proceduralism run into critics who allege that business
cannot replace government functions because its interests must be set
on making money and avoiding undue expenses. The wider public interest, in turn, gets subverted rather than supported.

Complexities arise when we look at the public sector, and not
only governments but also their linkages to non-profit organizations.
Depending on what provincial legislation allows, when it comes to
managing a redevelopment plan like we are seeing with Lawrence
Heights, local governments perform a mix of tasks that look different
depending on the context. A 2006 survey involving planning directors
in several Canadian cities produced a range of responses to what such
local government action looks like. Some argued that the primary role
of local authorities is to engage stakeholders. Others suggested that it
should focus on developing "community improvement schemes" (De
Sousa 2006, 399). With local government involvement in revitalization
schemes tending to vacillate between stakeholder engagement and community development suggests that there is a deep synergy between the
activities and personnel within the the City of Toronto, the TCHC, and
in LHION, with the implication being that they are inextricably linked.

A good deal of tenant involvement in the Lawrence Heights revitalization has been filtered through LHION, which itself is an addendum
of the local government. Tenants have little choice in this matter.
Community involvement is taken seriously so long as it melds with
bureaucratic proceduralism. Even within this prism, tenants themselves
can only affect the course of the planning in the ways that the local government will permit.

Indeed, tenant participation has tended to rest on three axes of activity — an SDP, housing, and community safety — all of which remain
tightly controlled by official decision makers. The objective here is to
explore how these processes of engagement played out on a human level
while bearing in mind the numerous tensions at work that twist and pull
the form and content of tenant involvement in the revitalization in multiple directions. Such tensions include the lasting hold of neoliberalism

on public policy, the influence of the neighbourhood-effects thesis on contemporary planning doctrines, and the undercurrent of anti-Black racism that reveals itself in planning activities.

This chapter unfolds over four sections. The first section documents several conflicts that took shape in the early planning days of the revitalization between tenants, planners, and those voices outside Lawrence Heights who were loudly opposed to the plan. The purpose is to provide a deeper sense of the varying opinions people voiced about the revitalization and how they serve as reminders of the persisting resentful treatment expressed by outsiders against the people living in Lawrence Heights. Empirically, this section relies on the presentation of archived letters, emails, posters, and references to news articles that document the content of outside resistance to the revitalization and how it was mobilized.

The remaining three sections discuss multiple angles through which Lawrence Heights tenants have been engaged in the revitalization planning. The point is to give a visceral sense of the committed work that community members have done to move the revitalization forward in ways intended to benefit them and their neighbours. Simultaneously, we learn how community involvement in planning actions gets filtered and hemmed into what public officials determine is feasible and gets rendered to fit with existing policy structures. A window is opened on how these working relationships operate along a continuum of negotiation, cooperation, and at times, conflict.

Grassroots Resistance to "Revitalization"

The feelings of the people living in and around Lawrence Heights fall along a spectrum from rejecting the plan outright to enthusiasm and hope. A member of the non-profit group Pathways to Education says the tenants in Lawrence Heights had little initial enthusiasm for the plan, with several young people fearing it was a conspiracy by Lawrence Manor residents to banish them from the area.

There was opposition on the other side as well. Many members of the Bathurst-Lawrence Four Quadrants Neighbourhood Alliance (4Q) expressed negative opinions about the plan, reasoning that more residential and vehicular traffic would put undue stress on existing infrastructure, threatening property values and quality of life. Rallies to block the revitalization were advertised through poster campaigns that pressured local politicians who were expected to approve the secondary plan. One archived email from 4Q that documented survey results showing that "not one respondent answered they strongly agreed that community groups in our district have been well consulted."

Some of the most vocal opponents of the Lawrence Heights plan were, it turns out, a familiar gang of antagonists. A March 17, 2010, email to Howard Moscoe came from a representative of the Committee to Save Lawrence Manor, an ad hoc network of homeowners and tenants. The email, written in a similar vein as those from the Lawrence Manor Ratepayers' Association from decades ago, appeals to Councillor Moscoe to make sure the Lawrence Heights "makeover" enhances rather than damages the "quiet, stable and pleasant neighbourhood in which we make our home" (Nitkin 2010). The message goes on to thank Moscoe and the city staff for listening to the "concerns raised by many residents" and making some adjustments to the plan, including lowering the planned future population of Lawrence Heights from an "increase of 7X to 6X over current levels," making sure there will be "no new traffic links to Yorkdale from surrounding neighbourhoods" and keeping the dead-ends at "Rondale, Kirkland, and Ridgevale" closed off to vehicle traffic, measures meant to stop excessive cars from moving through their surroundings (Nitkin 2010).

The opposition to the Lawrence Heights plan was indeed no small matter. News stories quoted Lawrence-Allen area residents and public officials who opposed the plan. A pair of staff members with the TCHC allege that these opponents, in Lawrence Manor and otherwise, were opposed to closer contact between themselves and the residents of Lawrence Heights:

> People say they are concerned about the increased density and concerns over traffic but that's not really why they are concerned. In 2007–2008, when revitalization conversations began, the greater Lawrence-Allen area was invited to hear about the vision, and the neighbours would come to these huge meetings that would happen at the local high school and there was a clear distinction where 'we are the fancy people that sit on this side of the gymnasium' and when these people start asking good and valid questions about how our neighbourhoods could be more integrated and our children

can play together in new parks and [these other] people were very clear that this wasn't their vision. I think some of these concerns around traffic and those sorts of things are masking the reality that 'we don't want to play with the people on this side of the fence for other reasons.' (Personal communication, November 26, 2019)

Through these statements, TCHC staff position themselves as the allies of Lawrence Heights. Ethically inclusionary planning works to the advantage of officials and other big moneyed interests by lending a human face to the process. Their language also mimics the expressions of public officials from the 1950s, who scolded members of the Lawrence Manor Ratepayers' Association for protesting the original Lawrence Heights plan on the basis that it would hurt their property values, increase vehicular traffic, and damage their area's aesthetics when in reality they "did not want to live next to foreign poor people."

Opponents of the revitalization say that city officials are making innuendos when responding to what they insist are purely practically minded objections to city planning decisions which should be taken at face value. The representative from the Committee to Save Lawrence Manor says as much in their email to Howard Moscoe, arguing that their organization takes strong exception to allegations made against them, for example, that their desire to keep Rondale, Kirkland, and Ridgevale closed to traffic "is a manifestation of racism and would amount to building a ghetto." Such an argument, they say, "is extremely offensive and clearly unfounded. Limiting road links between neighbouring communities is an urban design technique that helps keep neighbourhoods quiet and liveable and limits flow-through traffic."

It is true that unless these opponents say explicitly that they do not want to be forced into greater contact with public housing tenants, then any suggestion that they feel that way is more an insinuation than evidence of bigotry. But it is also misleading to think that these seemingly well-intentioned homeowners and renters are strictly concerned with "saving" their neighbourhood from the spectres of added density, traffic, and taller buildings obstructing their view. So long as they can find practical sounding reasons to reject the Lawrence Heights plan based on material considerations alone, rather than (alleged) bigoted fears of closer contact with public housing tenants, they will do that because it is more politically expedient. It is telling that the only time these relatively privileged Lawrence Manor residents have anything to publicly protest about Lawrence Heights is when it relates only to how it affects *their* lives. The protests, in other words, are never raised to demand more resources for the living conditions for people living in the so-called "priority neighbourhood" that is Lawrence Heights, even though they are their neighbours, albeit separated by a fence.

Another feature of inclusionary planning in Lawrence Heights is the community animator program. Community animators are Lawrence Heights tenants who work with planners to organize forums, enhance revitalization engagement, and work as translators for other tenants. When animators win accolades like the Urban Leadership Award from the Canadian Urban Institute, as they did in 2011, they provide another layer of legitimation for the plan.

These animators do essential work in informing other tenants who may otherwise be left less informed about important revitalization news and updates. But let us again quote the member of Pathways to Education:

> There's a dark side to the animators' program in the sense that after everything for the "revitalization" was passed by City Council, there's a sense that the animators' program just seemed to disappear into thin air. And that left a lot of residents wondering, did you just use us? (Personal communication, October 21, 2020)

Animators and other TCHC staff engaged widely with multiple communities, coordinating resources to get the necessary approvals. In this fashion, the planning process seems democratic, but it is also set on rigid goals of mediation and placation. The plan is considered too valuable to be hindered by the opposition, especially given all the benefits it affords to private builders, architects, state officials, and businesspeople.

An important goal for the planners involved in the Lawrence Heights revitalization was to develop a secondary plan that would win City Council approval, and tenant engagement was central to that effort. The TCHC has conducted over twenty-seven engagement sessions in the Lawrence-Allen area since 2008, which included over 2,500 residents and stakeholders. Among the concerns they voiced were intensification (added development leading to more residents, traffic, and stress on infrastructure), creating new parks and facilities, maintaining community character, and avoiding displacement. Survey results from a tenant consultation session revealed what residents prioritized and demanded from the TCHC in the new housing agreement. The listed priorities that tenants care most about included: 1) creating employment; 2) education; and 3) job training opportunities. The demands that tenants listed on the bulletin board were: 1) youth apprenticeships; 2) the integration of educational programs for residents; and 3) priority placement for construction jobs during the revitalization. Tenants also asked for assistance with moving during temporary displacement and into the new units, the right to stay in the community during construction, the right to select their new units, permitting variance in household size, and enhancing neighbourhood safety and tenant participation. These priorities crystallized into the approved secondary plan, putting the SDP into motion. Resident participation in forums and surveys is a way of holding the local government accountable, while the government, in turn, controls resident involvement because its planners draw up the surveys and set the boundaries around priorities.

Engagement Through LHION

The character and content of direct tenant participation in the Lawrence Heights plan during the years that this research was conducted (2019–2021) were persistently filtered through LHION as it is the main conduit for tenant participation in community matters. It can be credibly argued that the collaborative partnership between LHION, the TCHC and the City of Toronto is a product of the continued predominance of neoliberal policy trends and toolkits that became popularized after Ontario's move towards the Common Sense Revolution in 1995. The agenda of Mike Harris's administration, as typified through its push for amalgamation, austerity, and the privatization of public service delivery, represented an embrace of "new public management" (NPM). As Jennifer Brinkerhoff (2002, 19) says, "there is a growing popular consensus that the private sector— commercial and non-profit—is generally more efficient and effective than government, and that government should steer, or at least facilitate, and the private sector should row." The promotion of NPM by the provincial government of Ontario was actually less an embrace of a newfound idea as much as it was a slight rebrand of a longstanding proclivity by governments to cut costs and mirror the behaviours of private sector companies. It is through NPM, the cliché goes, that government is made to function "more like a business."

With NPM having been embedded within Ontario's public sector for so long, it has accrued a shield of common sense. It continues to hold broad appeal for the business community and really anyone who resents overbearing bureaucratic structures. Like with other "common-sensical" ideas, NPM has internal contradictions. It has drawn criticisms for re-engineering government — which is supposed to adhere to the principles of democratic decision making and institutional checks and balances — to treat citizens like passive consumers.

Critics of NPM have promoted greater expectations "of citizen involvement, either directly or indirectly, in defining service needs and holding deliverers accountable. This has placed the non-profit sector more prominently in the privatization agenda" (Brinkerhoff 2002, 20). Put in typical public administrative parlance, "non-profits assume a vast variety of forms, including voluntary associations, interest groups, and social-service agencies, all of which serve as important vehicles for civic engagement" (LeRoux 2007, 410). In their various forms, these organizations, particularly those who perform social service functions, typically are considered intermediaries between the public and governments.

Social service organizations serve as a "public voice for their clientele, many of whom lack access to political institutions or do not have the requisite knowledge or skills to participate in politics on their own" (LeRoux 2007, 411). Potential contradictions arise here, too, where non-profits, because they perform this function of mediator, can become replete with designated experts who, rather than being a conduit for their *clientele* when dealing with the government directly, end up mirroring the thinking and acting of public service professionals. The voices of the public get refined through what the non-profit professionals deem to be acceptable and good, holding the public in a firmly subordinate role. The clientele, moreover, become indistinguishable from consumers of governmental services rather than as active participants in government.

But these contradictions are not preordained, nor do they play out in a necessarily fixed fashion. Non-profits may fulfill their intermediary role in a way that delivers what the public wants. Members of the public, in turn, can gain a presence within non-profits, hold them accountable, and even turn their attention towards realizing substantive reforms when a true political mass movement remains out of bounds. The challenge can be significant in the case of the non-profits and assorted social service organizations in an urban revitalization. In such contexts, significant money and political support gets channelled into fulfilling what can be seen as a euthenics-based agenda, although of course they do not use those inflammatory words to describe it. The intent of such an agenda these days is to deconcentrate poverty by finding different ways to alter segregated, low-income environments in order that people there can be conditioned to adopt more prosperous lifestyles.

The writings of William Julius Wilson, author of the influential 1987 book *The Truly Disadvantaged*, provide examples of this view. Wilson (1991, 651) describes what he calls "concentration effects," arguing that in *environments* with "few legitimate employment opportunities, inadequate job information networks, and poor schools" persons are more likely to "turn to illegal or deviant activities." In a later article, Wilson (2010, 214) writes favourably about the Harlem Children's Zone (HCZ). Founded in 1990 by educator, activist, and author Geoffrey Canada, the HCZ was a multi-block project undertaken in central Harlem in New York City that comprised reform-oriented charter schools designed to guide youth from birth to college age to funnel them into prosperous careers. It featured numerous family health programs, youth dance classes, and after-school initiatives. Under Geoffrey Canada's guidance, says Wilson, the HCZ amassed significant money and political support, accruing a budget of $64 million from corporate donors. The Obama administration sought to develop a "promised neighbourhoods" campaign that was modelled after the HCZ. In this case, you have corporate leaders, social service providers, politicians and other public figures pooling resources and collaborating to intensively *re-program* youth living in disadvantaged communities. Non-profit groups, local organizers, and similar entities who possess finite resources and political influence in their work on behalf of long disadvantaged communities can understandably be encouraged to coordinate with, and ultimately get absorbed into, large urban revitalization agendas that are flush with private sector money.

In the case of the Lawrence Heights revitalization effort, LHION is a prominent example of tenants and other organizers being confronted with the challenges of collaborating with powerful partners. LHION has become woven into the machinery of local government while also comprising a large base of non-profit organizations, which have direct involvement with many Lawrence Heights tenants, along with civil servants and other volunteers. In its involvement with the revitalization, LHION has co-chairs and other elected officers, tenant leaders, etc. Tensions are at play with LHION being a conduit to realize tenant demands at the same time as it must negotiate with city officials to ensure that the revitalization continues in the way the formal public and private partners envision. As one report says, the non-profits that comprise LHION

> work together with the city, TCHC and local resident organiz-
> ations addressing community priorities through issue-specific
> workgroups including community safety, employment and
> training, education, food justice and youth outreach — all
> supported by a steering committee with representatives from
> each workgroup. (BePart Steering Committee 2010, 8)

LHION has been deeply involved with deploying the SDP as the main social infrastructure–based component of the revitalization plans, connecting tenants with prospective employers, job opportunities and training, scholarships, community art programs, and other tenant-led initiatives to be subsidized with public funding. Toronto City Council directed public administrators to develop the SDP in cooperation with LHION, the TCHC, tenants, and city divisions like TESS and Economic Development and Culture.

Neoliberalism and the Social Development Plan

Overall, LHION's involvement with the revitalization falls along the following three key dimensions: the SDP, housing, and community safety. The authors of the official 2012 report on the Lawrence Heights SDP frame their work as being a community-driven effort to help remedy the systemic disadvantages that Lawrence Heights tenants have long experienced. It is enveloped in the language of inclusivity, suggesting that everything is being driven by tenant activity. The report puts the voices of resident collaborators in the driver's seat: "From our perspective as residents, meaningful employment can significantly improve our economic and social well-being" (City of Toronto, TCHC and SDP Steering Committee 2012, 42). The document acknowledges that the community's identity is potentially threatened by revitalization but states that provisions included in the SDP can ameliorate this problem:

Ongoing stereotypes about our neighbourhood are fed by the current condition of the existing housing. Being isolated from the city, victimized, and stigmatized has created psychological barriers between the Toronto Community Housing buildings and the surrounding neighbourhoods. New housing types will help us get rid of these misconceptions and bring us together as a mixed community. (City of Toronto, TCHC and SDP Steering Committee 2012, 14)

Once Lawrence Heights becomes identified as being beset with the problems that these quoted statements suggest, the SDP is presented to tenants with promises of well-resourced and community-derived solutions so long as they commit to allowing their existing housing to be razed and rebuilt.

The formal solutions offered in the 2012 SDP report include the following:

- academically focused programs for children and youth;
- adult education with English language and literacy programs;
- opportunities for residents to share "good news" stories about the community;
- employment and volunteer opportunities for residents and leaders to promote community safety;
- satellite police station/support initiatives to end racial profiling;
- community animator program and resident involvement in the revitalization;
- food programs and community gardens;
- new pedestrian/bike lanes/parks; and
- local job hiring/connect employers with tenants/promote life skills and ESL training/resume building.

Regarding the SDP, LHION has demanded and taken control of important resources provided by the state for community building. What stood out during the community meetings I attended was the extent to which LHION holds public officials accountable while also maintaining productive working relationships with those present in the room. During a meeting on June 27, 2019, speakers discussed how revenue generated through the public-private partnership could deliver microgrants. These grants provide money to support resident-led enterprise projects since the TCHC cannot give funding in advance. Money has been distributed towards initiatives like those in the SDP, but the public-private partnership also has a revenue stream that gives microgrants outside public subsidies. LHION members voiced concern over how Ontario's then-recent budget cuts would impact their progress with financing their objectives. The group arranged to meet every Wednesday to spread the word about the SDP to tenants, performing door-to-door visits, linking employers with tenants, and compiling information for a TCHC report.

During another meeting at the Lawrence Heights Community Centre, on September 26, 2019, a government official announced the securement of $75,000 as part of the SDP to be devoted towards grassroots-led projects. In an earlier meeting, a LHION member questioned an official on the degree to which use of the money was to be free of government interference. The same official assured them that the money would be dispersed to the Career Foundation, a registered non-profit charity that the community chose as its trustee, once LHION nominates a neutral party to ensure the funding is going to where "the community wants it to" (LHION 2019, September 17). The same official followed up during a later meeting that took place in early 2020:

> We've gone through the priority setting, gone through the community consultations, going to events, going to interview people, the listening and learning from past documents that we created. Now we have put all that together, and now that money's been transferred to Career Foundations in North York, there's already been some hiring that's happened. (LHION 2020, March 18)

This example reveals some challenges when organizers and local officials work according to bureaucratic norms. Because both parties are large and complex, extra accountability layers are inevitably raised when a powerfully resourced local government provides money to a network of volunteers. At a gathering in Lawrence Square Plaza, one of LHION's co-chairs spoke of the network's commitment to bridging gaps between agencies like the TCHC and tenants in cooperating on planning initiatives.

Beyond the rhetoric of cooperation, LHION's volunteer members took proactive steps to realize the aims of the SDP. At LHION's General Membership Meeting (GMM), members and community animators insisted that tenants must be made aware of what the SDP offers them.

Meeting participants talked about promoting a job fair in October 2019 exclusively for TCHC tenants, including those in Lawrence Heights and in the nearby Neptune community east of the Allen Road. Speakers also talked about needing to promote the news that fifteen thousand retail jobs were being produced in Toronto, many in shopping centres with employers connected with the SDP, like those near Lawrence Heights — the Lawrence Square Mall and Yorkdale Mall — and Dufferin Mall in Brockton Village.

The volunteers within LHION are working to ensure that the network, in its dealings with the city, is fulfilling the promises outlined in the SDP. Toronto also has cooperative officials seated at the table; to be cooperative, genial, and effective mediators is precisely their role. Project managers and coordinators of the sort who were present at these meetings serve a similar function as do conventional city planners, smoothing out rancor between developers and the public to help secure approvals. During the GMM, members pressed the city's project manager to explain how much of the revitalization workforce would be Lawrence Heights tenants. These attendees were assured that tenants are to be given priority during hiring. This same manager described the government's approach to gauging the effects of the SDP between 2012 to 2018 as a process of "looking backwards and then forwards." Such reasoning implies that the local government would consistently be looking back to assess whether the policies implemented have fulfilled their original promises, while also keeping an eye to the future where the next round of policies are to be put in place, further remaking Lawrence Heights in its newly preferred image.

LHION has also done considerable work in Lawrence Heights for particularly marginalized groups living in the area. Such work gets touted by officials as a constitutive feature of the SDP. A 2020 City of Toronto report on the SDP and related community development initiatives points to "academic supports available to youth through homework clubs, tutoring programs, or scholarship opportunities, as well as the increase in seniors programming and community building opportunities available to support social development, wellbeing and reduce isolation" (City of Toronto 2020, 11).

The work done by LHION on these fronts, however, also compensates for the meagre government assistance available for seniors, youth, and other vulnerable groups in TCHC housing. During a forum on February 13, 2020, a LHION member said:

As you know, the province slashed most programming services. So, we did some research and our members talked about
what is affecting our community and we discussed what to do
about it since it is really affecting schools, parents, and others.
(LHION 2020, February 13)

The same speaker discussed LHION's work with seniors who live in
Lawrence Heights and others living on Neptune Drive and Lotherton
Pathway:

In 2019, we focused on seniors' isolation, encouraging them
to participate in community matters. We know a lot of our
seniors have mobility issues and some of them are home
bounded. So, they don't have good access to services … We
found that seniors returning from hospital can be lonely. They
might have been in the hospital for long periods and get separated from their communities. We go and visit them … We
have people doing phone calls, checking in on those seniors …
We invite all agencies in our communities to join in this effort.
[Unison Health and Community Services] is very active and
is the lone agency that is helping. Toronto Public Library has
been very active lately, but they don't have the people or the
resources. We'd like to see [the TCHC] participate actively in
our senior's initiative.

This speaker alerts us to pervasive hardships facing seniors in Lawrence
Heights, as well as the privation that confronts LHION when it works
to address community needs. With neoliberalism and austerity
having stripped out social programs for decades, the fact that LHION
has collaborated intensively in the revitalization plan becomes that
much more comprehensible given the promises it brings in terms of
the SDP, new housing, and facilities, much of which is being financed
with corporate dollars through the TCHC's partnership with Heights
Development.

History, Housing, and Neoliberalism

Observations drawn from community meetings can reveal more of the
gainful work done by LHION on behalf of tenants regarding housing
issues. One LHION member raised serious concerns over how the TCHC

dealt with Lawrence Heights tenants during temporary relocation during construction:

> People are being relocated without notice. Sometimes, they might get a letter or things like that and then they're being treated disrespectfully. They feel like they're being intimidated. They're not being spoken to like a person. They're being treated, and I'm sorry for using the expression, like *cattle*. (LHION 2020, March 12, emphasis mine)

A community animator said the temporary-displacement policy for the Lawrence Heights revitalization is messy because the TCHC is moving tenants into vacant units ahead of people on social housing waitlists. The problem is especially bad in a city that has a highly constrained supply of social housing units to begin with. Lawrence Heights tenants revealed concerns about being shuttled into units that are poorly equipped to handle their needs and numbers. The TCHC is moving over-housed tenants into appropriately sized units to reduce the number of bigger families waiting on available housing. Another speaker noted that the TCHC removed the option for tenants to choose where they want to live during their temporary displacement, and so they can wind up in an area that is not of their choosing:

> Trust has been eroded. Lots of people are saying people are being displaced without their choice being fulfilled because their doctor is here, the kid's school is here. And we hear this more and more. And that's why we want to put this on the table. (LHION 2020, March 12)

A LHION member responded that the network, in its capacity as a mediator between the public and the local government, would make the TCHC aware of these complaints to ensure tenants are better treated.

The problems of Lawrence Heights tenants and social housing waitlist applicants struggling to be housed in an environment with a low number of units available speak to the longstanding effects of austerity on social welfare in Toronto. Austerity is intended to bring down public deficits, reduce the burden on taxpayers to provide social services, and create a welcoming environment for the private sector to invest. But the effects of austerity in Toronto have widened gaps in well-being between the poor and wealthier taxpayers.

In early 2020, Social Planning Toronto and LHION hosted the City Budget Forum for the community at the Barbara Frum Library near Lawrence Heights, with over a hundred people in attendance. One researcher spoke about austerity's impacts:

> Look at Toronto after a decade of austerity. There are lots of reports from United Way, the Toronto Foundation, from the Metcalf Foundation, all of which point to the fact that there's a big gap that's growing every day between rich Torontonians and the rest of us. And we're seeing specific communities being left behind and so that trend has made everyday life difficult, especially for Indigenous, Black, Brown, and members of the LGBTQ communities, people with disabilities, seniors, all these people are seeing the biggest negative impacts. ...
>
> There is a lack of affordable housing, transit poverty ... We have had a decade of this political commitment to keep property taxes low and as a result we're spending about $200 less per person investing into the areas where help is needed. [Our data shows] climbing rents, increasing by thirty percent. The social housing waitlist has grown significantly. If you look at how much affordable rental housing we have built it does not keep up at all. Almost half of tenant households are paying more than 30 percent of their income on shelter, and the standard for what is considered livable is less than that. (Social Planning Toronto 2020, February 8)

These trends are difficult to reverse, and they set limits on what Lawrence Heights tenants can demand through the revitalization. At LHION's GMM, attendees talked about how their goals might be undermined by local and provincial budget cuts affecting social housing, public transportation, and K–12 education. During another community planning meeting, at the Unison building in Lawrence Heights, several speakers gave insights into shelter affordability challenges that low-income people in Toronto are facing, in large part because affordable housing supply is lacking (LHION 2019, September 17):

> Everywhere you look there are condos going up. There are supposed to be affordable units but [developers] are not doing

it because they are not mandated to do so. Should there be more affordable housing? More housing cooperatives? All of the above.

Now you have million-dollar housing in Lawrence Heights which makes it hard for people who've grown up in the community to keep living here. We need more affordable housing. We're not in a strong market area. People now see that affordable housing is not there in Lawrence Heights now. So, now they're looking elsewhere. There is a housing crisis in Toronto.

These statements show us some of the limits when it comes to what community volunteers can compel Toronto to do to help those who are struggling to secure affordable housing. LHION members understand that the answer to the city's housing crisis is to provide more affordable options. As more condo-style housing is built in the absence of apartment buildings and social housing, renters flood into the least expensive units available. As demand goes up and the vacancy rate lowers, landlords charge higher rents. While discussing the makeup of new socially mixed housing in the Lawrence Heights revitalization plan, a LHION member said that "all of it should be rent geared to income housing" (LHION 2019, September 17). These examples register the damaging impacts of long-running policy trends on disadvantaged individuals and families. Promoting expensive residential developments, suppressing subsidized housing construction, and retracting public money out of the budget that could alleviate housing affordability problems sets off mounting frustration among people who most need this help. Frustration, in turn, can foster greater solidarity and efforts to hold the government accountable.

Community Safety and Solidarity

When speaking about Lawrence Heights, public officials often make references to crime to justify the claim that a socially mixed redevelopment is the solution to enhance public safety. "Mixed-use developments [are] generally positive," says one unpublished TCHC report, "and will enhance [the] community's safety." Journalists and pundits have offered the opinion that the original structure of Lawrence Heights is to blame. The redevelopment architecture, says the *Toronto Star's* Christopher Hume (2018), "avoids the strictly utilitarian approach characteristic of social housing and offers a reassuring measure of pleasure. It addresses wants as well as needs." Former Toronto Mayor John Sewell once said: "Buildings in Lawrence Heights are set upon a sea of grass without any facing the street. Eyes on the street are what make a place safe" (Pratt 2004, B03). Sewell said, too, that Lawrence Heights failed because people living there were compelled by structural reasons to stay put rather than join the middle class and leave. Believers in social mixing say you must attract the middle class from outside, in part by rendering the buildings themselves more appealing and more expensive.

Addressing community safety is an important matter for tenants, as indicated by results from a TCHC survey. LHION, for its part, created a safety committee to work in tandem with TCHC employees and local government officials. These interactions carry tensions between a community and a police force that has been a persistent and often violent presence in tenants' lives for decades, especially when the drug trade gathered momentum in the 1980s and 1990s. In contrast, the TCHC's pamphlets project a strong police presence as creating safety for tenants rather than a threat. LHION pressed forward with demands for more public money to assist with public healing, safety, and improving related infrastructure. Working in cooperation with the local government, LHION organizers hosted multiple safety forums. In these meetings, they demanded better street lighting to reduce criminality. They discussed a healing project they initiated that is intended to offer solidarity and mentorship to tenants, especially young people. A city official explained that the city would introduce a grant stream specifically for communities undergoing revitalization to help at-risk people. One TCHC pamphlet for Lawrence Heights tenants exhorts them:

> Join your local Community Police Liaison Committee: The purpose of the committee is to: establish and maintain a meaningful community police partnership; to work together in identifying, prioritizing and problem solving of local policing issues; to be proactive in community relations, crime prevention and communication of initiatives, and to serve as a resource to the police and the community. (TCHC 2012)

Like with housing and the SDP, government officials taking part in public safety discussions present the image of dutiful public servants. But in their capacity as public representatives, they often engage citizens in ways that scramble this image. Society is a composite of hierarchies and wealth disparities between classes, with disproportionately negative effects inflicted upon low-income, racialized individuals and families. Disadvantaged neighbourhoods have seen access to public supports wither over time and get substituted by greater contact with police. Robin Maynard (2017, 109) says bluntly that the structure and application of "the law is neither colour-blind nor neutral." Lorna Akua Benjamin (2003, 12) argues that "Blackness must be seen to denote a system of marginality, powerlessness and subordination, one that is often experienced at the institutional level through systemic policies, processes and practices." In neighbourhoods like Lawrence Heights, the Toronto Police Service (TPS) comes into more frequent contact with residents than in affluent neighbourhoods. Settler colonial relations, far from evaporating over time, inform this relationship where authorities that enforce white supremacy keep people at the bottom of the social hierarchy under constant threat of punishment.

In such an environment, tenants, organizers, and non-profit organizations take steps to extend their hand to the police while also holding them accountable. At a meeting in early 2020, a member of a non-profit with deep ties to Lawrence Heights delivered the following statement:

> We used to have a staff sergeant who would come to LHION meetings, and at some point, they would get a call and would have to leave. I think it was more about placating the community more than it was being aligned with the interests of where we're going with residents and agencies. (LHION 2020, Feb. 13)

The speaker lauded the efforts of another staff sergeant who had attended a similar meeting but, unlike their counterpart, had listened considerately to the complaints levelled against them and the rest of the police force by aggrieved tenants. Afterwards, said the speaker,

> I invited [them] to my office. I said that as residents, and as agencies, when we see six officers who come to a community barbecue, and who are standing at the back and not really engaging, we as agencies need to risk inviting them to participate. Because they're afraid that they don't know if they have a place there ... That encounter with [the staff sergeant] started a transformative opportunity in Lawrence Heights ... [Her]

and another officer would walk through the neighbourhood and through the court every Wednesday night and talk to people … If there were police officers in the community who weren't quite getting this idea of community engagement they were transferred out. For a moment, we were seeing something amazing in terms of shifting the relationship … It is said that the price of democracy is eternal vigilance. The price of a good relationship with TPS is eternal vigilance. Because whenever there are personnel changes, and everything starts all over again, this work has to be ongoing.

These statements attest to a knowingness among Lawrence Heights residents that they are forced to live with a persistent police presence in their daily lives. As such, their focus turns on finding productive ways to accommodate that fact. Recognizing that these tenants believe strongly in the power of community, the speaker asks that they extend their hand to police as they would their neighbours. Such measures must be tempered by constant vigilance as incoming police personnel may seek to reverse any tide of reform and take a more aggressive stance with the community under the pretence of protecting public safety.

Meanwhile, when the government pursues reforms that are intended to address issues like public safety, contradictory effects can result. During one of LHION's Safety Committee meetings to discuss reforms, ten police officers attended, outnumbering the residents and agencies. At that meeting, officers discussed installing four new surveillance cameras at four entry points into the district. This raises concerns about how this may stigmatize tenants further under the pretence of generating safety, delivering conflicting messages by police and local government. Police officers, in essence, are seeking stronger bonds with tenants while simultaneously policing them intensely.

The government has tried to convince Lawrence Heights tenants that policing can be changed by having meetings with Lawrence Heights' Black youth on a regular basis. This strategy gained traction in the context of aftershocks during the summer of 2020 that followed the killing of George Floyd by a police officer in the United States. Apart from helping stimulate a great volume of what have been longstanding protests waged against police brutality upon Black communities, Floyd's death also shone a light on movements devoted to defunding police departments in favour of social services investments. Political dissatisfaction with policing reverberated into meetings conducted by LHION.

For instance, LHION teamed with Social Planning Toronto, the North York Community House, and others on research examining policing in the city and concluded that investments should be diverted to support social structures instead of law enforcement. At a LHION meeting, a member of Social Planning Toronto presented findings from its report, which was to be sent to local politicians, noting that Black and Indigenous Peoples are roughly four times more likely than non-racialized persons to be charged by police. Police officers, the report says, are being questionably deployed as "a Swiss army knife for all social problems" (LHION 2020, December 1). LHION has also encouraged the government to subsidize a Black Youth Action Plan meant to offer social assistance and to set up a Black youth composting initiative and culturally focused parenting initiatives, and to prioritize more broad goals like helping eliminate race-based disparities for young Black students.

The COVID-19 pandemic encouraged non-profits to try and alleviate the isolation and alienation that social distancing can exacerbate. As much as LHION has worked productively with the government during the revitalization, such as on issues like public safety, it has also resisted undue interference from forces that are external to the community. A speaker from an outside organization delivered a presentation to LHION members that promoted a pod program for use in Lawrence Heights. The pods are akin to local networks, the speaker said, organized "through WhatsApp groups, phone lines, and other ways to get communities to build latent infrastructure; neighbourhoods then use these networks to keep in touch and support their material and social needs" (LHION 2020, November 19).

More specifically, a pod program seeks to train tenants to do tasks typically done by bureaucratic agencies. These tasks include "phone check-ups with seniors, check-ins with people with special needs, getting people groceries, and providing financial supports for residents that are already engaging through volunteerism" (LHION 2020, November 19). A prominent LHION member responded:

> Residents [in Lawrence Heights] are already doing this without many resources. When I see this idea of pods, I look around my community and say we're already doing this work. It's really hard when people have been doing the work and then [others] come and say well we're kind of recreating

it again but we're not recreating it again. And many people have already had the training and they're doing it … I can understand the concern over what the residents' roles are and what are the agencies' roles, but we have to be very careful when there is power involved with policy people. (LHON 2020, November 19)

As the LHION member says, there is already a robust social network of people within Lawrence Heights who provide mutual care and solve problems. Such problems include helping alleviate food insecurity, combatting loneliness, and caring for the vulnerable in lieu of access to extensive public support from the government. Women form most of the tenant base, at 62 percent, including many single-parent households, Among the single-parent households, roughly 50 percent of residents are under the age of sixteen, and roughly 63 percent are under the age of twenty-six as of 2021. According to one Lawrence Heights organizer, "women play an integral part in the community through every facet of life. When it comes to leadership building, they step up to the plate, ensuring the community is held together" (LHION 2020, November 19).

People in Lawrence Heights have good reason to direct considerable ire at the Ontario government for its duplicity. In 2019, Doug Ford's administration cancelled "$14 million in funding promised by the former Liberal government for a new community centre in Lawrence Heights, putting the future of the project in limbo at a time when the neighbourhood has been overwhelmed by gun violence" (Pagliaro 2019, A1). Ford's image has been constructed around the idea of him being a populist foil to the so-called *downtown progressive elites*. Such elites are the source of resentment by voters who form a large part of Ontario's Progressive Conservative base.

About the funding cut for the proposed Lawrence Heights Community Centre, Ford said the former Liberal government's spending "put the province in bankruptcy" and joked that the Kathleen Wynne–led Liberal government also committed to "giving everyone a new car" (Wilson 2019). Councillor Mike Colle, playing the inner-city politician that Ford criticizes, voiced disapproval of the province's withdrawal of money for the community hub: "We've got to deal with the gun violence and the police in 32 Division up there are doing an incredible job, but the residents are going through hell … You got to have safe places for people to go to" (Wilson 2019). MP Marco Mendicino mentioned that he and Josh Colle were working to get the province back to the table to re-commit to funding the new centre. One LHION member said that they felt frustrated that "politicians are using the community like a political football." The neighbourhood faces the familiar risk of shouldering a greater burden for protecting tenants' safety with limited resources from the government, which is engaged in disputes and party politics. LHION organizers have repeatedly stressed that people living in Lawrence Heights have proven adept at finding solutions to everyday problems, despite whatever negative and prejudicial preconceptions others have about who they are.

Revitalization and Gentrification

In August 2018, CBC *News* published a feature story on a new project on display at the Gardiner Museum at Queen's Park in Toronto. *Reclaiming Artifacts — "What could a construction dig in 2050 find?"* displayed art pieces from teens living in Lawrence Heights depicting "elements of their neighbourhood that that they would like to see live on into the future." MPATHY, an organization that explores interdisciplinary work that intersects between "Design Research, Futures, and Systems" (2018a), posted an in-depth overview of *Reclaiming Artifacts* on its website (2018b). Participants in the project included young women of colour aged 15–18 who were first-generation immigrants from lower-income families. Regarding the revitalization, says MPATHY, these participants felt "no agency" and thinking about the future brought about serious fears in them.

When the CBC report and MPATHY talk about Lawrence Heights they both explicitly equate revitalization with gentrification. The CBC notes that the museum's exhibit "takes aim at the gentrification of one of the city's largest community housing projects." Likewise, MPATHY's website says that Lawrence Heights "has been undergoing sweeping revitalization efforts for over decade and is quickly gentrifying with original residents being displaced."

Cyclical patterns continue. Indigenous Peoples get dispossessed to make room for European farmers. By the end of WWII, the government decided that building public housing on certain tracts of these lands would be a productive investment. Decades passed, and these public housing sites are now being torn down and re-built. Eventually, new planning ideas will come into vogue, and it may get flattened and re-built once more. MPATHY's description of *Reclaiming Artifacts* refers to "youth creating clay artifacts from the year 2050 representing personal belongings a condo developer could find when digging for a *future wave* of 'revitalization'" (emphasis mine). The exhibit brings forward younger voices from Lawrence Heights who feel the earth moving out from under them and that they have little control over their future.

Gentrification is whirling through Lawrence Heights and remoulding it. But it is also true that conflicting tensions are present. Many within Lawrence Heights continue striving for futures that fit more with the visions they have in their minds, rather than having their fortunes dictated to them by others. Ute Lehrer, Roger Keil, and Stefan Kipfer give us a blunt assessment of Regent Park, which they describe as taking

> shape through political dynamics that were driven by housing administrators, downtown politicians, consultants, developers, and local ratepayer groups and included a micro-politics of engaging NGOs and select residents. The project (with its social development flank) is, in contrast to the original Regent Park, not a substantial territorial compromise, however. It tries to manage isolated resistance and preempt conflict, not grant material concession to organized housing movements. In fact, while during the 1970s and 1980s, diversity planning underwrote not only gentrification but also continued social housing production, today, it serves to break up and privatize existing housing districts without adding to the public housing stock (2010, 87).

Roughly the same outcomes are occurring at Lawrence Heights since the same model for change has been deployed there. Much of what has been said in the previous chapters affirms this claim. These people find themselves struggling against the colossal power of big money and bureaucracy. Once we acknowledge that these events are enflaming gentrification, which has such destructive effects, it can be tempting to fit nearly all related findings into the same negative premise.

The community animators and other organizers working in LHION may be targeted by critics for being *unwitting* contributors to the gentrification of Lawrence Heights. Does the animator program serve a useful purpose for the TCHC? Most certainly. It strategically sought those living in Lawrence Heights who fit the characteristic bill of being charismatic, compassionate, and possessed of deft negotiation skills. As one organizer said about the community animators program: "The key is to ensure the animators are from the soil, who are from the community and understand it, who can connect with people and share their vibe" (Brownsville Partnership 2021, 35:55). Such is standard practice in the age of competitive city politics in Toronto, with its continued embrace of a kinder, inclusionary form of neoliberal governance, where the city's programs directed towards "marginalized groups and communities has been reduced to a strategy of diversity management and community engagement aimed at containing potential conflicts arising out of the city's highly racialized and gendered situation of social polarization" (Desfor, Keil, and Wekerle 2006, 138). One person speaking during a community forum in early 2020 crystallized an ongoing problem with tenant participation in the Lawrence Heights revitalization, arguing that "it shouldn't be about agencies inviting residents to come and participate. It should be about residents getting agencies to come and participate with them as they work on building a future together" (LHION 2020, February 13).

Community animator programs can help ease frustrations that people might feel with being told that part of their neighbourhood is being re-zoned to make way for private housing developments, and wondering whether gentrification can be staved off. Nadine Kreitmeyr (2019, 289) writes that the "mutation of neoliberal tactics towards more inclusionary and consensual patterns seeks to ensure the survival of both neoliberalism and of authoritarian governance." Planning becomes more "inclusionary" as neoliberalism becomes paradoxically more vengeful, clearing spaces that capital has ignored on account of them being associated with poverty, crime, and racial segregation, and substituting them with higher end retail, services, and housing.

To suggest that people living in Lawrence Heights who have participated in the revitalization are unwittingly assisting the same forces that are intent on destroying their neighbourhood and culture might lead us to make unwarranted assumptions about the psyches of those involved. It can obfuscate how these people and those they engage with can just as plausibly feel empowered through this same work, even if it furthers the spread of gentrification more broadly. An organizer with LHION, speaking at a community forum, encouraged the attendees to celebrate the results of their work:

> I want to point to you, and you say: these are the fruits of our labour. We completed a collaborative research report where residents worked with agencies to build a community

where we could serve each other better. These are the fruits of our labour. We had the TCHC employment survey. We had ten priorities for revitalization that residents made with the Community Action Team. And then we had the SDP which a lot of us were on with other residents. This was the fruit of our labour … We had the feasibility study for the central hub. We had the Lawrence Heights heritage interpretation plan. These were the fruits of our labour. (LHION 2020, February 13)

The *Lawrence Heights Revitalization Learning Session* video on YouTube (Brownsville Partnership 2021) includes extensive coverage of its community animator program, with success stories about young participants who pursued related careers, thereafter attending school to learn about urban planning and social work, among other things. Participation required intense commitment. One TCHC planner explained the challenges of dealing with personnel turnover in the animator program, with some people being relegated to performing six-month stints. Animators would approach tenants with open-ended questions, such as "what does change mean to you?" These queries spurred debate among participants about what sort of change they wanted to see or not. One animator said of the program:

> We had some great times. We had some downtimes. Tragedies. But also, just, when you're building something from the ground up, people don't always see eye to eye. There is infighting. We stuck through it. We stuck through it, and we won awards. And at the end of the day, it was all worth it because we're standing here. (Brownsville Partnership 2021, 42:25)

Material and social advancements wrought through tenant participation with the community animator program and LHION can represent change that is responsive to what are, in part, a historically produced set of needs.

Consider the situation facing people in Lawrence Heights. As this case study shows, the local and provincial governments have for decades twisted the fates of the people living there. Tenants have been warehoused in what are now crumbling housing complexes while the government has over time alternately distrusted and over-policed them, strangling the area of resources and equitable economic opportunities. In this historical context, which is coloured by post-amalgamation gridlock, crises, and austerity, it is unsurprising that many organizers and tenants would be inclined to buy into the government's move to revitalize their district. In some respects, they demanded it. A TCHC planner recalls tenants applying pressure on Toronto City Council to set things in motion:

> When we went to the council to look for approvals, for the zoning changes, it was people from the community who spoke out and said: I'd like to live in a neighbourhood that looks like the one beside us, and further, I would like the opportunity to own my own home in my community. (Brownsville Partnership 2021, 48:30)

We could read the totality of these statements as comprising supportive evidence for multicultural and inclusionary approaches to city planning. They could appear to affirm the adage of "planning with the people," supporting the notion that positive neighbourhood effects can be reaped by empowering disadvantaged residents to do work otherwise left to governments and social service providers.

We should not forget that tenants, community organizers, and non-profits have little choice but to become engaged in these issues on terms that fit comfortably within existing policy regimes and planning schemes. It is thus advisable to keep an open mind when assessing the character and content of tenant involvement in these proceedings, whether that be organizing, the fulfillment of planning goals in collaboration with the local government, and even the mere expression of opinions about what is happening. Doing otherwise risks taking conflicting empirical findings, including those that describe the actions, feelings, and reflections of tenants, and not considering them carefully enough. Falling into this trap could lead us to lose a fuller sense of the real and passionate struggle for change, and often for a better life, on the part of these same tenants who are witnessing the neighbourhood they know and love being brought down entirely around them.

EPILOGUE

Visions and Dreams

This community needs new life; its residents are tired and want their just due and, in our society, everyone has the right to justice.

My current living condition is very despicable and if I can advocate to ensure that the quality of life improves for myself, my son and my neighbours that is what I will do.

We support the revitalization of Lawrence Heights because our community needs positive change and new opportunities that will transform our neighbourhood into a neighbourhood just like others in our city.

I urge you to pass this plan but most importantly, I implore you to refuse communities being segregated from one another. Please make sure that this plan will work effortlessly toward social inclusion where no one is left behind.

These statements from Lawrence Heights residents were drawn from a transcript of a North York Community Council meeting about the Lawrence-Allen Secondary Plan on November 2, 2011 (TCHC 2011c, 1–5). They form part of what were larger deputations made by these same four tenants in support of the revitalization. The entirety of their statements communicates a shared desire for justice and change and a mix of emotions about life in Lawrence Heights varying between affection, frustration, and despair. Such thoughts helped inspire the title that was eventually given to this book, which suggests that this long-forgotten neighbourhood is caught in a major storm. People cannot simply ward off a coming hurricane. They can only prepare for what is coming their way. Homes get destroyed, lives get turned upside down, and people

147

persevere and assist one another. Similarly, with the Lawrence Heights plan, people confronted with it have little power to stop it even if they wanted to. They may lament what is happening, but they are compelled to confront it. These statements work as a bridge for us to assess some potential lingering questions about this case.

One question concerns the issue of visions. A recurrent source of conflict is between the visions generated through institutional procedurialism, which align predominately with the interests of the wealthy and powerful, and visions for change that circulate among other various parties involved. These *unofficial* visions may be focused on objectives that do not necessarily align with what politicians, the business class, and other experts and decision makers deem to be reasonable, cost-effective, and non-threatening as regards prevailing policy regimes and planning dogmatisms. Unofficial visions might involve constructing wider numbers of public housing units rather than just replacing the existing supply and channelling more provincial and local government money into community programming as opposed to enhanced policing and security measures.

In other respects, official and unofficial visions for change merge. TCHC staff members point to the high level of community participation. The surveys and engagement sessions with Lawrence Heights residents revealed that these tenants want better quality housing, access to jobs, and improved infrastructure, all of which became prominent elements of the revitalization plan. Carrying through this plan involves generating potentially damaging consequences, gentrification among them, a gradual displacement of the existing tenant base, and the imposition of informal surveillance systems where newer affluent residents oversee and punish renters living in TCHC-controlled units. When questioned, officials with the TCHC and the city government retort that such risks are unavoidable due to practical limits on the content and scope of public policy. In the face of limited support from the other levels of government, rising costs for housing maintenance, and persistent demands to redress the negative effects of concentrated poverty, these official decision makers turn to revitalization as the commonsensical approach.

As this book shows, tenants in Lawrence Heights carry with them a long history of experiencing mistreatment, stigma, and anti-Black racism. Naturally, their efforts to improve the future of this neighbourhood are predicated on redressing these problems to the extent possible.

Lawrence Heights' tenant base was not always predominately racialized in the manner it is now; this book documents major political and economic changes that helped precipitate its demographic shake up, including the migration of industry-based jobs away from the inner city, which in turn transitioned towards a more heavily service-based economy. In addition, influxes of lower-income migrant workers were funnelled into narrow choices for lower-income housing in patterns that complemented a growing spatialization of poverty within Toronto's amalgamated inner suburbs. As Charles Green (1997) puts it, the "contemporary Black urban plight is a historical reality that is linked to their history of racial subjugation and exploitation throughout the world, which has been exacerbated by the present global economic transformation" (cited by Benjamin 2003, 44). The people trying to overturn this hegemonic situation are forced to address these problems in an environment where commonsensical revitalization rules the day.

Meanwhile, the official vision of revitalization, as promulgated by the City of Toronto, the TCHC, and its private partners, has been carefully curated over time, cementing its boundaries and content as it continues being deployed into action. Future Landscapes, a design studio that advertises client projects using photography, web design, and similar tools, has a webpage showcasing Lawrence Heights. Stephanie Braconnier, the founder of Future Landscapes, describes the Lawrence Heights plan as

> part of a new wave of change in Toronto as the central suburbs adopt new roles based on changing demands and growing populations. One of the critical new roles for these neighbourhoods is to absorb urban density and to generate new energy to vitalize and intensify the public realm. (2022)

This is the vision that caters well to interested parties in the investor class, developers, architects, and the council members who are willing to give the plan their stamp of approval. As the above passage indicates, Future Landscapes describes Lawrence Heights as having a new role that is being attributed to it from on high.

Recall that the Lawrence Heights plan was born during the reign of the former Ontario Liberal government under Dalton McGuinty, elected in 2003. At that time, the Ontario government instituted a "regional growth management framework" called Places to Grow, which complemented a regional greenbelt initiative called the Greater Golden Horseshoe, which began in 2006 and 2007. Places to Grow designates growth centres and non-growth centres, with an emphasis on limiting sprawl by focusing growth in "large contiguous sections of highly developed land," often bridging the typically conflictual political relations between "the dense urbanity of the metropolitan core and the sprawling suburbanity that lies beyond" (Keil and Addie 2015, 11–12). To this end, "many of Toronto's neighbouring municipalities have embraced planning and policy agendas centred on intensified urbanization" (14).

GTA-Homes, a real estate consultancy firm, identifies North York on its website as "one of Toronto's fastest growing municipalities," where between 2013 and 2017 it generated 40 percent of all non-residential developments within Toronto's Urban Growth Centre (UGC). The website says that since North York has been labelled a UGC, it continues to be targeted to support "Ontario's rapid residential growth and improve its transit-based employment." *The Local* published a piece in 2020 declaring that for

> a city in search of answers for how to turn its inner suburbs into healthy, vibrant communities, what happens in this neighbourhood is of the utmost importance. The future of Toronto as an equitable, liveable city begins in places like Lawrence Heights. (Huynh 2020, para. 4)

Post-revitalization Lawrence Heights is intended to be prototypical mixed-use development meant to absorb urban density and is being engineered to house and cater to workers who need to commute in and out of North York. These imperatives accord smoothly with Ontario's Official Plan. These elements help describe what has become a carefully crafted vision for change in Lawrence Heights, one underpinned by the ideological bent of neoliberalism and supporting policy toolkits. Even neoliberalism's loudest proponents may admit that its revolutionary sheen has worn off. We are long removed from when it first migrated out of academic circles into material political ones, starting with the American-backed capture of state power during the 1973 coup in Chile, the subsequent installation of the Chicago Boys' doctrine, and the elections of Margaret Thatcher and Ronald Reagan.

People often understand neoliberalism to mean "less government," but that is not entirely accurate. Governments are not eroded; they remain architects of change. This case study of Lawrence Heights helps document this process as it unfolded in Toronto through roll-back and roll-out phases where governance regimes were dissolved, restructured, and replaced. When Ontario forced amalgamation in the late 1990s, it perpetuated, rather than alleviated, intercity competition between Toronto and surrounding exurbs. That is, despite being brought under a new umbrella of regional governance, old conflicts persisted on the terrain of public finance. New services and infrastructure require financing and servicing, drawing on public coffers, and exurbanites care less about paying for inner city needs. New arrangements were made to make public financing schemes feasible.

Ontario thus made qualitative changes to provincial–municipal financial arrangements, making cuts to provincial transfer payments, changing its property tax system, and downloaded social housing responsibilities onto its cities. It also rolled back red tape, deregulated planning and development, facilitated privatization of municipal utilities, enacted workfare, and stripped back civilian oversight of policing (Kipfer and Keil 2002, 241–42). Consulting firms, development corporations, and public-private partnerships were rolled out, further privatizing the local government, which is prioritizing "signature projects" that contribute to altering the look and character of urban space (243). Private firms like Context and Metropia, which joined together to form Heights Development for the revitalization, helped make the financing of the first phase of the Lawrence Heights plan possible. But the pervasiveness of these partnerships, and trends associated with having privatized local governments, also produce contradictory effects. Struggling Torontonians see intensifying gentrification, rising living costs, austerity, and limited options for housing assistance, with the still-stagnant social housing supply being one example.

When groups of tenants have gotten involved with the Lawrence Heights plan through different vectors, including through the community animator program, voting on proposals put to them by the TCHC, pressuring City Council members, and expressing their opinions about to it to the press and others, they are apt to voice frustration as much as support. For instance, a long-time Lawrence Heights resident and project coordinator for the Lawrence Heights Revitalization Coalition, claimed at a TCHC-led Tenant Services Committee meeting in March 2021 to "see jobs allocated for residents going elsewhere" and that consultations with tenants over benefits have stalled since 2016 (TCHC 2021, 12). The speaker also argued that tenants "feel that their voices are being silenced and are only used when they want us to substantiate their initiative. No one is taking into consideration the trauma experience by revitalization" (TCHC 2021, 12).

Lawrence Heights tenants may feel at turns traumatized, disappointed, energized, or hopeful about the plan. Generally, calls for justice and for change, rather than stasis, underpin these emotions. Their respective visions may differ, but just as often they share commonalities, revealing resistance to the status quo as much as absorption by it. Visions expressed by tenants imagine a future Lawrence Heights that looks like any other neighbourhood in Toronto and where they could eventually own their own homes. Others may wish the housing was entirely publicly owned rather than a portion of it. There are endless possibilities, but all share a common demand for a better life.

Within these demands for change, there is also a common hope for preserving an existing culture and its traditions, as evidenced by the testimony of tenants and planners that has been documented in this case study whenever the spectre of gentrification is raised. As one TCHC staff member said about Lawrence Heights:

> There are challenges but also incredible assets … Incredible music and arts, athletics. Lawrence Heights is known for its basketball stars. Some big leaders in the community, cultural leaders as well. Spoken word artists. Incredible community history and legacy there. And a very strong sense of community. (Brownsville Partnership 2021, 20:55)

If gentrification runs roughshod over Lawrence Heights, wholly substituting the existing culture through the remaining phases of the revitalization, it would be fair to conclude that the capacity for neoliberalism to absorb challenges to its deployment will remain highly durable, despite it no longer having the benefit of being novel. Neoliberalism governs by bleeding into different areas of social life that traditionally are not designed to make money.

Tenants demand job training, new amenities and housing, an influx of retail businesses and other service providers, and a social development plan, simultaneously representing impassioned and valuable outcomes of organizing and the formidability of neoliberal policy regimes. Greg Albo

(2018, 6) spells out the way that neoliberal ideology gets codified into the devising of an individualized set of needs for people, who then get them satisfied either by capitalist firms or voluntary agencies. In this milieu, the domain of community organizing in Lawrence Heights gets fed into the neoliberal policy thresher, reconfiguring it into a locus of buy-and-sell transactions through the hiring of animators and housing cleaners, priority hiring schemes (for retail, moving services, etc.), and designating engagement work to non-profits (e.g., Pathways to Education). Tenants engaged in this work are forced to operate within the rules and limits set by the public-private partners in charge. Accordingly, when tenants themselves generate changes through negotiation or otherwise, they should be seen as hard-fought outcomes rather than framed merely as "concessions."

Another question we might ask is whether the Lawrence Heights revitalization is ripe enough to assess as a case, given that the plan has not yet entered its final phases, much less been completed. This study, nevertheless, draws out useful insights even at these liminal stages. Assessments of Lawrence Heights which occur only after the entire district has been transformed will naturally make conclusions based on the totality of events. This approach could colour how we evaluate available data concerning these early stages, potentially underappreciating their significant impacts for the people experiencing the events up close.

The rapidity and fragmentary nature of contemporary urban life suggests that grassroots political work operates in a multitude of societal creases. Research should not be limited to evaluating events that create lasting changes or that persist over a long enough expanse of time that they can be given a traditionally full retrospective account. To this point, the voices from tenants and organizers documented are just as concerned with addressing urgent everyday matters having to do with securing funding for programs and broader efforts like countering anti-Black racism in the media and in relations with government and its assorted agencies, to name a few. These affairs should be evaluated sympathetically and with appropriate comprehensiveness. If they are only viewed retrospectively, we risk making them into footnotes and composite elements of the larger fulfillment of the revitalization plan and all the negative effects it will engender for the people living in Lawrence Heights. The insights that this case study provides are meaningful because they suggest concerted efforts on the part of people in Lawrence Heights striving to break through the formidable wall of real estate development politics in Toronto, characterized by permanent austerity, competitive city-oriented policy strategies, and the widespread perceived success of the revitalization model being applied there.

We may also ask what the future holds for people in Lawrence Heights. Without being overly speculative, let us presume that the twenty-year re-construction plan concludes each of its phases, and that the local government, the TCHC, its private partners, and cooperating non-profit organizations follow through on their stated commitments to the Lawrence Heights' tenant body. We would likely hear from the government, the news media, and other prominent political commentators in the public sphere that the implantation of the Regent Park "revitalization" model in Lawrence Heights has been a successful venture, where the mistakes made in the Regent Park case were avoided.

By this metric, the process of conjuring and deploying neoliberal policy regimes to the ends of "revitalizing" Lawrence Heights will have absorbed potential roadblocks to their employment. Critics might conclude that the Lawrence Heights plan amounted to a successful following of the Regent Park script, arguing it does little to address the damaging effects that a neoliberal-charged capitalism has had on working people and families. Martine August, professor of planning at the University of Waterloo wrote about Regent Park as amounting to a

> one-time injection achieved by transferring public assets and resources to private actors who see the opportunity to profit from the transaction. As such, it holds questionable promise for addressing the key problems identified by tenants, all of which are traceable to ongoing issues like decreased funding for housing maintenance, a retracted social safety net, constrained labor-market opportunities, poverty, and racial inequality. (August 2014, 1330)

Public housing reformists use euthenics-charged language to continue hashing up fixes to the problem of improving housing conditions with socially mixed redevelopment projects (condos, apartments, townhouses, etc.), along with social development plans and infrastructure renewals now in vogue. Such strategies leave the underlying problems of eroded social safety nets, systemic inequality, and racism unaddressed in the way August describes.

This book repeatedly keys in on the need to assess grassroots activity in the Lawrence Heights case on its own terms. In other words, the aim of this type of research should be to consider the content and purpose of tenant-led activity through its vectors in non-profits, with the local government, and through general community engagement without being quick to simply box it into a conclusion that reduces it to one other manifestation of neoliberalism in action.

The CBC reported in November 2022 that Toronto awarded a $5.4 million contract to "CS&P Architects to design the new Lawrence Heights Community Recreation Centre and Child Care Centre, a project the city now says will be complete by summer 2027" (Pasieka 2022). It was welcome news to community organizers and grassroots leaders who had advocated for investment in the new centre for years. As documented above, the plans stalled when Doug Ford reneged on a promise to give funding, prompting local officials to cry foul. With the promise of funding secured, restless organizers continue insisting that the city commit to its other pledge, that neighbourhood members will have substantial input on what will be built: "Two pools, a gym, fitness studios, multi-purpose rooms, a community kitchen, administrative spaces, an active roof and an outdoor play area are part of the proposal. The childcare facility would accommodate 88 children" (Pasieka 2022).

Prominent voices in Lawrence Heights want to ensure that the new facility does not prioritize physical fitness, dining, and other utilities at the expense of losing the original community centre's function as a space for political organizing. The CBC report quotes a staff member with the North York Community House, who also grew up in Lawrence Heights, who says of the existing centre: "It's been a real caretaker for the community ... If you don't put those things in place or ensure those things could occur in a new space, then you're really taking those things away from the community." These voices are not merely content with the community centre being constructed. They are aware of the potential for diminishment of existing social bonds and the culture of Lawrence Heights through such re-investment, and they want to prevent that from happening.

The model for change being applied in Lawrence Heights is posed as the solution to the problems afflicting people living there. Simultaneously, it is part of the force of urbanization that flattens what previously existed to make it more closely resemble other affluent city districts, becoming another facet of everyday life that pressures people to conform. The tenants already living there are put in new contemporary-style housing with greater access to services and amenities. As has been stated repeatedly in this case study, fears that tenants have about the plan often circle back to gentrification, which can displace people by making them feel distant and unwelcome in their community. People's feelings of alienation get heightened because they no longer feel at home in a new gentrified environment. They feel strange and disembodied like one does in a dream. What you see in Lawrence Heights are many people who are committed to avoiding this predicament, while also struggling to create change within what the existing system of governance permits.

References

Albo, G. (2018). Introduction. In G. Albo, and B. Evans (eds.), *Divided Province: Ontario Politics in the Age of Neoliberalism* (pp. 1–39). McGill Queen's University Press.

Albo, G., and Fanelli, C. (2019). Fiscal Distress and the Local State: Neoliberal Urbanism in Canada. In M.P. Thomas, L.F. Vosko, C. Fanelli, and O. Lyubchenko (eds.), *Continuity and Change: Rethinking the New Canadian Political Economy* (pp. 264–298). McGill-Queens University Press.

Allen, D. (1970, October 20). Management of Public Housing by Tenants Urged. *Toronto Daily Star (1900–1971)*, 15. https://ezproxy.library.yorku.ca/login?url=https://www.proquest.com/historical-newspapers/page-15/docview/1406226547/se-2

August, M. (2014). Challenging the Rhetoric of Stigmatization: The Benefits of Concentrated Poverty in Toronto's Regent Park. *Environment and Planning A, 46*(6), 1317–1333.

August, M., and Walks, A. (2018). Gentrification, Suburban Decline, and the Financialization of Multi-Family Rental Housing: The Case of Toronto. *Geoforum* (89), 124–136.

Bacher, J. (1986). Canadian Housing Policy in Perspective. *Urban History Review/ Revue D'histoire Urbaine, 15*(1), 3–18.

Baldwin, J. (1961). *Nobody Knows My Name: More Notes of a Native Son.* Dial Press.

Benjamin, L.A. (2003). *The Black/Jamaican Criminal: The Making of Ideology.* Doctoral dissertation, University of Toronto.

Bennett, S. (2000). "The Possibility of a Beloved Place": Residents and Placemaking in Public Housing Communities. *St. Louis University Public Law Review, 19*(2), 259–307.

BePart Steering Committee. (2010). *Residents and Agencies Working Together: BePart Collaborative Research Report.* Toronto: Wellesley Institute.

Beradi, L. (2018). *Shots Fired: Experiences of Gun Violence and Victimization in Toronto Social Housing.* Dissertation, University of Alberta.

Beswick, J., and Penny, J. (2018). Demolishing the Present to Sell off the Future? The Emergence of 'Financialized Municipal Entrepreneurialism' in London. *International Journal of Urban and Regional Research, 42*(4), 612–632.

Boudreau, J.A. (1999). Megacity Toronto: Struggles over Differing Aspects of Middle-Class Politics. *International Journal of Urban and Regional Research, 23*(4), 771–781.

Braconnier, S. (2022). Lawrence Heights Revitalization. *Future Landscapes.* https://futurelandscapes.ca/lawrence-heights-revitalization

Bradford, N. (1999). The Policy Influence of Economic Ideas: Interests, Institutions and Innovation in Canada. *Studies in Political Economy, 59*(1), 17–60.

Brail, S., and Kumar, N. (2017). Community Leadership and Engagement after the Mix: The Transformation of Toronto's Regent Park. *Urban Studies, 54*(16), 3772–3788.

Brinkerhoff, J.M. (2002). Government-Nonprofit Partnership: A Defining Framework. *Public Administration and Development, 22*, 19–30.

Brownsville Partnership. (2021). *Lawrence Heights Revitalization Learning Session.* 1:50:17. https://www.youtube.com/watch?v=jfLVZcDTxek

Brushett, K.T. (2001). *Blots on the Face of the City: The Politics of Slum Housing and Urban Renewal in Toronto, 1940–1970 (Ontario).* Doctoral dissertation, Queen's University. https://www.collectionscanada.gc.ca/obj/s4/f2/dsk3/ftp05/NQ63408.pdf

Campbell, M. (2008, June 23). Community Redevelopment: Residents Wary about Lawrence Heights Overhaul Despite Two Years of Informal Consultations, Locals Remain Skeptical about Whether Planned Rebuilding Will Benefit the Community. *Globe and Mail*, A10. https://ezproxy.library.yorku.ca/login?url=https://www.proquest.com/historical-newspapers/community-redevelopment/docview/1371252270/se-2

Carson, J. (1969, May 1). Social Action in Lawrence Heights. *Globe and Mail*, W1. https://ezproxy.library.yorku.ca/login?url=https://www.proquest.com/historical-newspapers/social-action-lawrence-heights/docview/1242409297/se-2

Cart Before the Horse. (1954, December 10). *Globe and Mail*, 6. https://ezproxy.library.yorku.ca/login?url=https://www.proquest.com/historical-newspapers/cart-before-horse/docview/1290472928/se-2

Carter, J. (1972, June 8). More Goes on at Centre than Just Sewing — It Counters Loneliness in OHC Community. *Globe and Mail*, W3. https://ezproxy.library.yorku.ca/login?url=https://www.proquest.com/historical-newspapers/more-goes-on-at-centre-than-just-sewing-counters/docview/1240339103/se-2

Caulfield, J. (1994). *City Form and Everyday Life: Toronto's Gentrification and Critical Social Practice.* University of Toronto Press.

Chaskin, R.J., and Joseph, M.L. (2010). Building "Community" in Mixed-Income Developments: Assumptions, Approaches, and Early Experiences. *Urban Affairs Review, 45*(3), 299–335.

___. (2011). Social Interaction in Mixed-Income Developments: Relational Expectations and Emerging Reality. *Journal of Urban Affairs, 33*(2), 209–237.

City of Toronto. (2006, September 27). Completed Playground, Lawrence Heights Playground Building Event: Lawrence Heights Community Centre, 5 Replin Road. Toronto Municipal Archives, Fonds 219, Series 2311, File 2238, Item 651.

___. (2009, May 8). Housing Opportunities Toronto: An Affordable Housing Action 2010–2020. https://www.toronto.ca/legdocs/mmis/2009/ah/bgrd/background-file-21130.pdf

___. (2010a). Chapter 2: Setting the Context. In *The Revitalization Plan for Lawrence-Allen* (pp. 11–22). Toronto: City Planning Division. https://www.toronto.ca/legdocs/mmis/2010/ny/bgrd/backgroundfile-31040.pdf

___. (2010b, July 6). City Council Decision — Lawrence Heights Revitalization — Corporate Implementation Actions and Social Development Plan. https://secure.toronto.ca/council/agenda-item.do?item=2010.CD34.8

___. (2010c). Chapter 4: Planning Directions and Actions. In *The Revitalization Plan for Lawrence Allen* (pp. 33–46). https://www.toronto.ca/legdocs/mmis/2010/ny/bgrd/backgroundfile-31042.pdf

___. (2010d, June 8). Lawrence Heights Revitalization — Corporate Implementation Actions and Social Development Plan. https://www.toronto.ca/legdocs/mmis/2010/cd/bgrd/backgroundfile-31464.pdf

___. (2011, September). Lawrence–Allen Revitalization Study: Infrastructure Master Plan. https://www.toronto.ca/legdocs/mmis/2011/ny/bgrd/backgroundfile-41805.pdf

___. (2016). City Revenue Fact Sheet. https://www.toronto.ca/wp-content/uploads/2018/01/8ec1-Chart_MoneyComesGoes_full.pdf___. (2017a, November). 32: Lawrence–Allen Secondary Plan. https://www.toronto.ca/wp-content/uploads/2017/11/907d-cp-official-plan-SP-32-LawrenceAllen.pdf

___. (2019, July). A New Approvals Framework for Toronto Community Housing Corporation Revitalization Projects — Supplementary Report. https://www.toronto.ca/legdocs/mmis/2019/ph/bgrd/backgroundfile-135556.pdf

___. (2020, October 5). Lawrence Heights Phases 2 and 3 — Initial Development Proposal. https://www.toronto.ca/legdocs/mmis/2020/ph/bgrd/background-file-157267.pdf

___. (2021). Attachment 1 — Street Needs Assessment 2021. https://www.toronto.ca/wp-content/uploads/2022/11/96bf-SSHA-2021-Street-Needs-Assessment.pdf

City of Toronto, TCHC and SDP Steering Committee. (2012, June). Shaping Our Community Together: A Social Development and Employment Service Plan for Lawrence-Allen. https://www.toronto.ca/legdocs/mmis/2012/cd/bgrd/backgroundfile-48446.pdf

CMHC (Canada Mortgage and Housing Corporation). (1987). *Assessment Report: Public Housing Evaluation.* Ottawa: Program Evaluation Division. http://publications.gc.ca/collections/collection_2017/schl-cmhc/N5-560-1987-eng.pdf

CMHA/CRC (Canadian Mental Health Association and Community Resources Consultants of Toronto). (1979, October 17). [Letter to Ontario Municipal Board (OMB)]. Re: Hearing on North York Restricted Area By-Law 27223. Toronto Municipal Archives, Fonds 301, Series 1680, File 206.

Cochrane, R. (1962, November 23). Home Sweet (?) Home: More Than 30,000 In Metro Lack a Decent Place to Live. *Toronto Daily Star (1900–1971).* https://ezproxy.library.yorku.ca/login?url=https://www.proquest.com/historical-newspapers/page-17/docview/1426495157/se-2

Cole, D. (2022). *The Skin We're In: A Year of Black Resistance and Power.* Anchor Canada.

Colle, J. (2018, July 3). Josh Colle 'to' Chair Augimeri and Members of North York Community Council. *Subject: Lawrence Heights Revitalization 2.0.* [Letter.] https://www.toronto.ca/legdocs/mmis/2018/ny/bgrd/backgroundfile-118287.pdf

Colton, T.J. (1980). *Big Daddy Federick G. Gardiner and the Building of Metropolitan Toronto.* University of Toronto Press.

Computing in the Humanities and Social Sciences. (n.d.). Ethnic Origins for Census Tract #5250286 [data file]. http://www.chass.utoronto.ca

Cooper, A. (2007). Acts of Resistance: Black Men and Women Engage Slavery in Upper Canada, 1793–1803. *Ontario History, 99*(1), 5–17.

Corman, J.C. (1969). Law Enforcement in the Administration of Justice. *William and Mary Law Review, 10*, 579–585.

Crawford, J. (1984, December 3). [Letter to Howard Moscoe, Esq. Alderman, Ward 4 City of North York]. Toronto Municipal Archives, Fonds 301, Series 1680, File 997.

Crosby, A. (2023). *Resisting Eviction: Domicide and the Financialization of Rental Housing.* Halifax: Fernwood Publishing.

Crump, J. (2003). The End of Public Housing as We Know It: Public Housing Policy, Labor Regulation and the US City. *International Journal of Urban and Regional Research, 27*(1), 179–187.

Daly, R. (2005, February 12). The Big Fix; 7,500 People Will Be Uprooted and $1 Billion Spent on Regent Park's Remake but Plans for Mixed Housing Are Sending out Mixed Signals. *Toronto Star*, B01. https://ezproxy. library.yorku.ca/login?url=https://www.proquest.com/newspapers/ big-fix-7-500-people-will-be-uprooted-1-billion/docview/438782623/se-2

Daniels Spectrum. (n.d.). About. *Danielsspectrum.ca*. https://danielsspectrum.ca/ about-daniels-spectrum/

Darden, J.T. (2006). The Impact of Canadian Immigration Policy on the Structure of the Black Caribbean Family in Toronto. In E. Fong (ed.), *Inside the Mosaic* (pp. 146–168). University of Toronto Press.

De Sousa, C. (2006). Urban Brownfields Redevelopment in Canada: The Role of Local Government. *The Canadian Geographer, 50*(3), 392–407.

Dehli, K. (1990). Creating a Dense and Intelligent Community: Local State Formation in Early 19th Century Upper Canada. *Journal of Historical Sociology, 3*(2), 109–132.

Delagran, W.R. (1966). *Life in the Heights: The Tenants' Viewpoint.* Toronto Municipal Archives, Fonds 1001, Series 536, File 24.

___. (1967, April 10). *A Proposal for the Introduction of Social Services into Low-Income Neighbourhoods with Specific Reference to Public Housing Projects.* Toronto Municipal Archives, Fonds 220, Series 100, File 79.

Desfor, G., Keil, R., and Wekerle, G. (2006). From Surf to Turf: No Limits to Growth in Toronto? *Studies in Political Economy, 77*(1), 131–155.

Dewing, M. (2009). Canadian Multiculturalism (Background Paper). *Library of Parliament*(2009-20-E), 1–18. https://publications.gc.ca/site/eng/9.567286/ publication.html

Filc, D. (2021). Is Resistance Always Counter-Hegemonic? *Journal of Political Ideologies, 26*(1), 23–38.

Fine, J. (1980, December 19). [Letter to the Clerk of the City of North York by the Lawrence Manor Ratepayers' Association]. *Re: Summary of By-Law 27950.* Toronto Municipal Archives, Fonds 301, Series 1680, File 206.

Fleras, A. (2011). *The Media Gaze: Representations of Diversities in Canada.* UBC Press.

Fraser, J.C., Burns, A.B., Bazuin, J.T., and Oakley, D.A. (2013). HOPE VI, Colonization, and the Production of Difference. *Urban Affairs Review, 49*(4), 525–556.

Freeman, V. (2010). Toronto Has No History! *Urban History Review, 38*(2), 21–35.

Friedman, M., and Friedman, R. (1990). *Free to Choose: A Personal Statement.* Houghton Mifflin Harcourt.

Garside, P.L. (1988). 'Unhealthy Areas:' Town Planning, Eugenics and the Slums, 1890–1945. *Planning Perspectives, 3*(1), 24–46.

Gilroy, P. (1987). *'There Ain't No Black in the Union Jack': The Cultural Politics of Race and Nation.* London: Hutchinson.

Gramsci, A. (1971). *Selections from the Prison Notebooks.* (Q. Hoare, and G. Nowell-Smith, eds.) London: Lawrence and Wishart.

Grant, K. (2010, June 23). Lawrence Heights Redevelopment One Step Closer. *Globe and Mail*, A14. https://www.theglobeandmail.com/news/toronto/lawrence-heights-redevelopment-one-step-closer/article1211913/

Graves, E.M. (2011). Mixed Outcome Developments: Comparing Policy Goals to Resident Outcomes in Mixed-Income Housing. *Journal of the American Planning Association, 77*(2), 143–153.

GTA-Homes. (n.d.). North York Centre Growth Plan. https://www.gta-homes.com/real-estate-info/north-york-growth-plan/

Hackworth, J., and Moriah, A. (2006). Neoliberalism, Contingency and Urban Policy: The Case of Social Housing in Ontario. *International Journal of Urban and Regional Research, 30*(3), 510–527.

Haggart, R. (1958, October 20). How Two Reeves Stand as Housing Winds Roar. *Toronto Daily Star (1900–1971)*, 7. https://ezproxy.library.yorku.ca/login?url=https://www.proquest.com/historical-newspapers/page-7/docview/1425710246/se-2

___. (1964, February). Why Do We Build Public Housing? *Toronto Daily Star (1900–1971)*, 7. https://ezproxy.library.yorku.ca/login?url=https://www.proquest.com/historical-newspapers/page-7/docview/1427397366/se-2

"Happy with Lawrence Heights." (1958, November 7). *Toronto Daily Star (1900–1971)*, 8. https://ezproxy.library.yorku.ca/login?url=https://www.proquest.com/historical-newspapers/page-8/docview/1425980365/se-2

Hart, P.W. (1968). *Pioneering in North York: A History of the Borough.* Toronto: General Publishing Company Limited.

Harvey, D. (1989). From Managerialism to Entrepreneurialism: The Transformation in Urban Governance in Late Capitalism. *Geografiska Annaler: Series B, Human Geography, 71*(1), 3–17.

___. (2007). *A Brief History of Neoliberalism.* Oxford University Press.

___. (2015). Slums and Skyscapes Housing and the City Under Neoliberalism: Dangerous Times [Video File]. https://www.youtube.com/watch?v=M-3WcrQy8K4andt=759s

Hayes, D. (2016, December 8). *Inside Regent Park: Toronto's Test Case for Public–Private Gentrification.* DavidHayes.ca: https://davidhayes.ca/wp-content/uploads/2011/06/Guardian-INSIDE-REGENT-PARK-Dec8-2016.pdf

Heights Development. (2015). Lawrence Heights Phase One District, Public Art Plan. City of Toronto. https://www.toronto.ca/legdocs/mmis/2015/ny/bgrd/backgroundfile-82343.pdf

Hollobon, J. (1970, December 25). School Offers Room: Metro Community Unites to Get Clinic. *Globe and Mail*, 12. https://ezproxy.library.yorku.ca/login?url=https://www.proquest.com/historical-newspapers/school-offers-room/docview/1242275416/se-2

Housing Project Urged On. (1955, March 3). *Toronto Daily Star (1900–1971)*, 35. https://ezproxy.library.yorku.ca/login?url=https://www.proquest.com/historical-newspapers/page-35/docview/1433448670/se-2

Houston, C.J., and Smyth, W.J. (1990). *Irish Emigration and Canadian Settlement: Patterns, Links, and Letters.* University of Toronto Press.

How Could Anybody Live Here? Vancouver-Woman Says She'd Go Batty in Lawrence Heights; 6,000 People Is 5,200 More than in Her B.C. Project. (1970, June 18). *Globe and Mail*, W4. https://ezproxy.library.yorku.ca/login?url=https://www.proquest.com/historical-newspapers/how-could-anybody-live-here/docview/1242136593/se-2

How Metro Fails in Housing Needy. (1960, January 5). *Toronto Daily Star (1900–1971)*, 2. https://ezproxy.library.yorku.ca/login?url=https://www.proquest.com/historical-newspapers/page-2/docview/1425717427/se-2

HUD (U.S. Department of Housing and Urban Development. (n.d.). *About* HOPE VI. https://www.hud.gov/program_offices/public_indian_housing/programs/ph/hope6/about

Hulchanski, J.D. (1986). The 1935 Dominion Housing Act: Setting the Stage for a Permanent Federal Presence in Canada's Housing Sector. *Urban History Review, 15*(1), 19–39.

____. (2010). The Three Cities Within Toronto. Cities Centre.

Hulchanski, J.D., and Shapcott, M. (2004). Introduction. In J.D. Hulchanski and M. Shapcott (eds.), *Finding Room: Policy Options for a Canadian Rental Housing Strategy* (pp. 3–14). Centre for Urban and Community Studies, University of Toronto.

Hume, C. (2018, October 29). Lawrence Heights' Revitalization Aims to Weave the Community Back into the City. *Toronto Star.* https://www.thestar.com/news/gta/2018/10/29/lawrence-heights-revitalization-aims-to-weave-the-community-back-into-the-city.html

Huynh, T. (2020, January 28). Welcome to Lawrence Heights. *The Local(4).* https://thelocal.to/welcome-to-lawrence-heights/

Jacobs, J. (1961). *The Death and Life of Great American Cities.* New York: Vintage Books.

James, R.K. (2010). From 'Slum Clearance' to 'Revitalisation': Planning, Expertise and Moral Regulation in Toronto's Regent Park. *Planning Perspectives, 25*(1), 69–86.

Jones, F. (1970, June 18). 'People Power' Changes Housing to Homes in Lawrence Heights. *Toronto Daily Star (1900–1971)*, 26. https://ezproxy.library.yorku.ca/login?url=https://www.proquest.com/historical-newspapers/page-26/docview/1406201795/se-2

Kane, L. (2013, April 29). Lawrence Heights Developer Named For Revitalization. *Toronto Star.* https://www.thestar.com/news/gta/lawrence-heights-developer-named-for-revitalization/article_13f34cfe-ce07-54a2-b964-a2a271373ea7.html

Keil, R. (2000). Governance Restructuring in Los Angeles and Toronto: Amalgamation or Secession? *International Journal of Urban and Regional Research, 24*(4), 758–781.

____. (2002). "Common-Sense" Neoliberalism: Progressive Conservative Urbanism in Toronto, Canada. *Antipode, 34*(3), 578–601.

Keil, R., and Addie, J.P. (2015). 'It's Not Going To Be Suburban, It's Going To Be All Urban:' Assembling Post-Suburbia in the Toronto and Chicago Regions. *International Journal of Urban and Regional Research, 39*(5), 1–15.

Kelly, E., Manning, D.T., Boye, S., Rice, C., Owen, D., Stonefish, S., and Stonefish, M. (2021). Elements of a Counter-Exhibition: Excavating and Countering a Canadian

History and Legacy of Eugenics. *Journal of the History of Behavioural Sciences, 57*(1), 12–33.

Kids Run Free Like Bunnies. (1960, October 22). *Toronto Daily Star (1900–1971)*, 1. https://ezproxy.library.yorku.ca/login?url=https://www.proquest.com/historical-newspapers/page-1/docview/1426008939/se-2

Kipfer, S., and Keil, R. (2000). Still Planning To Be Different? Toronto at the Turn of the Millenium. *disP - The Planning Review, 36*(140), 28–36.

___. (2002). Toronto Inc? Planning the Competitive City in the New Toronto. *Antipode, 34*(2), 227–264.

Kipfer, S., and Petrunia, J. (2009). "Recolonization" and Public Housing: A Toronto Case Study. *Studies in Political Economy, 83*(1), 111–139.

Kreitmeyr, N. (2019). Neoliberal Co-Optation and Authoritarian Renewal: Social Entrepreneurship Networks in Jordan and Morocco. *Globalizations, 16*(3), 289–303.

Labour Community Services. (2019, September 18). We All Belong. https://twitter.com/Labour_CS/status/1174389936700710912

Lavee, E., and Cohen, N. (2019). How Street-Level Bureaucrats Become Policy Entrepreneurs: The Case of Urban Renewal. *Governance, 32*(3), 475–492.

Lawrence Manor Ratepayers' Association. (1956, February). [*Lawrence Manor Gazette*]. Toronto Municipal Archives, Fonds 301, Series 1680, File 1059.

Lehrer, U., Keil, R., and Kipfer, S. (2010). Reurbanization in Toronto: Condominum Boom and Social Housing Revitalization. *disP-The Planning Review, 46*(180), 81–90.

LeRoux, K. (2007). Nonprofits as Civic Intermediaries: The Role of Community-Based Organizations in Promoting Political Participation. *Urban Affairs Review, 42*(3), 410–422.

Leslie, D., and Hunt, M. (2013). Securing the Neoliberal City: Discourses of Creativity and Priority Neighborhoods in Toronto, Canada. *Urban Geography, 34*(8), 1171–1192.

Ley, D., and Smith, N. (2000). Relations between Deprivation and Immigrant Groups in Large Canadian Cities. *Urban Studies, 37*(1), 37–62.

LHION. (2019, June 27). Community Meeting Minutes.

___. (2019, September 26). Community Meeting Minutes.

___. (2019, September 17). Community Meeting Minutes.

___. (2020, March 18). Community Meeting Minutes.

___. (2020, March 12). Community Meeting Minutes.

___. (2020, March 18). Community Meeting Minutes.

___. (2020, March 18). Community Meeting Minutes.

___. (2020, December 1). Community Meeting Minutes.

___. (2020, November 19). Community Meeting Minutes.

___. (2020, February 13). Community Meeting Minutes.

LHTA (Lawrence Heights' Tenants Association). (n.d.). [*Constitution*]. Toronto Municipal Archives, Fonds 301, Series 1680, File 619.

Limit on Income May Be Abolished at Lawrence Heights Project. (1966, August 10). *Globe and Mail*, 8. https://ezproxy.library.yorku.ca/login?url=https://www.proquest.com/historical-newspapers/limit-on-income-may-be-abolished-at-lawrence/docview/1316555938/se-2

Liu, S., and Blomley, N. (2013). Making News and Making Space: Framing Vancouver's Downtown Eastside. *The Canadian Geographer/Le Geographe Canadien, 57*(2), 119–132.

Lorimer, J. (1978). *The Developers.* James Lorimer and Company.

Lucio, J., Hand, L., and Marsiglia, F. (2014). Designing Hope: Rationales of Mixed-Income. *Journal of Urban Affairs, 36*(5), 891–904.

Maley, T. (2019). The Democratic Imagination in Ontario and Participatory Budgeting. In G. Albo, and B.M. Evans (eds.), *Divided Province: Ontario Politics in the Age of Neoliberalism* (pp. 493–521). McGill-Queen's University Press.

Maynard, R. (2017). *Policing Black Lives: State Violence in Canada from Slavery to the Present.* Halifax: Fernwood Publishing.

Metcalf Foundation. (2021, December). *Regent Park: A Progress Report.* https://www.metcalffoundation.com/wp-content/uploads/2022/02/Regent-Park-2022-ONLINE-metcalf.pdf

Metropia Inc. (n.d.). Metropia Condo Developer. https://metropia.ca/about/

Micallef, S. (2020, January 28). Where the Spadina Expressway Didn't Stop. *The Local* (4). https://thelocal.to/where-the-spadina-expressway-didnt-stop/

Milczyn, P. (2018). Affordable Housing. *Legislative Assembly of Ontario. Edited Hansard, 129. 41st Parliament, 2nd session.* https://www.ola.org/sites/default/files/node-files/hansard/document/pdf/2017/2017-11/house-document-hansard-transcript-2-EN-30-NOV-2017_L129.pdf

Mississaugas of the Credit First Nation. (n.d.). *Treaty Lands and Territory.* http://mncfn.ca/about-mncfn/treaty-lands-and-territory/

Moscoe, H. (1983, May 20). [Letter to The Executive of the Lawrence Manor Ratepayers' Association]. Toronto Municipal Archives, Fonds 301, Series 1680, File 590.

___. (1984, November 14). [Letter to Jack Marks, Chief of Police]. Toronto Municipal Archives, Fonds 301, Series 1680, File 997.

Moscoe, H., O'Neill, P., and Foster, M. (1979, June 6). [Letter to Hon. C. Bennett, Minister of Housing (Ontario)]. Toronto Municipal Archives, Fonds 301, Series 1680, File 209.

MPATHY. (2018a). About Us. https://mpathy.ca/about/

___. (2018b). *Reclaiming Artifacts.* https://mpathy.ca/projects/reclaiming-artifacts/

Mullings, D., Morgan, A., and Quelleng, H.K. (2016). Canada the Great White North where Anti-Black Racism Thrives: Kicking Down the Doors and Exposing Realities. *Phylon (1960–), 53*(1), 20–41.

Murdie, R. (2002). The Housing Careers of Polish and Somali Newcomers in Toronto's Rental Market. *Housing Studies, 17*(3), 423–443.

___. (2008). Diversity and Concentration in Canadian Immigration: Trends in Toronto, Montreal and Vancouver, 1971–2006. *Centre for Urban and Community Studies, Research Bulletin*(42), 1–12.

Murdie, R.A., Preston, V., Ghosh, S., and Chevalier, M. (2006). *Immigrants and Housing: A Review of Canadian Literature from 1990 to 2005.* Ottawa: CMHC.

Murdie, R., and Teixeira, C. (2003). Towards a Comfortable Neighborhood and Appropriate Housing: Immigrant Experiences in Toronto. In P. Anisef, and C.M. Lanphier (eds.), *The World in a City* (pp. 132–191). University of Toronto Press.

New Look in Low-Rent Housing. (1961, May 27). *Toronto Daily Star (1900–1971)*, 7. https://ezproxy.library.yorku.ca/login?url=https://www.proquest.com/historical-newspapers/page-7/docview/1428735023/se-2

Nitkin, D. (2010a). [Letter to EthicScan: Ethics Consulting, Research and Education]. Toronto Municipal Archives, Fonds 301, Series 1680, File 1349.

___. (2010b, June 17). [Letter to EthicsScan: Ethics Consulting, Research and Education]. Toronto Municipal Archives, Fonds 301, Series 1680, File 1349.

North York Community House. (2019). About Us. https://www.nych.ca/about-us

North York Planning Board. (1980, May 28). [Committee Meeting on Alternate Residential Care Facilities — Group Homes and Crisis Care Facilities]. Toronto Municipal Archives, Fonds 301, Series 1680, File 206.

___. (1981, April 8). [Extract from the Minutes of Planning Board Held on April 8, 1981]. Toronto Municipal Archives, Fonds 301, Series 1680, File 206.

Ontario Coalition Against Poverty. (2021, November 8). *Statement on City's Shelter Infrastructure Plan and Shelter-Hotels.*

Owusu-Bempah, A. (2014). *Black Males' Perceptions of and Experiences with the Police in Toronto.* Doctoral Dissertation, University of Toronto. https://www.proquest.com/openview/334d9eaf8f57e32b0ee24963c3b47357/1?pq-origsite=gscholarand-cbl=18750

Pagliaro, J. (2019, August 8). Struggling with Violence, Lawrence Heights May Not Get the Community Centre it Was Promised. *Toronto Star.* https://www.thestar.com/news/gta/city-hall/struggling-with-violence-lawrence-heights-may-not-get-the-community-centre-it-was-promised/article_3fb862fc-40d3-5eea-8855-e0c57aa62ddd.html

Paikin, S. (1994, May 12). *Transcript: Mike Harris on the Common Sense Revolution.* TVOtoday: https://www.tvo.org/transcript/529615

Pasieka, C. (2022, November 13). Lawrence Heights Residents Demand More Input Into Neighbourhood's New Community Centre. CBC *News.* https://www.cbc.ca/news/canada/toronto/lawrence-heights-community-centre-coming-1.6649527

Plan Fight for Spadina Expressway. (1962, January 19). *Toronto Daily Star (1900–1971)*, 8. https://ezproxy.library.yorku.ca/login?url=https://www.proquest.com/historical-newspapers/page-8/docview/1426017888/se-2

Poisson, J. (2010, October 14). Two-Horse Race for Moscoe's Old Seat: The Voters, and How They Live: Development an Issue as Lawrence Heights To Be Torn Down, Rebuilt. *Toronto Star,* GT4. https://www.thestar.com/news/gta/two-horse-race-for-moscoes-old-seat/article_84430ec4-eca5-5466-8e42-bab6c2c32584.html

Powell, B. (2021, February). 'We Predicted Shootings to Happen and They Happened': In Lawrence Heights, Social Media Insults Leave Locals Bracing for Gunfire — And Looking for Blame. *Toronto Star.* https://www.thestar.com/news/gta/2021/02/15/we-predicted-shootings-to-happen-and-they-happened-in-lawrence-heights-social-media-insults-leave-locals-bracing-for-gunfire-and-looking-for-blame.html

Pratt, L. (2004, September 26). The Other Side of the Fence; A Chain-Link Divide in Lawrence Heights Residents Battle The 'Jungle' Stigma. *Toronto Star,* B03. https://ezproxy.library.yorku.ca/login?url=https://www.proquest.com/newspapers/other-side-fence-chain-link-divide-lawrence/docview/438751359/se-2

Prue, M. (2008). Budget Measures and Interim Appropriation Act, 2008. *Legislative Assembly of Ontario. Edited Hansard. 39th Parliament, 1st session.*

https://www.ola.org/sites/default/files/node-files/hansard/document/
    pdf/2008/2008-04/house-document-hansard-transcript-1-EN-07-APR-2008_
    L022A.pdf

Public Housing at Whose Expense. (1966, November 29). *Toronto Daily Star
    (1900–1971)*, 7. https://ezproxy.library.yorku.ca/login?url=https://www.proquest.
    com/historical-newspapers/page-a7/docview/1420243688/se-2

Public Housing Tenants Protest Harrassment. (1970, September 10). *Toronto Daily
    Star (1900–1971)*, B3. https://ezproxy.library.yorku.ca/login?url=https://www.
    proquest.com/historical-newspapers/page-83/docview/1411168608/se-2

Ralston, H. (1999). Canadian Immigration Policy in the Twentieth Century: Its Impact
    on South Asian Women. *Canadian Women Studies, 19*(3), 33–37.

Raphael, D., Steinmetz, B., Renwick, et al. (1999). The Community Quality of Life
    Project: A Health Promotion Approach to Understanding Communities. *Health
    Promotion International, 14*(3), 197–210.

Rosen, E. (1983, June 13). [Letter to Howard Moscoe, Alderman Ward 4]. Toronto
    Municipal Archives, Fonds 301, Series 1680, File 590.

Ross, D.G. (2017). *Remaking Downtown Toronto: Politics, Development, and Public
    Space on Yonge Street, 1950–1980.* Toronto: York University.

Saberi, P. (2017). Toronto and the 'Paris Problem': Community Policing in 'Immigrant
    Neighbourhoods.' *Race and Class, 59*(2), 49–69.

Sewell, J. (1993). *The Shape of the City: Toronto's Struggles with Modern Planning.*
    Toronto: University of Toronto Press.

Smith, N. (1995). Challenges of Public Housing in the 1990s: The Case of Ontario,
    Canada. *Housing Policy Debate, 6*(4), 905–931.

Social Planning Toronto. (2020, February 8). City Budget Forum. North York Public
    Library.

Sriskandarajah, A. (2020). Race, Space, and Media: The Production of Urban
    Neighborhood Space in East-End Toronto. *Canadian Ethnic Studies, 1*, 1–22.

Szende, A. (1970, March 11). The Poor Are Afraid to Speak Up, Principal Says. *Toronto
    Daily Star (1900–1971)*, 8. https://ezproxy.library.yorku.ca/login?url=https://www.
    proquest.com/historical-newspapers/page-8/docview/1416799231/se-2

TCHC (Toronto Community Housing Corporation). (2007). Regent Park Social
    Development Plan: Executive Summary. https://www.toronto.ca/legdocs/
    mmis/2007/ex/bgrd/backgroundfile-8820.pdf

___. (2011a, February 24). Josh Colle Community Panel [PowerPoint Presentation].
    Unpublished internal document.

___. (2011b). Community Feedback on the Housing Agreement from Community
    Forum [PowerPoint presentation]. Unpublished internal document.

___. (2011c, November 2). Lawrence Allen Secondary Plan Tenant Deputations.

___. (2012, September). Community Revitalization Update: What's Happening?
    Revitalization is moving ahead [Newsletter]. Unpublished internal document.

___. (2013, October). KPMB Community Design Workshop [PowerPoint Presentation].
    Unpublished internal document.

___. (2014, May 14). Lawrence Heights Revitalization: Phase One Overview Interior
    Unit Designs [PowerPoint Presentation]. Unpublished internal document.

___. (2017, May). Lawrence Heights Revitalization and Relocation Frequently Asked
    Questions [PowerPoint Presentation]. Unpublished internal document.

___. (2018, September). Lawrence Heights: Community Revitalization Update [Newsletter]. Unpublished internal document.

___. (2020d, September 17). Community Meeting Minutes.

___. (2021, March 24). Tenant Services Committee Meeting. https://www.torontohousing.ca/sites/default/files/2023-04/tsc_march_24_public_agenda_-_written_deputations1.pdf

___. (n.d.). *Lawrence Heights*. https://www.torontohousing.ca/lawrence_heights

Tempers Rise With Gas Bills. (1959, April 10). *Toronto Daily Star (1900–1971)*, 8. https://ezproxy.library.yorku.ca/login?url=https://www.proquest.com/historical-newspapers/page-8/docview/1425714082/se-2

Thobani, S. (2000a). Closing the Nation's Doors to Immigrant Women: The Restructuring of Canadian Immigration Policy. *Atlantis: Critical Studies in Gender, Culture and Social Justice, 24*(2), 16–26.

___. (2000b). Closing Ranks: Racism and Sexism in Canada's Immigration Policy. *Race and Class, 42*(1), 35–55.

Tong, V. (2021). Revitalization in Regent Park 12 Years Later. In S. Tsenkova (ed.), *Cities and Affordable Housing: Planning, Design and Policy Nexus* (pp. 129–139). Routledge.

Toronto City Council. (1999). *Provincial Local Services Realignment — Making It Work, and Towards a New Relationship with Ontario and Canada*. https://www.toronto.ca/legdocs/2000/agendas/council/cc/cc000704/pof9rpt/cl001.pdf

Tsenkova, S. (2022). Neighborhood Rebuilidng and Affordable Housing in Canadian Cities. *Urban Research and Practice, 15*(5), 773–788.

Vincent, Donovan. (2007a, May 15). Lawrence Heights' Plan Draws Anger; Proponents of the Renewal Get an Earful from Those Afraid They'll Be Squeezed Out. *Toronto Star*, E6. https://ezproxy.library.yorku.ca/login?url=https://www.proquest.com/newspapers/lawrence-heights-plan-draws-residents-anger/docview/439221557/se-2

___. (2007b, May 11). Massive Lawrence Heights Overhaul Planned; Huge Revitalization to Create Mix of Housing Raises Fears the Poor Will Get Swept Out. *Toronto Star*, B1. https://www.thestar.com/news/massive-lawrence-heights-overhaul-planned/article_ece3316e-3154-5b9f-af31-dd2547ef67ca.html

___. (2008, December 2). City Urged to Sell Housing to Pay for New Buildings; Report Calls for Unloading 370 Low-Income Units. *Toronto Star*, A8. https://www.thestar.com/news/city-urged-to-sell-housing-to-pay-for-new-buildings/article_4eae9eb1-5323-57e8-aaf8-4415f59a8259.html

___. (2010, February 25). 'Massive' Plan to Revamp Troubled Public Housing; Lawrence Heights Remake Plans Ready. *Toronto Star*, A1. https://www.thestar.com/news/gta/massive-plan-to-revamp-troubled-lawrence-heights/article_b2a79c08-1d87-514a-b318-1b6ad93bed8a.html

Viswanathan, L. (2010). Contesting Racialization in a Neoliberal City: Cross-Cultural Collective Formation as a Strategy among Alternative Social Planning Organizations in Toronto. *GeoJournal* (75), 261–272.

Walks, A., and Bourne, L.S. (2006). Ghettos in Canadian Cities? Racial Segregation, Ethnic Enclaves and Poverty Concentration in Canadian Urban Areas. *The Canadian Geographer/Le Geographie Canadien, 50*(3), 273–297.

Watson, D. (2019). Fordism: A Review Essay. *Labor History, 60*(2), 144–159.

Way Cleared for Start: Board Backs North York Housing. (1955, July 1). *Globe and Mail*, 5. https://ezproxy.library.yorku.ca/login?url=https://www.proquest.com/historical-newspapers/way-cleared-start/docview/1289865596/se-2

Wellman, B. (2006). Jane Jacobs the Torontonian. *City and Community, 5*(3), 217–222.

White, R. (2014). Jane Jacobs and the Paradigm Shift. In D. Schubert (ed.), *Contemporary Perspectives on Jane Jacobs: Reassessing the Impacts of an Urban Visionary* (pp. 31–56). Ashgate Publishing Limited.

Wilson, C. (2019). 'He Doesn't Get It:' Coun. Slams Ford Over Funding for Lawrence Heights Community Centre. *CP24*. https://www.cp24.com/news/he-doesn-t-get-it-coun-slams-ford-over-funding-for-lawrence-heights-community-centre-1.4543176

Wilson, W.J. ([1987] 1996). *The Truly Disadvantaged*. Routledge.

___. (1991). Another Look at *The Truly Disadvantaged. Political Science Quarterly, 106*(4), 639–656.

___. (2010). Why Both Structure and Culture Matter in a Holistic Analysis of Inner-City Poverty. *The Annals of the American Academy of Political and Social Science, 629*(1), 200–219.

Wolfe, P. (2006). Settler Colonialism and the Elimination of the Native. *Journal of Genocide Research, 8*(4), 387–409.

Wynn, G. (1979). Notes on Society and Environment in Old Ontario. *Journal of Social History, 13*(1), 49–65.

Yardhouse, N. (1960, November 16). From the Chairman of Council to the Minister of Public Works. The Municipality of Metropolitan Toronto Clerk's Department. Toronto Municipal Archives, Fonds 200, Series 100, File 78.

Index

*Note: page locators for images are in **bold***

affluent residents,
government favouring of, 19, 49
low-income tenants versus, 8, 48, 74, 103, 138
moral supervision by, 2, 52, 102, 148, 155
stimulating influx of, 2, 88–9, 108–9
affordable housing, 14
barriers to, 56, 58–9, 62, 119
calls for, 29, 135–6
production, 27, 86
shortage of, 13, 16, 23–5, 32–3, 53
African people,
immigration of, 56, 58–9
in Lawrence Heights, 60–3
Albo, Greg, 91, 152–3
alienation, 7–8, 140
capitalism/neoliberalism and, 5, 73
Lawrence Heights resident feelings of, 19, 21, 49, 156
Allen Expressway, 36–7
Lawrence Heights revitalization around, *see* Lawrence-Allen revitalization plan
splitting Lawrence Heights, 12, 19, 44–6, 132
anti-Black racism, 73
government policies and, 78–9, 81–2, 122
resistance to, 74–5, 148, 153
stereotypes, 53–4, 75–6, 80–1, 153
apartments, 37, 101, 136
construction of, 28, 41, 47, 96, 154
Lawrence Heights, 12-**13**, 18, **42**, 44
Lawrence Manor ratepayers' opposition to, 69–70

poverty concentration in certain, 58–9, 79
Asian people,
immigration of, 56, 58–9
as Lawrence Heights tenants, 8, 13, 60–1, 63
see also Chinese migrants
August, Martine, 154
austerity,
government commitments to, 19, 86, 91, 98, 126
impacts of, 4, 133–6, 146, 151, 154

Baldwin, James, 74–5
Ballantyne, Derek, 14, 21, 105
banking sector growth, 47, 57
Bathurst Heights Secondary School, 12, 45, 111
Black people,
government policies toward, 59–60, 73–4, 78–9, 122, 149
homicide victimization rate, 73
as Lawrence Heights tenants, 1, 8, 19, 61, 80–2, 139–40, 153
public housing over-representation, 19, 62, 135
racism facing, *see* anti-Black racism
resistance of, 74, 148–9, 153
state violence against, 15–16, 73–5, 79, 138–40
stereotypes of, 18, 74–6, 80, 148, 153
white supremacist hierarchies and, 53, 78, 82, 94, 138
youth initiatives, 139–40
Boudreau, J.A., 87
Bradford, Neil, 28

Brinkerhoff, Jennifer, 126
Britain, 28
    immigrants from, 13, 60–1
    settler colonialism of, 24–6, 56, 94
Brown people, racism and stigma facing,
    1, 15, 18, 53, 135
Bruce Report, 31–2, 41–2

Cabbagetown, 31–2
Canada Mortgage and Housing
    Corporation (CMHC), 71
    cheap purchase of Lawrence Heights
        land, 12, 21, 35–6
    Lawrence Heights project, 41–2
    public housing construction, 29, 89
capital,
    accumulation, 3, 16, 26, 82
    collectivization of, 34, 66
    labour needed for, 56–7, 60, 63
    needed for degraded housing, 91–2,
        98, 102, 106, 110
    for public works projects, 36, 38, 40,
        47, 85, 98
    real estate, 63, 88, 107
    for urban revitalization, 1–2, 8–13,
        78, 91–2
capitalism,
    hierarchies of race and class in, 4,
        22, 53, 83
    inequities of, 5, 17, 23, 26, 73
    Lawrence Heights tenants confront-
        ing, 3, 23, 153–4
Caribbean people,
    immigration policies and programs
        for, 59–60
    in Lawrence Heights, 60–1, 63
    in Toronto, 61–2
Caulfield, Jon, 47
Chaskin, Robert, 6–7
Chinese migrants, 8, 57–8
City Council, North York, 67–8, 99–100
City Council, Toronto,
    lack of financing for housing, 20, 40,
        90, 111
    pressure for more/better public
        housing, 8, 20, 146, 151
    public housing plans, 9, 94, 99–100,
        111, 125, 129

    seeking to mitigate violence, 116
    see also councillors, Toronto city
City of Toronto Act, 20, 87
class,
    difficulties of ties across, 14, 37
    dominance of business, 3, 38, 71, 88,
        96, 148–9
    hierarchies, 4, 22, 94
    stigmatization, 3, 5, 8, 71
    see also middle class; working class
commercial development, 83–5, 126
    efforts to attract, 2, 5, 34, 47, 90, 101
    homogeneity of, 108–9
    lack of, 1, 96
community animators,
    challenges of, 143–5, 153
    in Lawrence Heights, 9, 125, 130–1,
        134, 143–5, 151
community centres, 95, 99, 118
    Lawrence Heights, see Lawrence
        Heights Community Centre
condominiums, 70, 143
    alongside public housing, 1–2, 83,
        97, 103, 154
    building of downtown, 57–9, 107
    without social housing, 135–6
Cole, Desmond, 79, 94
Colle, Josh, 100, 109, 141–2
Context, 1, 106–8, 151
Cooper, Afua, 74
cooperative housing, 2, 29, 55, 59, 136
councillors, Toronto city, 25, 141
    action/opinions on Lawrence
        Heights, 13–14, 37–9, 44, 78, 100,
        109
    revitalization proponents, 1, 98
    tenant/resident complaints to, 15,
        37, 69, 123
    see also City Council, Toronto
COVID-19 pandemic, 20, 140
Creba, Jane, 79
crime, 96
    neoliberalism and, 73, 144
    news media portrayals of, 69, 71–4,
        97, 102
    social mixing theory and, 6, 14
criminalization,
    of Black people, 16, 53, 73–4

narratives of Lawrence Heights
tenants, 13–14, 54, 78–80, 136–7
culture, 7–10
destruction of, 2, 9, 23, 144
efforts to preserve, 59, 83, 140, 152,
155
Indigenous, 9, 23
lack of, 18, 48, 61
Lawrence Heights neighbourhood,
2, 111, 144, 152, 155
see also multiculturalism
Curtis Report, 29

Davis, James, 22
Davis, Rob, 100
Delagran, W.R. (*Life in the Heights*), 21,
43–4, 48–50
developers, private, 143
buying of Lawrence Heights land,
27, 39, 107–9
on Lawrence Heights revitalization,
3, 81–4, 90, 94–7, 120, 149
opposition to, 3, 69–70, 99–100,
135
reconstruction financing, 2, 16, 88,
106, 110–11, 114
tenants' involvement limited by, 3,
9, 100, 132
displacement,
government-fuelled, 2, 8, 58, 142,
148, 156
temporary, 104–5, 120, 126, 134
diversity, ethnic, 59, 100
government commitment to, 2, 5,
63, 84, 143–4
growth in, 8, 53, 61, 68, 79
neighbourhood, 8–10, 18
drugs, 102
trade in, 15, 54, 78, 104, 137
use of, 8, 71–2, 75

Eggleton, Art, 96
employment, 73
city initiatives for, 9, 23, 28, 86, 126,
150
Lawrence Heights tenant programs
for, 111–14, 117, 120, 129–30,
145

precarious, 23
relocation of blue-collar, 5, 57–8
see also jobs
entrepreneurial government strategies,
4–10, 90, 96
Etobicoke, 26, 34, 59, 79, 87
eugenics, 24
in government policies, 25, 31,
44–5, 79
euthenics, 63, 154
eugenics versus, 24–5
in government policies, 25, 31, 54,
77–82, 128
expressways, 5, 38
negative impacts of, 45–7
see also Allen Expressway; Spadina
Expressway

federal government,
funding for public/social housing,
19, 27–8, 34, 39–40, 106
housing policy, 29, 55–6, 59–60, 90
on immigration, *see* immigration
policy
on Lawrence Heights construction,
12, 35, 38, 66, 110
public housing program, *see* public
housing program (national)
transfer payments, *see* transfer
payment reductions
Filc, Dani, 10–11
financing, 34
bonds for public housing, 39–40
challenges with social housing, 29,
98, 110–11, 151
Lawrence Heights revitalization, 14,
105–6, 110, 131
Fine, Judith, 68–9
Flemington Road Public School, 1, 12,
64–6, 111
Ford, Doug, 141, 155
Ford, Rob, 100
Fordism, 28, 52
Foucault, Michel, 11
Friedman, Milton (*Free to Choose*), 86,
114
Future Landscapes, 149

gangs, 116
  narratives of violence of, 18, 70, 76
  policing intervention for, 79
Gardiner, Fred, fluctuation on public
  housing, 38–40
Garner, Fred, 32
gentrification, 97
  destructive processes of, 15, 58–9,
    62, 143, 148, 156
  government-fuelled, 2, 10, 57, 89,
    151–2
  narratives of, 8, 102, 142, 144
ghettoization of public housing, 5, 49,
  74, 124
Gilroy, Paul, 74
global city, Toronto as, 19, 56–7, 62–3,
  85, 88
Globe and Mail coverage, 71
  of Lawrence Heights, 21, 36, 39,
    48–50, 65–6
government,
  federal, see federal government
  mismanagement, 3, 102
  provincial, see provincial
    government
Gramsci, Antonio, 10
Great Depression, 27–8, 32
Greater Toronto Area, 13, 34, 93
Green, Charles, 149
green spaces, 5
  in Lawrence Heights, 41, 103, 109,
    113
  revitalization plans and, 5, 41, 83,
    113
gridlock, process of, 91–3, 146

Haggart, Ron, 49
Harlem Children's Zone (HCZ), 128
Harris, Mike, 20
  Common Sense Revolution, 19,
    85–6, 96, 126
  public service cuts, 20, 91–2, 97–8
  Social Housing Reform Act, 90–1
Harvey, David, 4, 5n1, 91, 108
hegemony, 10, 149
Heights Development, 120
  scholarship program funding, 75,
    111

TCHC development plan partnership, 1, 103, 106–8, 111, 133, 151
Hellyer Task Force (and report), 19, 55, 59
Henry, George S., 11, 26
hierarchies, social,
  government policies and, 9, 22–4,
    30, 82, 89, 94
  of migrants, 19, 60
  public housing and, 4, 52–3, 138
  racial, 51, 56–7, 74, 94
homelessness, 23–4, 29, 97
housing conditions, 125
  moral associations with, 16, 42, 154
  neoliberal policies and, 8, 23, 73
  oppressive, 9, 23, 53–4, 77
  substandard, 8, 24, 27, 59, 80, 93
Housing Opportunities for People
  Everywhere (HOPE VI) program,
    middle-class recolonizing through,
      7–8, 15, 89
    mixed-income housing in, 6–8
    neighbourhood-effects thesis, 6,
      15, 83
Housing Secretariat, Toronto, 14
Howard, Ebenezer, 41, 43
Hume, Christopher, 14, 136–7

immigrants, 142
  colonial violence against, 24
  European, 13, 56, 60–1
  housing for, 18, 58–9, 62–3, 117, 149
  Jewish, 57–8
  preferred versus non-preferred,
    56–7
  programs to attract, 59–60, 86
  racialized, 8, 56–62, 73
Immigration Act, 19, 56–7, 60
immigration pattern shifts, 13, 19, 53,
  56–61
immigration policy,
  ethnic diversity and, 8, 53, 61, 68,
    73, 79
  points system, switch to, 56–7
  relaxing of restrictions, 8, 34, 53–6,
    59, 73, 85
Indigenous Peoples, 29
  dispossession of land, 8–9, 11, 23–7,
    53, 142

erasure of, 24–6, 119, 135
government narratives of, 45, 51, 53,
    94, 140
homelessness, 23–4
as Lawrence Heights tenants, 13, 61
infrastructure,
    demands for improvements to,
        91–2, 94, 101–2, 122, 125, 137
    financing for, 34–6, 40, 98, 109–11,
        118, 151
    hard versus social, 1, 85, 99, 109–14,
        129
    investment, 11–12, 113, 148, 154
    Lawrence Heights, 1, 85, 92, 99–100,
        125, 137, 140
    Regent Park, 20, 118
inner city, 34, 42, 141, 151
    commuting to/from, 13, 34, 44, 47,
        64
    gentrification of, 5, 36, 62–3, 83,
        88–9
    public housing construction outside,
        5, 36, 63, 99, 108, 110
    racialized/lower-income people and,
        13, 35, 57–9
    shifting employment out of, 13, 63,
        149
investment, private, 13, 58, 95
    attracting, 5, 35, 134, 149
    companies, 107–8, 110, 114, 120
    foreign, 47, 87–8
    government prioritization of, 17,
        27–9, 39–40, 86
    gridlock and, 91–2
    HOPE VI program and, 6, 14–16,
        98–9
    Keynesianism and, 28
Irish, land settlement by, 25–7, 31

Jacobs, Jane, 32, 41, 45–6, 76–8, 81
James, Ryan, 32
Jamestown, 18, 79, 108
Jane-Finch neighbourhood, 18, 35, 79, 92
Jeanneret, Charles-Édouard, see Le
    Corbusier
jobs, 132
    programs for placements in, 4, 114,
        126

socially mixed housing and, 6
struggles to find decent, 54, 59, 86,
    148–9, 151–2
tenant commuting for, 13, 63
see also employment
Joseph, Mark, 6–7

Keil, Roger, 2, 11, 88, 143
Keynesianism, 7, 23, 28, 30, 73
Kipfer, Stefan, 2, 59, 143

lands,
    city financing sale of Lawrence
        Heights, 12, 14, 21, 35–6
    developer cheap purchase of, 27, 39,
        107–9
    stolen Indigenous, 8–9, 11–12, 23–7,
        53, 142
Lastman, Mel, 87, 97
Latin Americans, 56
    as Lawrence Heights tenants, 8, 13,
        60–1, 63
Lawrence-Allen revitalization plan,
    101–3, 106, 110, 113
    public engagement in, 111, 123–5,
        147
Lawrence Avenue, 12, 25–6, 37, 101
    history of name, 22
Lawrence Heights,
    boundaries and housing types of,
        12–13, 33, 41, 42–3, 44
    bussing kids out of, 44–5
    community engagement of, 20, 15,
        111–14, 126, 129–33, 145
    cost of land, 27, 39, 41, 107–9
    culture of, 2, 111, 144, 152, 155
    demographics of, 1, 8, 12–13, 19, 41,
        49, 60–3
    design and layout of, 2, 41–4, 48–50,
        52, 80
    disparagement of, 12–13, 23, 44,
        47–8, 77, 103, 122–5
    housing construction in, 18–20,
        23–4, 106–7, 118
    judo club in, 48–9
    as "jungle," 21, 50, 64, 71–2, 102
    loneliness and isolation in, 15,
        18–21, 50, 63–4, 78, 103, 130–3

pods in, 140–1
as "priority neighbourhood," 1, 48,
    53, 78–80, 93–4, 98, 125
settler-colonial history of, 11–12,
    22–7, 119
Turtle Island Road in, **118–19**
Lawrence Heights Community Centre, 1,
    64–6, 141
    meetings at, 50, **75**, 117, 131, 155
Lawrence Heights Inter-Organizational
    Network (LHION),
    community safety work, 137–40
    formation and aims of, 20, 117
    tenant engagement through, 120–1,
        126–9, 133–8, 140–2, 145
    work with city administration, 111,
        121, 128–32, 135, 143–5
Lawrence Heights tenants,
    challenging of government
        authorities, 15, 66–8, 122, 152
    community organizing, 64–6,
        136–42
    Lawrence Manor residents versus,
        12–13, 23, 68, 77, 103, 122–5
    limited revitalization involvement,
        9, 111, 121, 128–32, 135, 143–5
    as racialized, 53–5, 80–1, 94
    stigmatization of, 1, 13–15, 48–9,
        54–5, 71–2
    surveillance/control of, 3, 14–16,
        52–4, 63, 76–7, 82, 112, 140
    treatment by government, 12, 66–8,
        121, 131–3, 141–5, 148–50
    violations of rights of, 71–2
Lawrence Heights Tenants' Association
    (LHTA), 65–6
Lawrence Manor, 45, 66
    group home opposition, 68–9
    high-density housing opposition,
        55, 65, 69–71
    Ratepayers' Association opposition
        to Lawrence Heights, 37–8, 40,
        68–71
    residents shunning of Lawrence
        Heights, 12–13, 23, 77, 103, 122–5
    treatment by government, 39, 54–5,
        68, 77, 124
Le Corbusier, 32–3, 42–3, 63, 83

Lehrer, Ute, 2, 143
Liberal Party, 90, 92, 98, 100, 141, 149
Life in the Heights (Delagran), 21, 43–4,
    49
Lorimer, James, 96
low-income residents, 37, 72
    government housing programs for,
        22, 27–30, 40–1, 81
    in Lawrence Heights, 12, 64–5, 80
    migration and settlement patterns
        of, 49–50, 58–61, 79
    policies to control, 29, 44, 52, 93,
        98–9, 128
    racialized, 59, 62, 74
    revitalization narratives about, 41,
        84, 93–5
    social housing needs, 2, 12, 30–1,
        55, 135
    stigmatization faced by, 48–50, 53,
        68, 74, 138
    waiting lists for housing, 31, 67–8

Malvern, 18, 35
marketization, 3, 5, 8
market-rate housing,
    inability to afford, 30, 49, 76, 136
    increasing construction of, 47, 90,
        105–7, 117–18
    social mixing and, 2, 8, 14, 83, 103,
        110
markets,
    government empowerment of, 4–5,
        15, 112
    housing, 14, 27, 47, 59, 62, 86, 95
    Keynesianism versus, 28
    labour, 56–7, 154
    neoliberal free, 4, 5n1, 87, 91, 96,
        112
    real estate, 88, 96
Marxists, 4, 10
Maynard, Robyn, 16, 54, 138
McGuinty, Dalton, 92, 98, 149
Methodists, 11, 25, 61
Metropia, 1, 106–8, 151
    Metropolitan Toronto,
    amalgamation, 20, 87, 96
    census data, 19, 61–2
    Council of, 18, 38, 68

infrastructure funding and 34–6,
38–9, 68
municipalities of, 34, 96
public housing provision in, 31,
39–41, 47, 55, 60, 67
see also Toronto (city of)
Metropolitan Toronto Housing Authority
(MTHA), 30–1, 62, 65–6, 71
Micallef, Shawn, 46
middle class, 109
aim for low-income tenants to join,
49, 54, 66, 104, 114, 137
colonizing of public housing by, 7,
10, 15, 66, 81–3, 89, 118
growth of, 28, 33, 73
Housing Act amendments benefit-
ing, 30
revitalization dominance of, 93–4
sensibilities, notion of, 3, 8, 84, 102
supposed docility of, 32–3, 41
surveillance by, 14–16, 52–4, 76–7,
112
migrants,
hierarchy of, 19, 60
women, *see* women, migrant
see also immigrants
Milczyn, Peter, 92
Miles, Robert, 53
Miller, David, 98
Mississaugas of the Credit First Nation,
11, 24
modernist housing architecture, 5
Lawrence Heights as, 2, 24, 52, 80
movement of, 32–3, 59, 81–3
moral environmentalism, 16, 25, 42–3,
83
morality, 77
affluent resident hegemonic, 2, 10,
14, 81, 102, 109
conflation of slum dwelling with, 25,
42–3, 83
mortgages,
government insuring of, 30, 53
as middle-class affordance, 28, 33–4
Moscoe, Howard, 100
on bussing policy, 44–5
launch of Lawrence Heights
revitalization, 1, 13–14

on tenant/resident concerns, 67, 69,
78, 123–4
MPATHY, *Reclaiming Artifacts* exhibit,
142–3
Mulholland family, 25–7
multiculturalism,
federal narratives of, 5, 59–60
Toronto and, 82–5, 88–9, 98, 113,
119, 146
Multiculturalism Act, 19, 56–7, 60
Murray, John, 50

National Housing Act, 27
amendments, 29–30, 55
neoliberalism,
concept of, 4, 5n1, 86, 150–1
impacts on Black communities, 59,
73–4
"inclusionary," 98, 144
lasting policy influence of, 4, 82–3,
85–6, 88, 121–2, 126
Lawrence Heights revitalization,
82–3, 114, 133, 150, 152–5
narratives of, 6, 9, 86, 144, 152–5
rise of, 5, 16, 73, 81
urban planning and, 5–6, 9, 91,
96–8, 112
New Democratic Party (NDP), 69, 91
new public management (NPM), 126–7
news media, 65
analysis of themes in, 71–6, 78–80
anti-Black narratives in, 74–6, 153
coverage of local violence, 93–4, 116
public housing coverage, 49, 117
revitalization coverage, 20, 95, 98,
100–2, 116, 123–5, 154
stigmatization of Lawrence Heights,
13, 19, 54, 71–3, 116–17, 142
new urbanism, 5, 7, 83, 113
non-profit sector, 138
housing ownership by, 2, 29, 55, 59
neoliberalism and, 114–15, 126–7
public engagement through,
126–31, 140, 146, 153–5
revitalization planning/work, 7,
95–9, 117–18, 121–2
study of "at-risk" neighbourhoods,
79

North York, 1
    building infrastructure in, 36, 38–9,
        44–5, 87
    City Council 67–8, 97–100, 109, 147
    demographics of, 13, 18, 25, 150
    early racial homogeneity in, 18, 61
    farmers in, 57, 62
    history of, 11, 13, 25–6, 34 , 110
    housing construction in, 35–6, 47,
        59, 70
North York Community House, 155
    critiques of local policing, 75, 140
North York Planning Board, 37, 69–70
North York Welfare Department, 18, 21

Official Community Plan (Toronto),
    88–9, 97, 150
Ontario Federation of Citizens'
    Associations, 19, 66
Ontario Hospital ("999"), 50
Ontario Housing Corporation (OHC),
    50, 55
    management of public housing,
        18–19, 30, 62
    mistreatment of Lawrence Heights
        tenants, 15, 66–7, 71
Ontario Municipal Board (OMB), 37, 68
oppression, 113
    in living conditions, 9, 53, 80
    systemic, 3, 23, 74–5
Owusu-Bempah, Akwasi, 73

paternalism, government, 16, 32, 67, 76,
    86, 104
Pathways to Education, 92, 122, 125, 153
Petrunia, Jason, 59
Places to Grow, 149–50
planners, 132
    engagement of tenants, 4, 20, 97,
        104–5, 120, 124–6
    Lawrence Heights revitalization
        messaging, 21, 83, 85, 99, 109–11,
        152
    paternalism of, 32–3, 76–7, 104–5
planning, urban,
    democratic, 5–7, 17, 52, 88, 96–7,
        125–7
    euthenics-minded, see euthenics

monetary aims of, 16–17, 36, 83,
    120
neoliberalism, impacts of, 5–6, 9, 91,
    96–8, 112
theory of social mixing, see social
    mixing
police, 5n1, 66, 137
    anti-Black racism, 54, 73–5, 78–9,
        130
    minimal oversight of, 94, 138–41,
        145, 151
    see also Toronto Police Service (TPS)
political economy, 5n1, 27
    concept of, 22
post-industrialism, 5, 54, 57, 89
poverty, 66, 105, 135
    concentrated pockets of, 23, 81, 94,
        112–13, 148–9
    deconcentration of, 5–7, 83–4, 93,
        128
    media coverage of, 54
    racialized, 18, 62, 144
    as social ill, 6, 25, 78–9
    stigma attached to, 21, 23
    violence, association with, 18, 54,
        144
Powell, Betsy, 116
private sector, 59
    efficiency of, 17, 34, 126, 134
    profitability of, 17, 78, 83–4, 89, 99,
        112, 118
    revitalization project involvement,
        1, 19–20, 81–2, 93, 120, 128
    see also public-private partnerships
privatization, 86, 151
    government policies of, 19–20, 73,
        81, 98, 143
    new public management and, 126–7
Progressive Conservatives, 85, 100, 141
provincial government, 45, 73, 86, 93
    downloading of housing adminis-
        tration, 16, 19–20, 81, 85–91, 98,
        151
    on Lawrence Heights construction/
        revitalization, 12, 66, 121, 131–3,
        141–5, 148–50
    neoliberal policies, 19–20, 85–6,
        90–1, 95–8, 126–7

policing initiatives, 73, 79

public housing investment/cuts, 29–30, 34–5, 40–1, 55, 105–6, 110, 135

transfer payments, *see* transfer payment reductions

Prue, Michael, 91–2

public housing,
central intent of, 76–7
demolition of, 1, 6, 105
deterioration of, 8, 24, 27, 59, 80, 93
government dictating terms of, 18–19, 21–2, 30, 62
as machine for democratic living, 33, 52, 81–4
middle-class colonizing of, 7, 10, 15, 66, 81–3, 89, 118
program, *see* public housing program (national)
societal distain for, 5, 49, 54–5, 74, 117, 124

public housing program (national), 15, 53
creation of, 29–30, 34
reasons for failure of, 19, 33, 54–5

publicly subsidized units, building of, 1–2, 18

public money,
demands for more, 137
land sales in lieu of, 14
withdrawal of, 4, 91, 136

public-private partnerships,
government shift to, 5–6, 19–20, 35, 96, 111
in Lawrence Heights revitalization, 1–5, 14, 81, 106–10, 130–3, 151–4
portrayal of, 16–17, 94–5, 130, 149
prioritizing profitability in, 17, 78, 83–6, 89, 99, 112, 118
in Regent Park revitalization, 9, 20, 82, 94, 117–18

public works, 35, 40
money for projects in, 5, 36, 38, 47

racialization, 53, 57
of poverty, 18, 74, 138
settler colonialism and, 24, 89, 93–4

racialized tenants, 149
as outsiders, 57, 59, 144
stereotypes of, 53–5, 80–1, 94
surveillance/criminalization of, 3–4, 14–16, 73, 82, 140

racism, 100
anti-Black/Brown, 53, 74–82, 122, 148, 153
stigmatization and, 3, 5, 124
systemic, 10, 68, 154
see also anti-Black racism

real estate,
capital, attracting, 63, 78, 85, 99–101
corruption, 88, 97
development of, 11–12, 28, 57, 61, 68–9, 119, 154
market, 88, 96
services, 106–7, 109–10, 150
valuations, 41, 44

Rebellions of 1837/1838 (Upper Canada), 22, 26

recession, 28, 30
prolonged Toronto, 20, 59, 88, 96

Regent Park,
Lawrence Heights versus, 2, 14–18, 92, 105, 110, 118–19
model of, 20, 82, 97–8, 104–5, 154
postwar slum clearance in, 32–3, 143
racialized residents in, 59, 117
revitalization project in, 1, 8–9, 20, 94, 117–19, 143
right-of-return policy in, 104
Social Development Plan for, *see* social development plans (SDPs)
stigmatization of, 13, 44, 105, 116–17
We All Belong, 117, 119–20

rent-geared-to-income (RGI) housing, 14, 59
proposals for Lawrence Heights, 2, 103, 106, 110, 113, 136

resistance(s),
conceptual emergence of, 11
to public housing, 18, 34, 40
strategies of, 74, 119
tenant, 15, 122, 152
urbanist planning, 5, 143

revitalization, urban,
    concept of, 1
    hegemonic vision for, 3–4, 21, 83,
        85, 99, 109–11, 152
    limited tenant involvement in, 9,
        111, 121, 128–32, 135, 143–5
    media coverage of, 20, 95, 98, 100–2,
        116, 123–5, 154
    neoliberalism and, 82–3, 114, 133,
        150, 152–5
    recolonizing through, 7, 10, 15, 66,
        81–3, 89, 118
    research on, 4–6
Rexdale, 18, 35, 79
roadways,
    as bad environments, 41, 43
    funding for building, 34, 36, 40, 110
    Lawrence Heights, 1, 44, 63–4, 85,
        99, 109
Rose, Albert, 16, 29
row houses, 31, 43

safety, community, 38, 95
    concerns in Lawrence Heights, 72,
        75–6, 80, 109, 136–42
    organizing for, 136–42
    revitalization narratives and, 8, 78,
        129
    social development plans and, 9, 15,
        121, 126, 129–30
Saranac Neighbourhood, 69–70
Save Our Streets rallies, 100
Scarborough, 18, 34, 59, 62, 66, 79, 87
self-reliance,
    capitalist notion of, 3, 5–8
    racialized tenant lack of, 16, 41
seniors, 29, 80
    community support for, 132–3, 135,
        140
    opposition to apartment building
        for, 69
service sector,
    emergence of, 13, 19, 56
    jobs, 59, 62
settler colonialism,
    British, 24–6, 56, 94
    Lawrence Heights land and, 11–12,
        22–7, 119

public housing redevelopment and,
    7–10, 15, 66, 81–3, 89, 118
white supremacy and, 23–5, 53, 94,
    138
Sewell, John, 76–7, 137
slum dwellers, 81, 104
    euthenic narratives about, 24, 33,
        41–2, 66, 79
    see also low-income residents
slums,
    clearance of, 31–2, 41, 84
    enclosure of, 63, 77, 83, 99
    as producing immorality, 16, 41–3,
        104
social development plans (SDPs), 137,
    152, 154
    Lawrence Heights, 15, 111–14, 126,
        129–33, 145
    Regent Park, 9, 111
    LHION involvement in, 111, 121,
        129–33, 145
social housing, 143
    assumptions about, 18, 63
    concept of, 2, 29
    downloading of administration for,
        16, 19–20, 81, 85–92, 98, 151
    funding for, 4, 19–20, 94–8, 105–7,
        117–18
    programs, 29, 34–5, 55, 73, 134
    revitalization and, 4, 16, 92, 105,
        109
    Toronto provision of, 1, 29, 81, 92,
        102, 134–6
Social Housing Reform Act (SHRA), 20,
    89–91
social infrastructure, 110, 114
    Lawrence Heights, 1, 85, 99, 109,
        111, 129
socialism, 27, 38, 96
social mixing, 78, 154
    control through, 3–4, 14–15, 93,
        102–4
    theory of, 2–3, 83–4, 95, 109, 112,
        136–7
Social Planning Toronto, 135, 140
social reformers, 32, 80, 98
    moral environmentalism of, 16, 25,
        42–3, 83

social services,
    calls to improve, 55, 71–2, 80
    cuts to, 81, 97, 112
    financing of, 47, 87, 134
    public housing and, 35, 47–8, 95–6
Spadina Expressway, 19, 45–6
    campaign against, *see* Stop the
        Spadina movement
stock, public housing, 29
    degradation of, 14, 92, 97–9, 143
    pressure to grow, 28, 55, 70
Stop the Spadina movement, 45–6
Strong Neighbourhood Taskforce, 93–5
St. Stephen's Community House, 95
subsidized housing,
    cuts to, 59, 86, 136
    demand for, 29, 34–5
    public-private partnerships for, 38, 78
    social mixing of, 1–2, 14, 40
    stigma of, 18, 49, 77
suburbs,
    financing development in, 87–8, 110
    housing investment in, 28, 30, 44–5,
        89
    living conditions in inner, 2, 11, 18,
        47, 62–3, 79, 149–50
    migration to, 5, 34, 47, 57–8
    public housing in, 2, 18, 33–6, 55, 70

Task Force on Race Relations and
    Policing, 73
taxes, 151
    allocation to public housing, 34, 36
    cuts to, 19, 28, 49, 98, 121
    income base for, 34–5, 69, 88–91
    property, 87, 89, 118, 135
    revenues from, 35, 86–90, 96–7
technocratic managerialism, 5, 28, 88, 98
tenants,
    Lawrence Heights, *see* Lawrence
        Heights tenants
    racialized, *see* racialized tenants
Thobani, Sunera, 56–7
Toronto (city of),
    budget, 89–90, 135
    Council, *see* City Council, Toronto
    former boroughs of, 11
    as global city, 19, 56–7, 62–3, 85, 88

    Metropolitan, *see* Metropolitan
        Toronto
    Official Community Plan, 88–9, 97,
        150
    as primary business/financial centre,
        5, 35, 47, 134, 149
Toronto Community Housing
    Corporation (TCHC), 149
    community safety priorities, 136–8
    Lawrence Heights revitalization
        work, 21, 98–9, 101, 103–10,
        112–13, 151–4
    mistreatment of tenants by, 15, 93,
        104–5, 133–4, 148
    project financing challenges, 14, 85,
        90–1, 98–9, 105–10
    public-private partnerships, 1–2,
        83–4, 94, 99, 105–10, 120
    Regent Park revitalization work, 1,
        9, 94, 97, 104–5, 117–18
    social development plan involve-
        ment, 15, 111–14, 126, 129–33,
        145, 151–2
    social housing of, 2, 18, 91, 97–9
    tenant engagement with, 4, 98–100,
        120–6, 143–6
Toronto Daily Star coverage, 45
    of Lawrence Heights, 33, 67, 71–2,
        102
    of public housing in city, 30–1,
        39–40, 49
Toronto District School Board, land
    ownership of, 107, 110–11
Toronto Employment and Social Services
    (TESS), 111, 114, 129
Toronto Police Service (TPS), 78, 148
    relations with Lawrence Heights
        tenants, 14–15, 117, 50, 54,
        69–72, 137–40
Toronto Star coverage, 71, 97
    of Lawrence Heights, 14, 100, 107,
        116, 136
tourism, 17–18
    focus on attracting, 5, 62–3, 88
townhouses, 83, 97, 154
    in Lawrence Heights, 2, 12, 99, 103
transfer payment reductions, 7, 88, 91,
    97, 151

Truly Disadvantaged, The (Wilson),
6, 128
Tsenkova, Sasha, 117–18

unemployment, 128
city initiatives to address, 27, 29, 154
insurance, 28
rising, 26–7, 88, 96
Unison Health and Community Services,
1, 103, 133, 135
United Way (Greater Toronto), 79, 93,
135
urbanization, 5, 18
objective of, 2, 155
Toronto's, 47, 150
see also new urbanism
urban renewal, notions of, 32–3, 41, 84

veterans, housing demands of, 28–30, 32

Walcott, Rinaldo, 73
walkability, community, 5, 7, 83, 109, 113
welfare,
conference on social, 50
cuts to benefits, 86, 97
dependence on, 59, 134
narratives about those receiving, 30,
55, 88, 114
notions of, 28, 49
welfare state, 28, 73
weakening of, 4, 7–8
white Europeans,
colonization and land dispossession
by, 23, 25, 53
immigration of, 8
whiteness, 52, 62, 94
Canadian immigration policy and,
56, 60
middle-class sensibilities and, 3,
84, 93
white supremacy,
government policies and, 78–9, 89
policing and, 74–5
resistance to, 4, 74
settler colonialism and, 23–5, 53,
94, 138
Wilson, William Julius (*The Truly
Disadvantaged*), 6, 128

women, migrant,
community role of, 141
racialized, 59–60, 142
single-parent, 59, 141
working class, 8, 18, 33, 49
World War II, post-, 25, 36, 56, 61, 142
Keynesianism, 4, 23, 27–8
Wrigglesworth, George, 42
Wynn, Graeme, 25
Wynne, Kathleen, 141

Yonge Street, 17, 58
Yorkdale Shopping Centre, 1, 111, 123
prompting immigration/settlement,
61–2, 107, 132
as tourist locale, 18